Edward John Still
Representing Algerian Women

Mimesis

Romanische Literaturen der Welt

Herausgegeben von
Ottmar Ette

Band 68

Edward John Still

Representing Algerian Women

Kateb, Dib, Feraoun, Mammeri, Djebar

DE GRUYTER

ISBN 978-3-11-073641-0
e-ISBN [PDF] 978-3-11-058610-7
e-ISBN [EPUB] 978-3-11-058386-1
ISSN 0178-7489

Library of Congress Cataloging-in-Publication Data 2018963417

Bibliographic information published by the Deutsche Nationalbibliothek
The Deutsche Nationalbibliothek lists this publication in the Deutsche Nationalbibliografie; detailed bibliographic data are available on the Internet at http://dnb.dnb.de.

© 2020 Walter de Gruyter GmbH, Berlin/Boston
This volume is text- and page-identical with the hardback published in 2019.
Printing: CPI books GmbH, Leck

www.degruyter.com

Contents

Avant-Propos —— VII

Acknowledgments —— IX

1   **Introduction – Une dissymétrie s'évoque** —— 1

2   **Kateb Yacine – Nedjma as Woman** —— 17
2.1   Painful Beginnings —— 19
2.2   Mythical Interpretations —— 25
2.3   Masculine Perspectives on the Feminine Image: Desiring Objects —— 33
2.4   Rivalrous Relations —— 40
2.5   National Possibilities —— 45
2.6   Fragile Emancipation and Pessimistic Representation —— 51

3   **Mohammed Dib: From one Gender to an Other** —— 60
3.1   Realist Plenitude and the Coming Revolution —— 62
3.2   Feminine Voices, Articulating Change —— 74
3.3   Gendered Frontiers —— 81
3.4   Maternal Melancholy —— 84
3.5   For whom the Texts? —— 95

4   **Mouloud Feraoun – Humility in the Representation of Women?** —— 100
4.1   Masculinist Structures and Women's Participation —— 102
4.2   Breaking the Chain —— 112
4.3   Cacophonous Narration —— 123
4.4   Ventriloquism, Factitiousness, and Failure —— 129

5   **Mouloud Mammeri – A Dissenting Masculine Perspective** —— 135
5.1   Kabyle Sociology, Masculinist Structures, and Women's Suffering —— 137
5.2   Lévi-Strauss, Matrimonial Strife, and Positive Change —— 143
5.3   Masculine Blindness, Perspective and Scopophilia —— 149
5.4   Supplements, Activity, and Pessimistic Uncertainty —— 157

6	**Assia Djebar – Movements Towards Self-reflexive Representation** —— 167
6.1	A Representative Scribe? —— 172
6.2	Socio-historical Progression? —— 177
6.3	Psychic/Subjective Progression and Emancipatory Learning —— 183
6.4	Shattered Mirrors —— 188
6.5	Ideological Evolution —— 193
7	**Conclusion – Women's Postcolonial Representation** —— 200
8	**Bibliography** —— 211
8.1	Primary Sources —— 211
8.2	Secondary Sources —— 212

Name Index —— 219

Index of Theoretical Terms —— 221

Avant-Propos

Approaching in five separate though interconnected chapters the late-colonial texts of Kateb Yacine, Mohammed Dib, Mouloud Feraoun, Mouloud Mammeri, and Assia Djebar, while situating them within a complex Algerian history of women, this work represents a contribution to and development of wide-reaching scholarship on these authors' works carried out by critics like Jean Déjeux, Charles Bonn, Christiane Achour, Jane Hiddleston, and Nicholas Harrison, while it constitutes somewhat of a radical expansion of and departure from the few studies that exist which treat the specific issue of Algerian women's literary representation in my period of study. Where critics like Winifred Woodhull (*Transfigurations of the Maghreb*) and Miriam Cooke (*Women and the War Story*) have tended to present the texts of my corpus as producing representations of women that are symptomatic of the masculinist psychic approaches and social structures of their historical context, problematising in particular a perceived marginalization or instrumentalisation of women in their narratives, my study argues that these texts act, in part, precisely as attempts to critically articulate and remedy these associated symptoms. The meat of my work and the principal contribution it makes to francophone scholarship rests on an appreciation of my corpus' capacity to circumvent, to highlight, and to undermine the perils of realist form and the potentially masculinist psychic and sociological structures it might convey, in its representation of women. It is my sincere hope that my efforts have generated a useful and thought-provoking study that might generate new perspectives on Algerian literature and on the more wide-reaching issues concerning women's representation that it has sought to address.

Acknowledgments

The development of my analytical perspectives during my time as a doctoral student at St Catherine's College, Oxford, required the contributions, past and contemporaneous, of a great many great people, from tireless library staff to indefatigable publicans. For lack of space, I shall simply thank a few whose support immediately springs to mind. I should like to thank Dr. Dominic Davies for the example of industriousness that he set and the washing-up that he did during my DPhil. I should like to thank Mr. Paul Brandilly for his offer of accommodation in aid of my research into Djebar's early novels at the BNF, Paris. I should like to thank Mr. Llewelin Siddons for his belief in my abilities. I should like to thank my mother, father and sister for their faith and fortification. Finally, I should like to thank my DPhil supervisor, Prof. Jane Hiddleston, who provided an endless amount of assistance, feedback and helpful criticism during my time at Oxford, and who encouraged me to understand the fact that words on a page that mean something to the writer do not necessarily mean something to the reader.

1 Introduction – Une dissymétrie s'évoque

La fausse vierge toute nue
   On lui voit les genoux
      Si délicate
         Elle doit taper sur les machines d'où sortent les procès les discours et les guerres – Kateb Yacine[1]

The complicity of *vertreten* and *darstellen*, their identity-in-difference as the place of practice can only be appreciated if they are not conflated by a sleight of word. – Gayatri Spivak.[2]

Frantz Fanon, in his oft-cited work on the Algerian insurgency and its struggle for independence from French rule, *Sociologie d'une révolution (L'An V de la révolution algérienne)* (1959), comments on a "repatterning" of Algerian women engendered by their embodiment of unprecedented revolutionary roles in the conflict.[3] He describes a phenomenological and symbolic transformation, a disruption of the feminine incarnation and symbolization of traditional meanings which would frame women as repositories for honour and national identity, relegating them to regulated private space. For Fanon, this transformation depends on women's establishment of a bodily connection with a revolutionary public space, on their leaving behind rigid psychogeographical and traditionalist conceptual divisions as they take on new, traditionally "masculine" roles outside of the private sphere. Moreover, Fanon describes a rupture in traditionalist social norms initiated by an understanding of the necessity of women's inclusion in revolutionary struggle. He famously writes, for example, in reference to women's public engagement that "le père lui-même n'a plus le choix. Sa vieille peur de déshonneur devient tout à fait absurde, eu égard à l'immense tragédie vécue par le peuple".[4]

Certainly when one reads Fanon's description of a feminine "unveiling", despite occasional inaccuracies and reproductions of a masculine gaze,[5] alongside

---

1 Kateb Yacine: *Le Polygone étoilé*. Paris: Éditions du Seuil 1966, p. 30.
2 Gayatri Spivak: Can the Subaltern Speak? In: Rosalind Morris (ed.): *Can the Subaltern Speak: Reflections on the History of an Idea*. New York: Columbia University Press 2010, p. 31.
3 I borrow this description from Rita Faulkner in her article Assia Djebar, Frantz Fanon, Women, Veils and Land. In: *World Literature Today* Vol. 70 No. 4 (Autumn 1966), p. 847–855.
4 Frantz Fanon: *Sociologie d'une révolution (L'An V de la révolution algérienne)*. Paris: Maspero 1972, p. 94.
5 Fanon's description of the Algerian veil, the haïk, and its restriction of bodily movement, for example, has been rejected by commentators like Marnia Lazreg who argues that Fanon's em-

both reports of women's involvement in the fight against colonialism and affirmations made by representatives of the Algerian state to come, one begins to appreciate the late-colonial period and especially the period of the Algerian war (1954–1962) as productive of a picture of progressive social change that promised greater gender equality.[6]

On August 2nd, 1956, the FLN, (Le Front de Libération Nationale, the predominant independence movement that then formed the Algerian state government), issued the Soummam Platform which outlined women's new roles as:

> a) Providing moral support to fighters and resisters; taking care of intelligence, liaison, food supplies and sanctuary.
> b) Helping families and children left behind by those at the front, in prison or in detention camps.[7]

Indeed, we know that women's active involvement in the war of independence went far beyond these parameters as thousands took responsibility for the implementation of key revolutionary tactics in both urban and rural settings. The details of women's involvement in the war have been meticulously inscribed in the works of historians and critics like Natalya Vince, Fadéla M'Rabet, Marnia Lazreg and Djamila Amrane-Minne, with Amrane-Minne seeking in particular to redress a lack in the documentation of women's revolutionary engagement:

> Ayant personnellement pris part à la guerre de libération nationale, j'ai gardé en mémoire l'image de toutes ces militantes que j'ai connues pendant la "bataille d'Alger", au maquis et dans les prisons. Et il m'a paru d'une injustice profonde que l'histoire de ces sept années de guerre s'écrive en faisant abstraction d'une moitié du peuple algérien : les femmes.[8]

Through personal testimonies, photographic and anecdotal narration, and statistical evidence, Amrane-Minne gives important flesh to our understanding of women's crucial role in the war, detailing the wide variety of responsibilities over which women took charge: the supervision of hiding places and food col-

---

phasis on women's struggle to adjust to public space without the veil is "overwrought". See *The Eloquence of Silence: Algerian Women in Question*. New York: Routledge 1994. p. 127.
6 I identify the "late-colonial" period as the period between the end of the Second World War and independence in 1962, because most cite the Algerian nationalist protests and the massacres of those who protested at Sétif and Guelma in 1945 as the beginning of the political *prise de conscience* that led to the dismantling of French rule.
7 Chérifa Benabdessadok: *Pour une analyse du discours sur la femme algérienne*. University of Algiers (Diplôme d'Etudes Avancées en Linguistique) 1977, p. 206.
8 Djamila Amrane-Minne: *Les Femmes algériennes dans la guerre*. Paris: Plon 1991, p. 13–14.

lections; the collection of funds, medicine and ammunition; acting as guides or liaisons; nursing; cooking and washing; terrorism. Amrane-Minne crucially emphasises the fact that women were important agents in the violence carried out by the armed insurgency. In discussing, for example, the historical events that took place during the battle of Algiers (1956–1957) prior to the seizure of the iconic revolutionary Ali La Pointe, inscribing the actions of revolutionary women such as Maliha Hamidou and Hassiba Ben Bouali, she writes that "il est incontestable que les femmes, outre leur rapport déterminant dans les liaisons et l'intendance, jouèrent un rôle actif et décisif au sein même des groupes armés".[9]

With the creation and fulfillment of these decisive and unprecedented revolutionary roles came new forms of respect and praise for feminine figures. Miriam Cooke informs us that "the women fighters, like Hassiba Ben Bouali [...] and Djamila Bouhired, were revered" whilst "those who had not only fought but had also experienced prison and torture – like Djamila Boupacha and Zohra Drif – became revolutionary heroines".[10] [11] Moreover, in the introduction to *Les Femmes algériennes dans la guerre,* Amrane-Minne, having noted the dearth of historical texts that cover women's involvement in the war, begins her work by impressing upon the reader the importance of Djamila Bouhired as a revolutionary figure, citing the films, books and songs dedicated to her whilst attributing to her the status of "le symbole de tout un peuple en lutte".[12]

---

[9] Ibid, p. 109–110.
[10] Miriam Cooke: *Women and the War Story.* Berkeley: University of California Press 1996, p. 122.
[11] Cooke's assertion that those who underwent torture and confinement acquired greater respect and recognition is further supported by the notoriety of the case of Djamila Boupacha. In 1960, Gisèle Halimi, her lawyer, requested that Simone de Beauvoir help her publicize the details of her case with a view to achieving full legal representation for her in a French court of law. The French had implemented various sickening forms of torture, having illegally imprisoned her in a detention centre: She was kicked in the chest by a group of soldiers and had a rib permanently displaced, had electrodes affixed with transparent tape to her nipples, legs, face, anus, and vagina and was given electric shocks, was burned with cigarettes, and was "deflowered" with a beer bottle as they sought information on the FLN's movements. So harrowing was de Beauvoir's description of Boupacha's suffering that her *Le Monde* article was censored, Robert Gauthier requesting that the euphemism 'belly' be employed in her detailing of the rape that took place. Interestingly, Ranjana Khanna reports that Boupacha's case was depicted by de Beauvoir as unexceptional in itself (her being arrested on suspicion of having planted a bomb in a university canteen) and therefore, to some degree, her actions and suffering can be considered as representative of the lived experiences of a number of Algerian women. See Ranjana Khanna: *Algeria Cuts: Women and Representation, 1830 to the Present.* Palo Alto: Stanford University Press 2008, p. 83–85.
[12] Djamila Amrane-Minne: *Les Femmes algériennes dans la guerre*, p. 13.

Lazreg informs us that revolutionary women and men referred to each other as "brother" and "sister" and Alistair Horne claims that, "on the whole the FLN woman was treated with respect never experienced before – either from her menfolk or from even the most liberal French emancipators".[13] Moreover, once independence had been obtained and the FLN took power following the signing of the Évian accords in 1962, Lazreg indicates that the new administration's early post-war stance on gender equality promised much with Algerian socialism purporting to "pursue the gains made by women in encroaching on the collective conscience of their countrymen".[14] Indeed, President Ben Bella was apparently "wont to threaten men who harassed women on the streets with forced labour in the Algerian desert!".[15] And, if one looks at speeches made by the party in these years, examples of their progressive rhetoric would indicate that the socialist FLN central discourse on women purported to establish them as meriting equal standing in the new state. In his inaugural speech at the July 1964 FLN Congress, President Ben Bella said that "[l]a libération de la femme n'est pas un aspect secondaire qui se surajoute à nos autres objectifs, elle est un problème dont la solution est un préalable à toute espèce de socialisme".[16] Then, for example, on International Women's day 1966 Houari Boumédiène, following his coup in 1965, stated: "Notre politique, particulièrement dans le domaine de la femme, est une politique claire, elle ne peut être celle de la ruse, de la fourberie et de l'intrigue [...] Notre révolution ne sera une révolution entière que lorsque tous les membres de la société y prendront part, et lorsque la femme y participera d'une manière efficace".[17]

What is clear, however, is that though FLN rhetoric and legislation appeared in part to seek to legitimate the new status-construct of the revolutionary Algerian woman, the nature of the historical, cultural and political context, of the socio-symbolic background to our period for study, ensured that she occupied a singularly conflictual conceptual space in late-colonial and post-colonial Algeria. [18] [19] As Anne McClintock puts it, "the Manichean agon of decolonization

---

13 See Marnia Lazreg: *The Eloquence of Silence*, p. 133 and Alistair Horne: *A Savage War of Peace*. New York: Viking 1977, p. 402–403.
14 Marnia Lazreg: *The Eloquence of Silence*, p. 142.
15 Ibid, p. 142.
16 Fadéla M'Rabet: *La Femme algérienne: suivi de les algériennes*. Paris: Maspero 1983, p. 12.
17 Ibid, p. 239–240.
18 New legislation included a policy which purported to ensure that couples were married on a basis of mutual consent. See Zahia Smail Salhi: Algerian Women, Citizenship, and the 'Family Code'. In: *Gender and Development* 11.3 (2003), p. 27–35.
19 By "socio-symbolic" background or order, I understand the partial fixing, the fleshing out of a trans-individual Lacanian Symbolic order of unsteady signification, through shared social dis-

[was] waged over the territoriality of female, domestic space".[20] A discussion of Algerian women's socio-political representation must thus carefully acknowledge the oppositional nature of socio-symbolic relations between colonised and colonial communities and authorities in this context and the impact of these relations upon socio-political rhetoric and discourse concerning women and their societal roles. If one focuses on one side of this symbolic conflict, on French colonial concerns, one notes that the fight for control over the Algerian woman, often conceived of as the manipulation of her self-identification,[21] had long been viewed as a potentially decisive battleground, gaining an even greater degree of importance in a period of counter-revolutionary struggle. To again refer to Fanon, he determines an aggression implicit in the colonial relationship towards the Algerian woman thus:

> Convertir la femme, la gagner aux valeurs étrangères, l'arracher à son statut, c'est à la fois conquérir un pouvoir réel sur l'homme et posséder les moyens pratiques, efficaces, de déstructurer la culture algérienne.[22]

Many critics have discussed the reactions that aggressive assimilatory practices provoked and it is likely that in perceiving certain "liberatory" acts and stances as colonial, having been brandished tactically by the French, a cleaving to retrograde traditionalist and masculinist conceptions of women's roles took place, both prior to and during the establishment of an Algerian nation. [23] [24] As McClintock remarks, referring to Benedict Anderson's work *Imagined Communities*, nations are "not simply phantasmagoria of the mind; as systems of cultural representation whereby people come to imagine a shared experience of identification with an extended community, they are historical practices through which social difference is invented and performed".[25] Concordantly, one can argue that the

---

course and the production of imaginary identifications and relations. This will become clearer as the monograph progresses.
20 Anne McClintock: No Longer in a Future Heaven: Gender, Race and Nationalism. In: Anne McClintock/Aamir Mufti/Ella Shohat (eds.): *Dangerous Liaisons: Gender, Nation, and Postcolonial Perspectives*. Minneapolis: University of Minnesota Press 1997, p. 90.
21 In the case of the French, identification with "modern", Western mores.
22 Frantz Fanon: *Sociologie d'une révolution*, p. 20.
23 The prime example of a tactical "liberatory" act is the public demonstration of Algerian women's unveiling on May 13, 1958 which included invocations to "être comme la femme française". See Winifred Woodhull: Unveiling Algeria. In: Reina Lewis/Sara Mills (eds.): *Feminist Postcolonial Theory: A Reader*. New York: Routledge 2003, p. 574).
24 I understand "masculinist" to mean "of a character which would support a maintenance of a conceptual gendered hierarchy, of an agential dissymmetry in socio-symbolic representation".
25 Anne McClintock: No Longer in a Future Heaven, p. 89.

identity of a notional Algerian state was, for those invested in its establishment, to be articulated in part through the performance of those conceptual and real sites that stood in opposition to the colonial Other, with the conceptual space devoted to women being chief among them. Lazreg, for example, goes so far as to suggest that the FLN were willing to compromise their own espoused political approach to women's freedoms due to the provocation of policies and attitudes of assimilation characterised by the action described in footnote 23, writing that "responses to colonial policies focusing on women [...] were consciously distorted by casting women's civil rights as a Quranic issue" despite the fact that the religious establishment was seen as "a native arm of colonial domination of the Algerian people".[26]

However, to whatever extent one considers the calibration of Algerian women's status to be a function of oppositional socio-political relations, relating above all to French colonial discourse and policy, both in pre and post-independence Algeria, the question of women's emancipation and whether promises of greater gender equality were broken is certainly a fraught one. Some, like Khalida Messaoudi, report that the typical experience of a moudjahida entailed a stymied emancipation that began before the end of the war. She records what is, according to her, a representative statement from one such fighter who argues that "[o]ur return to the 'inside' didn't begin in 1962, but, rather, before independence. Little by little, during the war, the FLN removed us from the real fighting zones and sent us to the borders or overseas. Our role was defined from that movement on. We didn't have any place in the world of the 'outside'".[27] Other writers, like Natalya Vince, might argue that class structures in fact played a decisive role in determining women's capacity to acquire and maintain social power and that the period can be understood as a site of uneven social development, as indicated in her chapter '1962: Continuities and Discontinuities' in *Our Fighting Sisters*.[28] What one can certainly argue is that there existed a gendered deficit of influence with regards to the structural planning and discursive interventions staged by the FLN. Detailed in many accounts is the lack of women in the FLN's leadership (0.5% inside the country, 0% in exile in Tunis), in particular in forums dedicated to position papers and policy development.[29] And, supporting this claim, Marie-Aimée Hélie-Lucas writes that "even in the hardest

---

[26] Marnia Lazreg: *The Eloquence of Silence*, p. 132.
[27] Khalida Messaoudi/Elizabeth Schemla: *Unbowed: An Algerian Woman Confronts Islamic Fundamentalism*. Philadelphia: University of Pennsylvania Press 1998, p. 51.
[28] See Natalya Vince: *Our Fighting Sisters*. Oxford: Oxford University Press 2016.
[29] Marnia Lazreg: *The Eloquence of Silence*, p. 125 + 140.

times of struggle, women were oppressed, confined to tasks that would not disturb social order in the future. Although these tasks were essential, they should not have absorbed all female energy. One woman bore arms, none was in a decision-making position!".[30]

Upon independence, as will often be alluded to throughout this monograph, women as a whole did not acquire the status that progressive rhetoric and active involvement in the war had appeared to augur. As one example amongst many, Hélie-Lucas indicates that "official agencies did not encourage women to register [as veterans]" and testimony provided by Djamila Amrane-Minne from her early study *La Femme algérienne et la guerre de libération nationale (1954–62)*, which is cited in Hélie-Lucas' writing, testifies to women's post-war exclusion from veteran status, indicating, for example, that only one woman per logistics unit was allowed to register after the war.[31] Moreover, a lack of support for women soldiers is further alluded to by the inclusion in Hélie-Lucas' essay of Amrane-Minne's admission that from her early study's sample of some 2,500 women, only one woman stated that she had been an armed fighter.[32] On the question of post-colonial political leadership, Amrane-Minne informs readers of *Les Femmes algériennes dans la guerre* that "[s]ur 194 membres, la première Assemblée nationale constituante compte 10 femmes, toutes anciennes militantes: elles ne sont que 2 sur les 138 membres de la deuxième Assemblée. Au parti, aux syndicats, aucune n'a un poste de responsabilité".[33] In part because of this lack of political transformation and citing a perceived lack of a feminist movement, state-run or independent, following the war, Miriam Cooke goes so far as to question whether women themselves gained a feminist consciousness at all during the years of conflict, writing:

> So much for Fanon's and others' myth of Algerian women liberated along with their country. Only later did women acknowledge the participation of other women and perceive its potential significance to feminist consciousness.[34]

---

30 Marie-Aimée Hélie-Lucas: Women, Nationalism, and Religion in the Algerian Struggle. In: Margot Badran/Miriam Cooke (eds.): *Opening the Gates: A Century of Arab Feminist Writing*. Bloomington: Indiana University Press 2004, p. 107.
31 See ibid, p. 105–106.
32 Ibid, p. 107.
33 Djamila Amrane-Minne: *Les Femmes algériennes dans la guerre*, p. 264.
34 Miriam Cooke: *Women and the War Story*, p. 161.

Lazreg, on the other hand, counters assertions of this nature, writing:

> The prevailing feminist view, according to which Algerian women, like so many other women before them, were duped into joining the nationalist movement by unscrupulous men who later did not share with them the spoils of independence, must be rejected for its derogatory connotations that deprive women of will and agency, and its lack of understanding of the dynamics of Algerian nationalism.[35]

It would be my suggestion that the testimonies of women such as Djamila Amrane-Minne at the very least demonstrate a transformation in consciousness of a substantial number of Algerian women, and that studies like Natalya Vince's produce a credible and nuanced picture of women's transition into independence, highlighting the disparities in experience and the lack of wisdom in unitary circumscriptions of Algerian women's "consciousness" or "betrayal". Nonetheless, in wishing to conceive of the period as a whole and the structural bases for gender relations in post-colonial Algeria, it seems to me that the failure to create a post-colonial nation that would not just extol but actualize gender equality, despite an expansion in women's freedoms and their involvement in the public sphere during the war, should be conceived of as a function of a fundamental gendered symbolic division which was insufficiently undermined for a radical order of emancipation to take place.

The nature of the gendered symbolic division that this book envisages takes its cue initially from the work of Pierre Bourdieu in his analyses of Amazigh society in *La Domination masculine* where he describes the following:

> [L]a dissymétrie fondamentale, celle *du sujet et de l'objet, de l'agent et de l'instrument*, qui s'instaure entre l'homme et la femme sur le terrain des échanges symboliques [...] les femmes ne peuvent y apparaître qu'en tant qu'objets ou, mieux, en tant que symboles dont le sens est constitué en dehors d'elles et dont la fonction est de contribuer à la perpétuation ou à l'augmentation du capital symbolique détenu par les hommes.[36]

In his work Bourdieu demonstrates the procedures which produce habitus, unconscious physical and psychic dispositions, both masculine and feminine, while ensuring masculine hegemony over symbolic capital as they fix the structures of society (labour, ritual, amorous relations etc.). [37] He outlines the univer-

---

35 Marnia Lazreg: *The Eloquence of Silence*, p. 118.
36 Pierre Bourdieu: *La Domination masculine*. Paris: Éditions du Seuil 1998, p. 65.
37 As will be expanded upon throughout this book, symbolic capital represents a value of esteem, of social agency/import or honour which accrues to individuals in their mastery of social exchanges.

sal mastery that an androcentric world view holds and its predication on binary couplings (up/down, above/below, dry/moist) whose apparent cosmological "naturalness" is applied to human roles, positions and corporeal constitutions in such a way that "le principe masculin est posé en mesure de toute chose".[38] For Bourdieu, the symbolic separation of masculine and feminine exists not just at a conscious level but "s'achève et s'accomplit dans une transformation profonde et durable des corps (et des cerveaux)".[39] He writes:

> L'effet de la domination symbolique (qu'elle soit d'ethnie, de genre, de culture, de langue, etc.) s'exerce non dans la logique pure des consciences connaissantes, mais à travers les schèmes de perception, d'appréciation et d'action qui sont constitutifs des habitus et qui fondent, en deçà des décisions de la conscience et des contrôles de la volonté, une relation de connaissance profondément obscure à elle-même.[40]

Beyond his establishing the foundations of masculine domination of the symbolic field, Bourdieu's analysis of the exchange of symbolic goods is particularly pertinent for this study where it highlights the heteronomous nature of the affirmation of male identity in its relation to the opposite sex. Taking as his starting point Lévi-Strauss' conception of the incest taboo, his building block of the order of culture or, in Lacanian parlance, the Symbolic order, Bourdieu outlines the primordial nature of gift exchange, women's exclusion from agency in this exchange, economies that spring from it, and the politics of domination inherent to these economies. What is central to the orders of exchange described is honour, which one can interpret more broadly as symbolic capital. It drives the interactions as the telos sought by both parties who affirm each other's status as negotiations develop. Bourdieu writes of "un échange agonistique visant à accumuler [...] du capital symbolique, donc des pouvoirs et des droits durables sur des personnes [...].[41] He then goes on to allude to the importance of notions of representation to the acquisition and preservation of symbolic capital/honour, writing:

> La division sexuelle est inscrite [...] dans la division des activités productives auxquelles nous associons l'idée de travail ainsi que, plus largement, dans la division du travail d'entretien du capital social et du capital symbolique qui assigne aux hommes le monopole de toutes les activités officielles, publiques, de *représentation*, et en particulier de tous les échanges d'honneur [...][42]

---

38 Ibid, p. 29.
39 Ibid, p. 40.
40 Ibid, p. 58–59.
41 Ibid, p. 68.
42 Ibid, p. 71 (Bourdieu's emphasis).

What's perhaps particularly interesting for the historical context of this book is that Bourdieu's exchanges are predicated on an idea of "une relation essentielle d'égalité en honneur" that despite its dependence on a notion of parity produces an agonistic relation.[43] If we transpose Bourdieu's symbolic agon into the colonial domain we can infer that in a profoundly unequal male–male relationship, that of colonised and coloniser, the necessity to reproduce "le jeu et les enjeux [...] les conditions de l'accès à la reproduction sociale", in essence to reproduce the fundamental structures of a gendered symbolic division, takes on a particular unconscious importance that rather than being undermined, is in fact strengthened once the satisfaction of national self-affirmation is achieved.[44]

And, if one turns to Gayatri Spivak's seminal essay *Can the Subaltern Speak?* and focuses on her discussion of Marx's *Eighteenth Brumaire of Louis Bonaparte* which attempts to problematise notions of representativity, in particular the capacity of authors to represent the radically dispossessed, the *subaltern*, one can better understand the specific importance of representation in the continuation of symbolic division and hegemony over symbolic capital. For Spivak importantly and provocatively investigates both the split in the meaning of representation between representation-as-proxy (*Vertretung*) and representation-as-portrayal (*Darstellung*) and the status and impact of the *Vertretung* representative, the writer or spokesperson, when he/she acquires an authority of determination in *Darstellung* representations.

Dissymmetry and discontinuity stand as the most important factors for our reading of Spivak: dissymmetry between the symbolic capital generated and held by the writer, the proxy, and the lack of symbolic authority accrued to the subjects discussed, and discontinuity in interests and experience between these two groups and within the groups themselves. For when we figure forms of representation in our colonial domain as acts of *Vertretung*, Spivak's Marxist commentary on social incoherence allows us to consider writings that act to speak *for* women on women, that produce an image of women that claims to know them in their historical ontology and essential being, as actions of symbolic domination that mask their own inability to represent, in both senses. Spivak writes:

> The event of representation as *Vertretung* (in the constellation of rhetoric-as-persuasion) behaves like a *Darstellung* (or rhetoric-as-trope), taking its place in the gap between the formation of a (descriptive) class and the nonformation of a (transformative) class.[45]

---

43 Ibid, p. 68.
44 Ibid, p. 68.
45 Gayatri Spivak: Can the Subaltern Speak?, p. 31.

For my purposes I will constitute Algerian women under French rule as pertaining to the position held by class in this structure, acknowledging in so doing their lack of a shared interest, of a solid feeling of community. Spivak cites Marx who writes:

> In so far as millions of families live under economic conditions of existence that separate their modes of life...*they form a class.* In so far as...the identity of their interests fails to produce a feeling of community...*they do not form a class.*[46]

In the context of Algerian decolonization, it is my argument that women formed a group or class in their shared poverty within the symbolic economy. Without self-inscription allowing for a collective transformational consciousness, the dissymmetry of representation in this milieu ensured the continuation of symbolic hegemony, with men determining the parameters of womanhood as representatives in social symbolisation. Furthermore, symbolic hegemony is to be understood as partly independent from cognition, from intent, as a structural outcome. As Marx writes in *Capital:*

> My standpoint, from which the development of the economic formation of society is viewed as a process of natural history, can less than any other make the individual responsible for relations whose creature he remains, socially speaking, however much he may subjectively raise himself above them.[47]

As was alluded to above, within the organized resistance of the FLN, the figureheads through whom representation (*Vertretung*) was to take place were almost exclusively male. Limiting our scope to political rhetoric, one can thus understand how, despite a number of positive discursive interventions from members of the political class, the imbalance in control over the stakes of symbolic conflict represented a structural imbalance that stymied continued representative progress in gender relations. When one turns to literary output, one notes a concomitant imbalance and thus, by the same structural logic, one might imagine that the literary should support the political/discursive in its reproduction of a representative imbalance.

For, the famous writer of Algerian history, Benjamin Stora, writes that "[o]f the overall figure of works dealing with the "first" Algerian war (revolutionary as opposed to civil), barely 10 percent are by women (approximately 240 out of 2200). The description of the world of war thus remains the privilege of the

---

[46] Ibid, p. 31 (Spivak's emphasis and suspension marks). Indeed, I would be inclined, like De Beauvoir in *Le Deuxième Sexe*, to theorise women as a "caste" rather than a "class".
[47] Karl Marx: *Capital, Vol. 1.* London: Penguin Books 1992, p. 92.

men who made it".⁴⁸ Stora also indicates a lack of representativity within the female writing body itself, drawing our attention to the fact that all of the cited 240 works were written in French and that in the period between 1954–62, more than half of the 101 novels (52) were written by Algerians of French descent.⁴⁹ He goes on to affirm that in the early post-revolutionary period "Assia Djebar is practically alone as she pursues her writing [...] and the reader wonders what happened to these women once peace was regained; silence in this post-1962 period gives the impression of a flight".⁵⁰

Unhappily, this silence during and after the war is often adjudged to characterise the feminine literary landscape of revolutionary Algeria as is a dearth of texts, among the few women's works that one could cite, that positively portray the lived reality of Algerian women and that might thus favorably impact upon the distribution of symbolic capital. Contrasting writers such as Djamila Debèche, Taos Amrouche, and Djebar with other women's literary movements that have taken place against the background of conflict (Beirut Decentrists, Palestinian writers), Miriam Cooke argues that Algerian women who did write, "wrote alone and without commitment to a women's cause that could stand side by side along with, but not under, the nationalist cause".⁵¹ She also cites Hélie-Lucas who adds that "[i]n Algeria many, including myself, kept silent for a whole decade after independence. We gave those in power the time to strengthen and organize and enforce discriminatory laws against women [...] Of course we congratulated ourselves on the freedom that women had gained during the struggle. We were inside the myth talking about the myth".⁵²

However, despite women's exclusion from writing the myth of the nation and inscribing its metonymic agents, a structural imbalance does not necessarily preclude the possibility of the era's literary representation of women eschewing interpellation into masculinist ideology, rejecting the symbolic coordinates that define women's worth as supplementary or inferior. Nor does it mean that the writers whose works this monograph will analyse did not have an appreciation of and a will to display and critique modes of representation and conceptual and subjective approaches that might contribute to the continuation of masculine domination and its necessary failure in women's representation. Indeed, what

---

48 Benjamin Stora/R.H. Mitsch: Women's Writing between two Algerian Wars. In: *Research in African Literatures* No. 30.3 (1999), p. 79.
49 Ibid, p. 81.
50 Ibid, p. 87.
51 Miriam Cooke: *Women and the War Story*, p. 161.
52 Ibid, p. 118.

this book will to a large extent endeavour to illuminate is precisely that the canonical writers of the period, who were mostly male, both textually acknowledge their inability to articulate the experiences and subjectivity of the feminine Other, to *represent* women, and deploy a remarkable variety of formal and conceptual innovations in an attempt to tentatively produce evocations of Algerian femininity that seek to highlight or upset the structural imbalance of masculinist symbolic hegemony, in literary and socio-political milieux.

The five authors whose work this monograph will focus upon can, to a large extent, be considered the principal representatives of Algerian Francophone literature, not just with regards to their era but indeed, in a general canonical sense, and consequently one can conceive of their depictions of Arab and Amazigh women as parts of predominant literary edifices. Kateb Yacine, Mohammed Dib, Mouloud Feraoun, Assia Djebar and, perhaps to a slightly lesser extent, Mouloud Mammeri, are names that have acted in Algeria and elsewhere, viewed through differing political and conceptual prisms, as national representatives, as figures of *Vertretung*. This book makes the claim that each deploys literary form in a fashion particularly worthy of study for its implications for women's representation. Thus, though it is not always useful to think of representational modes as ineluctably bound to their authors – indeed, in particular in the works of Dib and Djebar, one may track a development in their texts towards a greater appreciation and more skilful treatment of the importance of feminine inscription – this book is divided into five chapters each investigating identifiable characteristic particularities of an author's late-colonial writing in respect of the representation of Algerian women.

Though it was noted above that this book seeks to elucidate the productivity of the texts to be analysed in their potential to subvert a masculinist symbolic hegemony, its analyses will not seek to avoid elucidating aspects of representation that fail to subvert a masculinist depiction of women, that contribute to a literary determination that reproduces the pernicious aspects of the Bourdieusian and Marxian divisions outlined above. Principally, criticisms will be levelled at works where claims to depict women through a realist mode of representation are undermined by the effects of the fundamental ideological underpinning of reality production, as the subject seeks to comprehend the world and its players, a factor that marks in particular the early novels of Mohammed Dib. As Slavoj Žižek skilfully outlines in books like *The Plague of Fantasies* and *The Sublime Object of Ideology*, ideology, like an intractable coloured lens, precedes conscious comprehension, conditions, as a primordial form of narrative, the nature of subjective reality. To simply apply the consequences of this theoretical understanding to writers of the late-colonial period and in particular to Dib, we can sometimes view the pictures of women generated by his texts as reproducing models and stereotypes that exist as a product of masculinist ideology or as overlooking feminine existences that this ideology ignores or cannot see.

What then constitutes a radical and productive break from the pitfalls of realism is the deployment of literary strategies that undermine the notional voice of representation, both in the sense of a narrator and in the sense of agents understood to hold power over the representation of women. It is perhaps helpful to split these strategies of undermining into three principle strands, though others could be cited: psychoanalysis of agents, principally masculine, formal decentring of the voice of representation, and literary forms of a productive conceptual "pessimism". It should also be stated that these strategies constitute a progressive representative mode activated by the acceptance and highlighting of failure, that they are limited to an *indirect* activation of feminine literary agency. However, though I am suggesting that the potency of this literature is revealed in the texts of my authors as stemming from a kind of productive negativity, this is not to say that a number of the authors do not produce feminine characters who can be understood as constructive agents existing in a metonymic relation with others working in a symbolic establishment of specific communities and the nation as a whole. This is particularly important considering the writings on literature and the postcolonial nation conducted by critics like Elleke Boehmer which illuminate the contrast between men's "metonymic", contiguous role in nationalist representation and women's "metaphoric or symbolic role".[53] Nonetheless, since from the feminist perspective of my work the central issue for my authors is an evocation of a feminine Other from the problematic position of a *Vertretung* (proxy) representative, their ability to boldly though tentatively negotiate this issue remains, for me, the principle contribution of their work.

From the evocation of obsessional desire in Kateb's *Nedjma*, to Dib's depictions of a precarious masculine subjectivity, to Feraoun's allusions to death drive, Thanatos, to Mammeri's depictions of the male gaze, it will be seen that the texts of my corpus invite psychoanalytic readings which destabilise the homeostasis of a masculinist perspective. As such this monograph will perform readings with the aid of the psychoanalytic notions developed by Sigmund Freud and Jacques Lacan and redeployed by readers and theorists like Jane Gallop, Slavoj Žižek, and Julia Kristeva. And, if the literary evocation of problematic subjective approaches to women along with the articulation of concordant socio-symbolic structures undermines the agents within the novels and their worldly

---

[53] Elleke Boehmer: Stories of Women and Mothers: Gender and Nationalism in the Early Fiction of Flora Nwape. In Susheila Nasta (ed.): *Motherlands: Black Women's Writing from Africa, the Caribbean and South Asia*. London: The Women's Press 1991, p. 6.

referents, simultaneously placing emphasis on women's marginalisation as supplements in masculinist psychosexual and socio-symbolic economies, the formal innovations perhaps most readily perceptible in the work of writers like Kateb, Feraoun and Mammeri work to undermine the texts themselves by placing emphasis on the hollow representative mastery that the describing subject embodies, in literary and social symbolisation. Thus this book performs close textual readings of the myriad formal innovations employed in the service of representing women from a deliberately undermined narrative position, seeking to convey and develop aspects of a literary complexity worked on previously by critics like Charles Bonn, Jean Déjeux and Jacqueline Arnaud.

In reference to the third principle subversive strand embodied by the texts of the period that this book explores, productive "pessimism", it is certainly true that potential failure hangs as a kind of protective warning spirit, a gloomy guardian angel that attempts to drive debates over women's representation and emancipation into a state of perpetual self-reflection in private and public spheres beyond the text. Whether it's the failure of the masculine narrator at the end of *Qui se souvient de la mer* to find his wife and end his quest for discursive mastery, or the cyclical narratives composed of competing nuggets of progressive and problematic discourse and action that Kateb's work generates, or the maintenance of traditionalist misogyny in the crucible of revolution that Djebar's *Les Enfants du nouveau monde* stands for, or Mammeri's repeating evocations of masculine epistemic blindness or indeed, whether one looks at Feraoun's illumination of a breakdown in communication between the scribe and his feminine object, the writers of the period produce formally innovative texts that embody both the necessity for a continual reassessment of social praxis and the limitations imposed on its feminine agents, and a rejection of complacency, of phallic certainty in representation in a postcolonial domain.

Though the writers whose works this book treats did not subscribe to an artistic manifesto, their shared reflexivity, their unique tendency to problematise notions of representation, invites a particular, quasi-melancholic perspective on pre and post-independence politics. Their evocations of Algerian femininity and of others' evocations of Algerian femininity stand in stark contrast to the unitary political projects of post-independence Algeria, their capacity to unpick fantasies of representative mastery contrasting with subsequent attempts to rigorously define identity through linguistic policy and nationalist identity politics. Indeed, at their core, the works of my corpus, despite generous helpings of literary brilliance and audacity, incorporate a stance of humility in the face of representation, in their attempts to create and describe subjects, in particular women, whose being had long been and indeed continues to be subject to definition by a socio-symbolic order predicated on a principle of gender inequality.

As such, it is my belief that they represent important contributions both to humanity's literary heritage and to our attempts to conceive of a productive and progressive communal *mode de vie*.

2 Kateb Yacine – Nedjma as Woman

At a 2014 workshop held in Oxford and entitled "Rethinking the Political through Intercultural Aesthetics" acclaimed Algerian author Salim Bachi, most famous for his oneiric novel *Le Chien d'Ulysse* (2001), affirmed the preeminence of the œuvre of Kateb Yacine in the literary history of Algeria and alluded to its continuing influence on Algeria's literary field, remarking that "il est vrai qu'il pèse toujours un peu lourd sur la littérature algérienne". Similarly, Kateb's *Cycle de Nedjma*, as circumscribed by critics like Ismail Abdoun and Christiane Achour, represents for this, a study of the representation of Algerian women in francophone texts of the late-colonial period, an unavoidable literary landmark whose enduring reputation as a container for both the Algerian national novel (*Nedjma*) and for the most notable literary sites relating to mythical frameworks of Algerian femininity, ensures its positioning at the commencement of this study.[54] This is not to say that one should treat its texts with a misplaced reverence for their canonical status but is rather to suggest that their reputation denotes an influence in reception that accords a privileged status in a study of the establishment and subversion of representative articulations of femininity. Moreover, the texts' complexity, richness and perspicacity demand a multifaceted analysis whose potential for reapplication to other literary sites in their historical context will be manifest.

The object of Kateb's *Cycle* – Nedjma in her many guises – is a singularly intricate puzzle, a protagonist in whom innumerable significations can be read. Kateb's texts can be seen to encode her with resonant symbolism that continually invites interpretation and subsequent incorporation into an understanding of women's meaning and representation, as perceived at the time of their creation. Furthermore, beyond the myriad symbolic facets of their chief female protagonist, the works allude to socio-symbolic and psychic structures upon which conceptions of women are contingent, both in the specific historical moment of late-colonial Algeria and in a more fundamental, universal sense.

Although, as this chapter will later investigate, the *Cycle de Nedjma* can be argued to evince signs of implication in processes of objectification and essentialisation – Nedjma is famously for the most part, especially in her eponymous novel, a silent, singular representative – I argue that the texts clearly demonstrate an awareness of these types of reductive procedure that is key to their exculpation and their genius. The pitfalls of representation, the potential for literary and discursive forms to deny agency and propound myth, are highlighted,

---

[54] The *Cycle de Nedjma* is agreed to comprise *Nedjma* (1956), *Le Cercle des représailles* (1959), *Le Polygone étoilé* (1966) along with fragments collated in *L'Œuvre en fragments* (1986).

often through a representation of masculine subjectivity that establishes the coordinates in which such missteps are born. The reader is encouraged to examine the psychic bearings and historical and universal structures behind pernicious masculinist representation, and thus to perform readings which benefit from an appreciation of the sociological and psychoanalytical structures and notions of thinkers such as Pierre Bourdieu and Jacques Lacan.

Furthermore, Kateb's texts undermine attempts to embrace totalising and therefore objectifying representation with a form that radically opposes the teleology and, in the words of Charles Bonn, "l'endoctrinement" that the Western Romanesque style can embody.[55] Instead, while maintaining a perspective on a contemporary actuality of women's representation and the potential for this to change, Kateb's texts open literary spaces which invite conceptual expansion and the formulation of epistemological structures that might support feminine emancipation.

This chapter will thus, while maintaining an appropriately critical approach towards those aspects of the texts that might undermine their feminist credentials, seek to demonstrate the "pouvoir libérateur" of Kateb's *Cycle de Nedjma*, of its poetic inscription of Algerian womanhood through its chief female protagonist, Nedjma.[56] Simultaneously, however, Kateb's opposition to a totalising narrative form will be read as a function of a form of productive "pessimism" that will be seen to characterise much of my corpus. In producing literary spaces that reject a fixity of meaning or telos, Kateb will be shown to generate sites of conflictual significance which confront the reader with the possibility of a failure of emancipatory reconceptualization and the necessity to continue signifying processes which might subvert women's symbolic determination into a post-colonial future.

In contrast to other chapters where a greater separation will be maintained between texts, here Kateb's work, namely the *Cycle de Nedjma*, will be considered as a singular literary body comprised of interdependent texts, approaching them thematically while appreciating the importance of their chronology, including, for example, the fact that *Le Polygone étoilé* (1966) was published at a point beyond the timeframe of this study, though based on text produced in the late-

---

[55] See pages 20–22 in *Kateb Yacine: Nedjma*. Paris: PUF 1990, for Bonn's description of the problems of the "tradition romanesque" especially with regards to descriptions of colonial sites.
[56] See Kateb's comments on the "pouvoir libérateur" of poetry on page 47 of *Le Poète comme un boxeur: Entretiens 1958–1989*. Paris: Éditions du Seuil 1994.

colonial period.⁵⁷ In this way the chapter will follow Kateb's own conception of his work:

> Je crois bien que je suis l'homme d'un seul livre [...] À l'origine, c'était un poème qui s'est transformé en romans et en pièces de théâtre, mais c'est toujours la même œuvre que je laisserai comme je l'ai commencée [...]⁵⁸

Moreover, exceeding the purely novelistic material of the other chapters of this monograph, the *Cycle de Nedjma* will be seen to incorporate poetic and theatrical forms that augment Kateb's representational project, illuminating in unique fashion literature's capacity to display and negotiate the difficulties of *Vertretung* representation highlighted in my introduction.

2.1 Painful Beginnings

Kateb was born on the 6th August 1929 in Constantine, Algeria, where he was raised by his father, an *oukil judiciaire*⁵⁹ well read in both French literature and Quranic verse, and by his mother, whom Kateb regularly cites as being the generative force behind his literary persuasion, stating for example that "[e]lle était à elle seule un théâtre".⁶⁰ At twelve he entered the Collège de Sétif as a boarding pupil and it was his subsequent exclusion from this school due to his involvement in the demonstrations of the 8th May 1945 that led to his meeting the girl who is cited as being the worldly model for the literary Nedjma. Charles Bonn tells us that "[i]l s'agit d'une cousine plus âgée et mariée, fille d'une juive constantinoise convertie à l'islam, que son père lui donne comme correspondante alors qu'exclu du collège de Sétif il est désormais inscrit au lycée de Bône".⁶¹ Kateb was arrested and tortured for his involvement at Sétif, where the French gendarmerie shot a number of protestors, having attempted to remove banners expressing nationalist and anti-colonial sentiment, and the importance of this event in Kateb's formation as a writer and as a man is evi-

---

57 *Le Polygone étoilé* was formed through a creative remolding of fragments excluded from the original text of *Nedjma*.
58 See the back cover of Anne-Yvonne Julien/Colette Camelin/François-Jean Authier (eds.): *Kateb Yacine et l'étoilement de l'œuvre*. Rennes: Presses Universitaires de Rennes 2010.
59 A type of legal defence counsel.
60 Jean Déjeux: *Littérature maghrébine de langue française*. Sherbrooke: Naâman 1978, p. 211.
61 Charles Bonn: *Kateb Yacine: Nedjma*, p. 13.

denced by frequent references to it throughout his work.[62] In *Nedjma*, the involvement and imprisonment of Lakhdar and Mustapha is represented in detail, including Mustapha's illegal penal mistreatment, *Le Cadavre encerclé*, the first play in the famous collection *Le Cercle des représailles*, relates to Algerian suffering at the event from its opening scene, depicting a severely injured Lakhdar declaring: "Ici est la rue des Vandales. C'est une rue d'Alger ou de Constantine, de Sétif ou de Guelma [...]", and Kateb's poetry contains numerous allusions to and direct invocations of the 8th May.[63]

This traumatic historical event can be seen to coincide affectively with another site of trauma, albeit of a less grave order, that of Kateb's subsequent estrangement from his cousin. In the poem *Keblout et Nedjma*, one notes, for example, the transposal of emotional response from one site to the other as in a plaintive text, filled with expressions of anguish at his failed love: "Nous étions deux à sangloter // Sous la pluie d'automne // Je ne pouvais fuir // Tu ne pouvais me suivre", Kateb writes: "Et mon dard à sa gorge // M'emplit d'ivresse au sortir de la prison // J'apportais *l'ardeur des Sétifiens...*"[64] One can thus appreciate an unusually intense affective importance accorded to the split by the author and the yoking of the two moments as nuclei in his work. Kateb affirms his personal turmoil in an interview of 1967 in *Jeune Afrique*, stating with regards to his state of mind whilst writing the *Soliloques* of 1946: "Je suis amoureux de Nedjma. Nedjma est mariée, ça ne colle pas, je fous le camp après avoir imprimé ma première plaquette de vers [...]".[65] Indeed, though Nedjma is often to be perceived as a composite, ephemeral and thus irreal figure, it should be born in mind that she has an origin in Kateb's lived experience through a connection defined by its severance and by its proximity to the site of trauma that the demonstrations and aftermath of Sétif represented. The consequences for her representation are readily discernable in Kateb's early poetry.

In Jacqueline Arnaud's collection of Kateb's literary fragments, *L'Œuvre en Fragments*, she brings to light a previously unpublished poem entitled 'Loin de Nedjma', that she believes closely predates 'Nedjma ou le poème ou le couteau', a work that, according to Arnaud, Kateb saw as being "comme la matrice

---

[62] In the months that followed the initial demonstration, "perhaps as many as 15,000 Muslims died in violence which spread to several towns in the Constantine region". Martin Stone: *The Agony of Algeria*. London: C. Hurst & Co., 1997, p. 35.
[63] Kateb Yacine: *Le Cercle des représailles*. Paris: Éditions du Seuil 1959, p. 15
[64] Jacqueline Arnaud (ed.)/Kateb Yacine: *L'Œuvre en fragments*. Paris: Actes Sud 1986, p. 83.
[65] Kateb Yacine: (Interview) Les Intellectuels, la révolution et le pouvoir. In: *Jeune Afrique* (26th March 1976), p. 28.

de son œuvre".⁶⁶ These two early works emphasise the significance of loss, of an order of division and dispossession that came to define Kateb's relationship with the real Nedjma and that can be interpreted as informing the subsequent production of the literary figure. Kateb writes in 'Loin de Nedjma':

> Nedjma si je t'ai bue
> Tu fermentais
> C'est une excuse
> Maintenant
> Je suis esclave⁶⁷

He continues:

> Le temps se trouble
> Et j'erre
> Autour du centre
> Par Nedjma renié⁶⁸

And, as the poem continues, through a more elegiac tone characterised by the use of the 1st person plural pronoun and reference to the narrator and Nedjma as "amants", we see glimpses of a resentment and a frustration that come to be connected with their separation. Kateb's poetic subject seethes:

> Aussi
> Suis-je
> Violent avec les fleurs
> Et doux avec les vaches
> J'aboie sans perfidie
> Contre des voleurs amis⁶⁹
>
> Or
> Vivant
> De rancune
> De mes poings
> Sur ma bouche⁷⁰

This sense of frustration is repeated in 'Nedjma ou le poème ou le couteau' where one detects a logical movement that assigns to Nedjma a burden of culpability.

---

66 Jacqueline Arnaud (ed.)/Kateb Yacine: *L'Œuvre en fragments*, p. 434.
67 Ibid, p. 53.
68 Ibid, p. 56.
69 Ibid, p. 59.
70 Ibid, p. 65.

While Kateb/the narrator agonises: "j'ai beau jeter ton coeur il me revient décomposé";[71] "Coupez mes rêves tels des serpents",[72] Nedjma smiles and sleeps: "Nedjma fit un sourire trempa les fruits dans sa poitrine";[73] "Nedjma dormait comme un navire".[74] Finally, the poetic subject pleads: "ne sois pas inhumaine !"[75]

Ali Merad writes that "[i]l ne serait pas exagéré de dire que Kateb a surtout voulu nous parler de lui-même: du tout jeune enfant qu'il fut, puis du potache, enfin de l'adolescent jeté précocement à la rue [...]" and Assia Djebar recounts in *Le Blanc de l'Algérie* how Nedjma accompanied him until death, and how after his passing she remained in physical proximity:[76]

> [D]ans cet ultime voyage de retour, une femme veillait et descendit avec le corps : c'était la cousine qui, jeune fille, prêta sa beauté et son aura à l'héroïne de Kateb Yacine, la Nedjma bien réelle que le poète aima adolescent, lui qui ne fut jamais vraiment guéri de ce premier amour.[77]

Though of course one should be wary of conflating author and poetic narrator, his own comments on his work as well as those of friends and critics suggest that Kateb's œuvre, in particular his early poetry, can be seen as profoundly subjective and autobiographical. The figure of Nedjma retains, despite her potential to be read as a metaphorical marker for the Algerian woman, a remnant of the real. Due to the couching of his relationship in the pain of separation, this remainder is perhaps most evident in moments where Kateb, or the narrator, expresses grief or frustration at the wounding caused by the separation, or at Nedjma's non-espousal of his wish to remain together. Kateb's anguish, his refusal to conceal the affective wound with which Nedjma has afflicted him holds importance as it forms a textual acknowledgement of her representation's predication on a male standpoint while it begins to allow his work to resist her potentially pernicious mythologisation wherein she is accorded a symbolic burden, becoming merely a canvas for attributes. As the next section will investigate, the figure of Nedjma, especially in *Nedjma* and *Le Polygone étoilé*, holds a symbolic weight that, as has been intimated by critics like Winifred Woodhull, might threaten to make of her the embodiment of a circumscribed class, a treasure-house of fem-

---

71 Ibid, p. 70.
72 Ibid, p. 72.
73 Ibid, p. 72.
74 Ibid, p. 72.
75 Ibid, p. 72.
76 Ali Merad: Nedjma (review). In: *IBLA* No. 76 (1956), p. 438.
77 Assia Djebar: *Le Blanc de L'Algérie*. Paris: Albin Michel 1995, p. 177.

inine meaning. Perversely then, perhaps I would argue that the moments in Kateb's work where Nedjma is an expression of Kateb's subjectivity, of his affective response, allow for a degree of individuation to be maintained that allocates Nedjma a singular agency, extant beyond the text, and can thus be cited as the beginning of Kateb's works' capacity to undermine the mythical constructs that it beautifully erects. For, firstly, his affective response forms an acknowledgment that a real singular agency is the generative force behind its own inscription. Kateb writes the literary Nedjma, a sometimes plural, contradictory figure, in part because of a contact with the real Nedjma, a specific individual referent related in part through traumatic psychic residue that can be read in moments of distress within the texts. And secondly, as a real Nedjma is related through her traumatic inscription, Kateb's work implicitly acknowledges the indomitable nature of the object of representation for the author, she remains beyond the text while her presence is inferred through Kateb's subjective scars.

In the plays *Le Cadavre encerclé* and *Les Ancêtres redoublent de férocité*, the longest in the collection known as *Le Cercle des représailles*, whose oneiric narratives re-examine the colonial and gendered conflicts of Kateb's novels and poetry, numerous interactions can also be seen to be marked by the rupture that Kateb experienced. In the former it is the character of Lakhdar who embodies Kateb's position relative to Nedjma, stating for example that "[c]omme un récif, ton sein me paralyse. Je nage à peine, par brasses retenues, vers le sommeil de la grotte. Et maintenant je viens te rendre l'âme."[78] In the latter it is the Vautour, into which Lakhdar has metamorphosed, whose laments regarding Nedjma, in the guise of *la femme sauvage*, bare the trace of his separation: "Ce cœur d'acier qui se détraque, j'en ai perdu la clé // Aux mains de cette magicienne qui vous exhorte".[79]

However, though one should recognise the importance of a singular agent, a referent for the text, being established through an underpinning in affect, one should not leave aside a critical analysis of the representations generated as a result. Indeed, though later sections will focus on Kateb's critical depictions of frustrated desire, rivalry and of the interdependence of male subjectivity, here one should acknowledge that Kateb's texts perhaps do not completely escape limiting, potentially sexist depictions engendered by the unconscious association of Nedjma with emotional pain.

Many critics have noted the strong influence that the works of Flaubert have had on Kateb and the direct references to *Salammbô* which abound in his work,

---

[78] Kateb Yacine: *Le Cercle des représailles*, p. 29.
[79] Ibid, p. 134.

most notably in *Nedjma*. However, Denise Brahimi, in her article 'Nedjma, Complexités du Personnage' argues that "il y a aussi l'équivalent de la jeune Emma Bovary dans la portrait de Nedjma la jeune bourgeoise de Beauséjour, dont les traits de bovarysme ne sont pas difficiles à déceler [...]".[80] She goes on to link Nedjma, in her representation, to the figure of the *garce*, of the bourgeois seductress who plays perversely with her male lovers. It is my contention that one could read the presence of this template of the *garce* as a restaging of Kateb's relationship with the real Nedjma. Indeed, Louis Tremaine, in his article 'The absence of Itinerary in Kateb Yacine's Nedjma' which studies Nedjma's resistance to idealisation, articulates a view of Nedjma's representation that supports the presence of this type. He highlights how in *Nedjma*, she treats Mustapha, one of the four masculine protagonists whose quests the book presents – the others being Lakhdar, Mourad and Rachid – somewhat haughtily, "*non seulement comme un commissionnaire, mais comme un mécréant, à qui l'on signifie qu'on n'a rien de commun avec lui, évitant de lui parler dans la langue maternelle*" and how Rachid complains that she is "l'adversité faite femme", while Mustapha writes of her "n'ayant que ses jeux taciturnes, son goût de l'ombre et des rêves jaloux ".[81] Similarly, Brahimi points to Nedjma's infidelity to her husband and her "désir de séduire, d'avoir des amants, rêves ou rêveries romanesques [...]" and writes that "on sent flotter dans le roman une sorte d'accusation latente selon laquelle Nedjma aurait plus ou moins causé la perte des quatre personnages principaux".[82] However, though I find Brahimi's intertextual argument interesting and cannot deny the impact of Nedjma's unpredictable nature on the four protagonists, I should make three points that would undermine the implication that Nedjma's similarities to Emma, to the figure of the *garce*, constitute a defining, sexist/masculinist aspect of her representation:

First, her position as "notre perte, la mauvaise étoile de notre clan", as an unfathomable seductress, is established by protagonists to whom Kateb assigns problematic traits, her amorous motivations are not criticised by an omniscient, unproblematic authorial voice.[83] Second, on one of the very few occasions in the novel where we are invited to penetrate Nedjma's thoughts, her pathetic distress at her married situation is outlined, legitimating her desire to experience extramarital love: "*Ils m'ont isolée pour mieux me vaincre, isolée en me mariant [...]*".[84]

---

80 Denise Brahimi: Nedjma, complexités du personnage. In: Anne-Yvonne Julien/Colette Camelin/François-Jean Authier (eds.): *Kateb Yacine et l'étoilement de l'œuvre*, p. 39.
81 Kateb Yacine: *Nedjma*. Paris: Éditions du Seuil 1956, p. 79 (Kateb's emphasis), 191, 199.
82 Denise Brahimi: Nedjma, complexités du personnage, p. 39, 35–36.
83 Kateb Yacine: *Nedjma*, p. 202.
84 Ibid, p 74.

Third, I would argue again that the sense of an "accusation latente" contained within a depiction of her amorous situation (her marriage and her position as the object of affection of frustrated others) can be considered a partial reflection of an individual agency that once wounded the author. The *Cycle de Nedjma* conveys that there is a part of Nedjma, and by extension of Algerian women more generally, that remains extrinsic to the amalgam of mythical, historical and sociological signifiers that she/they can be argued to incorporate. Though, as we shall now explore, Nedjma is a central, composite protagonist whose status may therefore be elevated to universality, Kateb's texts ensure that her representation does not efface the presence of an individual ontology that drives their attempts at an articulation of femininity in their bearing of traumatic affective scarring.

2.2 Mythical Interpretations

Jacqueline Arnaud in her doctoral thesis, *Recherches sur la littérature maghrébine de langue française: le cas de Kateb Yacine* famously argues in her section on *Nedjma* that "Nedjma n'est plus une femme mais un mythe de la femme".[85] Though, as the previous section in part demonstrates, I would argue that Arnaud's statement cannot be uniformly applied to the entirety of our corpus, it does make clear the preeminent position of myth in the construction of Nedjma throughout the *Cycle*. An exploration of her mythical composition is indeed integral to any study of Nedjma's role in the texts and is thus key for this study of the representation of Algerian women. Of course, Nedjma's mythical framework comprises pillars borrowed from a collective memory; we read a reinscription of numerous established mythologies of femininity, interpreting both milieu-specific narratives and imaginaries and mythologies of non-Algerian origin. At the same time, however, new mythical content is generated, Kateb's texts contribute fresh narratives for interpretation that broaden the mythical potential of Nedjma and of the Algerian woman she represents. Furthermore, the formal panache of Kateb's reinscriptions is such that new spaces within the writing of gender identity are opened for exploration. In their combination, juxtaposition, undermining and reworking, a focus on myth is produced that works to dismantle conceptions of mythical significations as fixed.

---

[85] Jacqueline Arnaud: *Recherches sur la littérature maghrébine de langue française: le cas de Kateb Yacine*. Université de Paris III (Doctoral Thesis) 1978, p. 722.

To begin, it will be useful to outline some of the mythological strands that are woven together and to discuss their significance as Kateb's writings make use of their symbolic content. One might first argue that the incorporation of myths of femininity is necessarily problematic because of the reproduction of essentialising narratives that it often implies.[86] Moreover, as Nedjma's position as a feminine representative is so dominant, with very few other women to challenge her presence, the essentialising potential of these established narratives is further heightened. However it is my argument, as will be noted in subsequent chapters, that it is the manipulation of literary form as it produces the inscription of symbolic content that truly dictates whether a text reinforces or questions the essentialising potential of myth. Notwithstanding, one can identify areas of representation that invoke narratives which, in themselves, can be seen as problematic, even pernicious.

Following the first description of the villa Nedjma in *Nedjma*, Mustapha, who is one of the novel's four central masculine protagonists and who is presented as being enraptured by "l'apparition" that precedes and represents Nedjma's description in the narrative, thinks: "*Pays de mendiants et de viveurs, patrie des envahisseurs de tout acabit... pays de cagoulards et de femmes fatales* [...]".[87] Immediately after this description that establishes the fundamentals of Mustapha's socio-topographical imaginary, we receive our first direct description of Nedjma, who is depicted as follows:

> Étoffe et chair fraîchement lavées, Nedjma est nue dans sa robe ; elle secoue son écrasante chevelure fauve, ouvre et referme la fenêtre [...][88]

Thus, from our first novelistic meeting with Kateb's chief female protagonist, a connection is forged between her and the literary myth of the *femme fatale*. Loubna Benhaimi argues that this designation was first employed by Théophile Gautier in 1872 in his *Guide de l'amateur au musée du Louvre*, regarding Bernardino Luini's painting *Salomè con la testa del Battista* and that "pour l'homme du XIXe siècle finissant, elle [woman] fut essentiellement présente sous les traits de la femme fatale et ce sont les mythes représentant des femmes dangereuses qui ont retenu notre attention".[89] Indeed, though there is not space here to detail the

---

[86] One only has to think of Simone de Beauvoir's famous deconstruction of masculinist myths in her section "Mythes" in *Le Deuxième sexe 1*. Paris: Gallimard 1986.
[87] Kateb Yacine: *Nedjma*, p. 73–74 (emphasis in bold added).
[88] Ibid, p. 74.
[89] Loubna Benhaimi: Le Mythe de la femme fatale dans Nedjma de Kateb Yacine. In: *Synergies Algérie* No. 13 (2011), p. 130.

evolution of the figure of the *femme fatale* throughout history, it should be said that her conceptual origins almost certainly predate the 19th Century. Mireille Dottin-Orsini goes so far as to equate the biblical Eve with "la cocotte contemporaine" to demonstrate the duration of the myth.[90] References to *la femme fatale* and to figures who might represent this type abound throughout Kateb's texts, with perhaps the most readily noticeable literary reference being that of Flaubert's Salammbô.[91] In *Nedjma*, for example, Rachid writes of his relationship with the eponymous object of his desire:

> [J]e devais revivre pour une Salammbô de ma lignée l'obscur martyrologe; il me fallait tenter toujours la même partie trop de fois perdue, afin d'assumer la fin du désastre, de perdre ma Salammbô [...][92]

Moreover, while Denise Brahimi associates Nedjma with Antinéa, the dangerous seductress of Pierre Benoit's *L'Atlantide*, Khedidja Khelladi sees in her a panoply of referents who might represent the figure of *la femme fatale*, including Balkis, Cleopatra and Bettina, whilst focusing on the figure of Mélusine and arguing that "les correspondances sont encore plus explicites avec la poésie surréaliste où la place de la femme est envoûtante, magique, comme celle de Nedjma qui est parfois sorcière, maîtrisant le pouvoir de ses 'sortilèges'".[93]

Beyond those mythical referents that can be seen to evoke potentially masculinist narratives of the treacherous inscrutability of feminine desire and magic, many other figures of differing significance can be seen to invest Nedjma. For example, in focusing on the scene in *Nedjma* of the eponymous protagonist bathing in the Nadhor, the tribal homeland, and Rachid's subsequent interior monologue, Mireille Calle-Gruber sees numerous charged referents implicated in the scene, writing that "Nedjma, c'est Vénus naissant de l'écume de la mer et du sperme de Zeus et c'est Diane non moins dont le bain sous la lune est interdit

---

90 Mireille Dottin-Orsini: Femme Fatale. In: Pierre Brunel (ed.): *Dictionnaire des mythes littéraires*. Monaco: Éditions du Rocher 1988, p. 277.
91 In Flaubert's novel, the eponymous Carthaginian female protagonist represents an inaccessible object of obsession and the ruin of the character Matho, who takes the sacred veil of Carthage, prompting Salammbô to attempt to steal it back.
92 Kateb Yacine: *Nedjma*, p. 188.
93 Khedidja Khelladi: Archétypes et paradigmes littéraires dans l'œuvre de Kateb Yacine. In: Anne-Yvonne Julien/Colette Camelin/François-Jean Authier (eds.): *Kateb Yacine et l'étoilement de l'œuvre*, p. 176.

à tout regard".⁹⁴ Whether specific mythic referents or mythical types, one could go on to list a myriad of figures whose defining characteristics and attending narratives compound the principle problem associated with their mythical nature: the accordance of essential, masculinist representative characteristics, produced in acts of non-representative *Vertretung* representation. Indeed, Calle-Gruber goes so far as to state that "Nedjma est la construction la plus extraordinaire des phantasmes masculins et machistes à l'égard de 'la femme'".⁹⁵

However, she also then argues that this construction is relentlessly exposed to what she terms the "puissances inconnues de la littérature".⁹⁶ Concordantly, it is precisely the argument of this chapter that Kateb's texts work to resist allowing their mythical content to dominate, to retain mastery over the representation of Nedjma and, by implication, the worldly referent of the Algerian woman. If we turn to Kateb's application of mythical content that springs from a North African literary tradition, we can begin to explore the manners in which his texts undermine the essentialising potential of myth as a part of authorial representation and contribute to a production of a radically non-limiting order of representation.

One of the key terms used to describe Nedjma throughout the texts is "ogresse". In *Nedjma,* she is described as "l'ogresse au sang obscur comme celui du nègre qui tua Si Mokhtar, l'ogresse qui mourut de faim après avoir mangé ses trois frères [...]".⁹⁷ In *Le Vautour*, the final part of *Le Cercle des représailles*, the Vautour asks:

> Mais puis-je
> M'empêcher
> De fumer sous les dents
> D'une si pure ogresse
> Et vierge
> Par surcroît ?"⁹⁸

Kateb's second poetic novel, *Le Polygone étoilé*, which was formed in part from reworkings of material excluded from *Nedjma*, also contains a key passage which deploys the term as we read that "[t]outes les chimères qui prennent le

---

94 Mireille Calle-Gruber: Comment en toucher un mot? La Voix féminine de Kateb Yacine ou le pari de la littérature, une lecture de Nedjma. In: Anne-Yvonne Julien/Colette Camelin/François-Jean Authier(eds.): *Kateb Yacine et l'étoilement de l'œuvre, p. 66*.
95 Ibid, p. 61.
96 Ibid, p. 61.
97 Kateb Yacine: *Nedjma*, p. 192–193.
98 Kateb Yacine: *Le Cercle des représailles*, p. 163.

masque ardent de Moutt, l'ange de mort subit, sont des ogresses pour lesquelles dépecer un babouin vivant n'est guère plus cruel que de faire craquer entre ses dents une crevette».[99] The recurring figure of the ogress takes as its model the *teryel*, battled in Kabyle mythology by the hero Mcquides, or M'Quidech, as Mouloud Feraoun transcribes in *Le Fils du pauvre*.[100] Camille Lacoste-Dujardin has highlighted the potential for the ogress figure to be read as a scapegoat of feminine defiance to social order that must be expelled for the good of the community.[101] Kateb's inscription of his "ogresse", however, can be seen to invite associations with uncontrollable and indomitable violence, contrasting with both her need to be quelled in the original mythology and the seductive allure implicit in the *femme fatale* model. Jane Hiddleston writes that "[h]er violence and her wildness [...] are not merely manifestations of a certain mystique, but emerge as perplexing hints at a form of feminine desire that will continue, in its voraciousness rather than its passivity, to resist mastery, explanation, and control.[102] As ogress, Nedjma refuses to be incorporated into the self-serving narratives that misogynistic myths deploy. Of course, one must be careful of embracing any signifier that could be interpreted as rendering Nedjma and, by implication, Algerian women more generally, inscrutable or profoundly "other". Indeed, one might conceive of an uncontrollable violence that points to a peculiarly feminine and inexplicable desire as potentially detrimental, for though her ogress characteristics may indicate a non-conformity to the expectations of masculine desire, they could also be determined to justify conceptual exclusion from "normal" socio-sexual activity, therefore reinforcing masculine hegemony.[103]

It is important, therefore, that in its redeployment, the ogress myth be textually challenged and Kateb's inscription does this repeatedly. First, if we look again at the above citations, it is of note that though an authorial voice establishes Nedjma as ogress in *Nedjma*, it does so in a key passage about Nedjma's parentage which, through a particularly and deliberately obtuse rendering of the amorous competition for Nedjma's mother, alludes to the predication of her consumption of her three "brothers" on pernicious masculinist competitive structures. Moreover, the two other citations are also taken from scenes where what

---

99 Kateb Yacine: *Le Polygone étoilé*, p. 77.
100 Mouloud Feraoun: *Le Fils du pauvre*. Paris: Points 1995, p. 55.
101 Camille Lacoste-Dujardin: *Le Conte Kabyle: étude ethnologique*. Paris: Maspero 1970, p. 95 – 107.
102 Jane Hiddleston: That Obscure Object of Desire: France, Algeria, and the Circumscription of the Feminine in Kateb Yacine's *Nedjma*. In: *French Forum* Vol. 38, No. 3 (2013), p. 137.
103 See Shoshana Felman: *What Does a Woman Want?* Baltimore: Johns Hopkins University Press 1993 for more on feminine desire and conceptions of it as inscrutable.

is at stake are masculine preoccupations. The first of these demonstrates the potential for the ogress signifier to stem from anger, attaching itself to the conception of the *garce* previously discussed, as Lakhdar in the form of the Vautour curses the violence of his lover, whilst the second comes after a scene which one is compelled to read as a Freudian male nightmare, a point of fantasmatic panic conveying castration anxiety. Moutt, as Nedjma's feminine substitute in this scene, is said to be "intriguée par le ver solitaire qui sort parfois sa tête" who would not wish to "attirer ver lui, méchant ténia de race borgne, la frénétique volaille qui perce à coups de bec [...]".[104] Thus while Nedjma is established as the ogress who, in Hiddleston's words "resist[s] mastery, explanation and control", her representation as such is problematised within the texts themselves.

Moreover, Charles Bonn, in reference to this scene, highlights the importance of parody, which can be argued to carry out a similar function to that which he ascribes to the profusion of signifying figures, as it "récuse [...] les séparations trop faciles d'avec l'Autre qu'opère le discours officiel" by undermining the solemnity of the description of difference between masculine self and feminine Other.[105] Bonn sees Moutt as an obscene parody of la Kahina, the legendary Amazigh heroine with whom Nedjma is also associated. This parodying, this inclusion of an absurd double, serves to radically undermine la Kahina's mythic role and Nedjma's embodiment of it, preventing her representation from being subsumed into a totalised figure, established by a *discours officiel*.

Indeed, there is also a direct parodic link detectable between Moutt and Nedjma herself owing to a clear parallelism between the respective scenes that introduce them: In both cases it is the character's domain that is first established as where once we were introduced to our chief female protagonist through la villa Nedjma, we now read about Moutt initially through her château; in both cases we are introduced to a home elevated in its position relative to arriving visitors: "Elle avait un château suspendu à un câble élevant ses amants [...]",[106] where in *Nedjma* we meet a rich description of the grounds surrounding the property, in *Le Polygone*, we are greeted with "un jardin dévasté par la flamme verte".[107]

The parodying of this scene is also important when one considers how Kateb constructs a mythical narrative that is singular to Nedjma. For while Kateb redeploys and rewrites certain myths, combining them with references to more established mythical content, he also accords Nedjma her own narrative that one can

---

[104] Kateb Yacine: *Le Polygone étoilé*, p. 76.
[105] Charles Bonn: *Kateb Yacine: Nedjma*, p. 102.
[106] Kateb Yacine: *Le Polygone étoilé*, p. 75.
[107] Ibid, p. 75.

conceive of as mythical as it presents an intensity of symbolism for both national and feminine identity and is staged in a particular historical moment whilst retaining a kind of eternal resonance. In *Nedjma* we can identify different sites in a particular mythical narrative, beginning with her early years:

> Incontestablement la fatalité de Nedjma provenait de l'atmosphère dont elle fut entourée petite fille, alors que s'allumaient les jeux déjà ravageurs de la vestale sacrifiée en ses plus rares parures.[108]

From her particular upbringing, to her seclusion in the la villa Nedjma, to her progression to the Nadhor, *Nedjma* provides mythical stages for its feminine protagonist to play out her own myth. We might conceive of these different scenes as analogous to the symbolic set-pieces that play a foundational role in religious myth. One thinks perhaps of the New Testament with the geographical/situational fixing of the sermon on the mount, the rejection of money lending in the Temple, and the last supper, as examples of the central importance of geographical locality to myth.

Added to this, Nedjma is given particular signifiers that establish her new mythical status with perhaps the most important mythical marker being contained in the title of Kateb's second poetic novel, *Le Polygone étoilé*.[109] Variations on an astral theme abound throughout the texts of the *Cycle de Nedjma*, with Nedjma, of course, meaning "star" in Arabic. As with l'ogresse, one can detect a historical primary influence for the myth of the star. Woodhull in her article 'Rereading Nedjma' tells us that the name "evokes the modern "warriors" – Algerian immigrant workers – who in the 1930s formed the secular anti-colonial movement called the *Étoile Nord-Africaine*".[110] Her astral quality does therefore point to her implication in the politics of revolution and in the representation of a new Algerian state, a study of which will follow in a later section. However, whether as Rachid's "mauvaise étoile",[111] "l'étoile de sang jaillie du meurtre",[112] "la mauvaise étoile de notre clan",[113] Lakhdar's "étoile" in *Le Cercle des repré-*

---

[108] Kateb Yacine: *Nedjma*, p. 198.
[109] One might also argue for the equal importance of *la femme sauvage* in *Le Cercle des représailles*.
[110] Winifred Woodhull: Rereading "Nedjma": Feminist Scholarship and North African Women. In: *SubStance* Vol. 21, No. 3, Issue 69: Special Issue: Translations of the Orient: Writing the Maghreb (1992), p. 50.
[111] Kateb Yacine: *Nedjma*, p. 189.
[112] Ibid, p. 192.
[113] Ibid, p. 202.

sailles' *Le Cadavre encerclé*[114] or the "étoile de sang noir" mentioned in *Le Polygone*,[115] the signifier of the star in her myth most strongly represents plurality and chimeric indeterminacy in its myriad rays diffusing from a magmatic core. Just as "L'adversité faite femme – Nedjma l'Andalouse, la fille de la Française"[116] eschews identification with a singular geographical origin, her mythical make up is such that one is invited to pose the question, as Calle-Gruber does, "dans ce tissu touffu de relations indécidables, *où couper* pour qu'il y ait *le* sujet ?"[117] The flood of mythical references that rushes through the texts, both new and old, ensures that, though we are invited to consider their significations, Nedjma escapes over-identification with any of them. We are left with a fabric that is ripe for individual interpretation, allowing for a constant renovation of meaning through combination, criticism and even subversion and shattering. For, as has been shown above, Kateb's texts are prepared to undermine their mythical referents even while they constitute them as key signifiers. A delicious example of this comes in *Le Polygone*, where the chief symbol of Nedjma's very indeterminacy, l'étoile, is playfully and ironically redrawn, through Nedjma's own speech:

> 'Je t'offre mon corps en étoile de mer, mes yeux sombrés et le sel de ma langue', disait-elle.[118]

This section began by alluding to Arnaud's declaration that Nedjma comes to constitute "un mythe de la femme". Charles Bonn also shows his concern for the potential of Nedjma's "betweenness", a term that Woodhull employs,[119] to make of her merely a "chimère [...] figure double [qui] médiatise la quête d'identité des héros'.[120] Questions certainly remain to be answered regarding an evocation of Nedjma's agency and her reliance on masculine perspective, and these will be addressed in subsequent sections. However, while providing Nedjma with her own myth, her own narrative, Kateb produces cracks in the façade of fixed identity, assigning an indomitable profusion of meaning that undermines mythical narrative and refuses to articulate the creation of a manageable notion of womanhood, whether in line with a Fanonian "revolutionary" woman or other

---

114 Kateb Yacine: *Le Cercle des représailles*, p. 115.
115 Kateb Yacine: *Le Polygone étoilé*, p. 148.
116 Kateb Yacine: *Nedjma*, p. 191.
117 Mireille Calle-Gruber: Comment en toucher un mot?, p. 64.
118 Kateb Yacine: *Le Polygone étoilé*, p. 24.
119 Winifred Woodhull: Rereading "Nedjma", p. 52.
120 Charles Bonn: *Kateb Yacine: Nedjma*, p. 77.

traditional types.[121] Kateb's texts are constantly in the process of denying meaning, of destroying mythical monuments, even as they build them. This results in a realm of radical possibility for literary representation where the undermining of meaning lays the groundwork for its poetic inscription, developing symbolic possibility within an allusion to the male writer's representative deficit, his incapacity to fully articulate the coordinates of womanhood. And indeed the following sections will precisely investigate how Kateb's texts display the impact of a male subject position, of masculine perspective, on representations of Algerian women, principally Nedjma, within the text's fictional world.

2.3 Masculine Perspectives on the Feminine Image: Desiring Objects

Kateb's texts incorporate masculine perspectives, dominant in both textual space and narrative mastery, that force one to acknowledge their presence and consider their role in the representation of Nedjma and the conceptions of femininity for which she stands. Almost without exception, where Nedjma or one of her substitutes (la femme sauvage, Moutt etc.) is present, her ontology and symbolism is outlined by masculine others granted more space for notional self-identification, for the outlining of their own ontological contours.[122] Consequently, the *Cycle de Nedjma* invites us to inspect the nature of these perspectives, their psychic and historical grounding, and to interrogate their impact on the representation of Algerian women in literature and society.

To comment initially upon the historical and milieu-specific factors which the texts connect with problematic conceptualisations of women, Miriam Cooke in *Woman and the War Story*, though perhaps in rather sweeping terms, impresses upon her readers the importance of the change in women's roles and status during the revolutionary period for their representation. She writes in reference to the male writers of the period that "[t]hey infused all women's actions and their temporary change in status with significance. They wrote not so

---

121 I surround the term "revolutionary" with quotation marks, here and elsewhere in my work, to imply an expanded significance that incorporates the social and subjective revolutions that accompanied military insurgency.
122 Charles Bonn writes in *Kateb Yacine: Nedjma*, p. 13, for example, "elle est dite, elle ne dit pas. Elle peut être lue dès lors au centre du roman comme une sorte de noyau vide". Indeed in the entirety of the novel I can identify only five separate pronouncements made by Nedjma herself, four aloud and one, to which I have previously referred in 2.1 Painful Beginnings, as an interior monologue.

much out of admiration as of dread. The reader senses the fear that women are gaining control and that the danger they pose to social order, their *Fitna* (an Arabic word that means both women's physical attraction and political unrest), is about to be unleashed".[123] Indeed, this concept of *fitna* is almost omnipresent in writings about prevalent perceptions of femininity and social cohesion in an Algerian context, in particular in commentaries on the socio-symbolic influence of certain interpretations of Islamic tradition.[124]

Within its socio-historical context, one can understand a fear that Nedjma generates amongst male protagonists as partly a product of an association of social change, uncontrollable progression, with a monadic conception of femininity as *fitna*. Cooke notes that in *Nedjma*, the male protagonists are indeed aware of her belonging to a new order of womanhood, linked closely to new and developing socio-political roles for women. She cites Mustapha's description of her wearing *"une ample cagoule de soie bleu pale, comme en portent depuis peu les Marocaines émancipées"*, his detailing of her teenage dream to escape Bône and acquire personal independence, and her description as the "amazone".[125]

One could list numerous citations demonstrating Nedjma's anxiogenic nature for her enraptured protagonists but a particularly useful description for this study comes from Mustapha who describes Nedjma as "stérile et fatale, femme de rien, ravageant dans la nuit passionnelle tout ce qui nous restait de sang, non pour le boire et nous libérer comme autant de flacons vides, non pour le boire à défaut de le verser, mais seulement pour le *troubler* [...]".[126] This description comes in a section of his *Carnet* in which one senses, in a highly emotive and poetic passage, an unbridled consternation generated by dramatic social change embodied by Nedjma:

> Il n'en reste qu'un éboulement au pied du vieux principe : mâle et femelle prêts à s'unir jusqu'au point du jour, mais c'est la débandade au lever de l'aurore [...][127]

Furthermore, in this passage concomitant allusions are also made to a will, generated in part by a particular historical transformation or perception thereof, to maintain control of an image, of a steady conception of womanhood in opposi-

---

[123] Miriam Cooke: *Women and the War Story*, p. 129.
[124] See, for example, Fatima Mernissi: *Women's Rebellion and Islamic Memory*. London: Zed Books 1996, or the works of Rachid Boutayeb or Winifred Woodhull.
[125] Kateb Yacine: *Nedjma*, p. 79 + 92 + 86.
[126] Ibid, p. 201 (emphasis added).
[127] Ibid, p. 199.

tion to *fitna*. Indeed, Kateb's texts display more generally, in the writing of the perspectives that convey Nedjma's ontology and symbolism, an emphasis on her functioning as object/image for mastery. A desire to contain, to take control of her outline is all-pervasive in the male protagonists' approaches to her.

Benhaimi, for example, has commented on the presence of Ekphrasis in *Nedjma* and femininity is often represented in Kateb's work in terms that frame it as a pre-established representation.[128] Nedjma is described as "ce tableau vivant",[129] Moutt and her "féminine armée" as "ce tableau"[130] while Rachid states of *le nègre* with regards to Nedjma that he was "ni même un esthète capable d'apprécier le tableau".[131] However, it is another citation from *Le Polygone* that alludes most intriguingly to the form of representation I wish to continue to address:

> On réduit l'être à un objet, et on le hisse hors de soi, vers une *mystérieuse possession* qui pourrait bien n'être qu'un songe.[132]

Coming in a long passage at the beginning of the poetic novel in which the narrator again laments a separation from Nedjma, stating that "je n'emporte pas *ton portrait*", the above citation indicates how Nedjma's description as a tableau, a portrait, alludes to a psychic preconstruction that can be connected with a will for mastery.[133] Though she is described at great length, many of her descriptions can be understood not as attempts to articulate her particular characteristics, to engage with her subjectivity, but rather as self-serving tableaux of aspects ascribed to her through the psyches of the protagonists. This nature of description thus emphasises both the incapacity and the lack of desire amongst the masculine agents of description to excavate the potentially troubling parameters of a feminine subjectivity that fascinates them. Indeed, though Nedjma is framed as an agent whose "griffe" leaves a mark, it is interesting how one may view her presence as evoking Lacanian conceptions of desire and its object causes as she serves as a catalytic shell, driving their quests as subjects.[134]

---

[128] Michèle Aquien and Georges Molinié write of Ekphrasis in *Dictionnaire de rhétorique et de poétique*. Paris: Le Livre de Poche 1996, p. 140: "une Ekphrasis est une description d'une œuvre d'art [...] cette représentation est donc à la fois elle-même un objet du monde, un thème à traiter, et un traitement artistique déjà opéré [...]".
[129] Kateb Yacine: *Nedjma*, p. 71.
[130] Kateb Yacine: *Le Polygone étoilé*, p. 75.
[131] Kateb Yacine: *Nedjma*, p. 147.
[132] Kateb Yacine: *Le Polygone étoilé*, p. 22 (emphasis added).
[133] Ibid, p. 26–27 (emphasis added).
[134] Kateb Yacine: *Le Cercle des représailles*, p. 30.

In Lacanian thought, the imaginary Phallus, the entity that the proto-subject sees as being the object cause of desire for the mother is splintered at castration, at the point where the child enters the Symbolic order forming objets petit a.[135] Lionel Bailly evokes the metaphor of "the mirror of the Snow Queen in the fairy tale, which breaks into a thousand pieces that lodge themselves in objects and people".[136] These fragments are the object cause of desire and are sought by the subject, driving endeavour. They are themselves, however, "un fantasme qui est en réalité le *soutien* du désir, ou un leurre".[137] They hold no fixed parameters and cannot thus be truly embodied by the desired subjects who bear them. Furthermore, they are products of the psyche of the desiring subject, with their own attendant symbolism, the signifiers that facilitate desire.

Throughout the texts, one notes many references to a hollowness that defines Nedjma, tallying with her description as the *Polygone étoilé* and the structure of her articulation through perspectives external to her own subjectivity. For example, in *Nedjma*, Lakhdar refers to her as "*la forme sensible, l'épine, la chair, le noyau, mais non pas l'âme, non pas l'unité vivante* [...]" and one sees in this an ignorance of Nedjma as a potential active subject, and a focus on what is desired within her, what constitutes Lakhdar's object of desire, his *objet petit a*.[138] Indeed, in Kateb's work and particularly in *Nedjma*, manifestations of masculine protagonists' psychic configurations in relation to Nedjma's desirability can be read as symptomatic of an obsessional form of desire.

Bruce Fink articulates the root of the obsessional mode by reference to the classical Freudian example of the infant's initial separation from the mother and the generation of objects of desire:

> In the obsessive's fantasy (and I shall refer to the obsessive here as "he", since the majority of obsessives are male), separation is overcome or made up for as the subject constitutes himself in relation to the breast, which functions as the cause of his desire; unity or wholeness is restored to the subject by addition of the object. But the obsessive refuses to acknowledge that the breast is part of or comes from the mOther, or bears any relation to the actual woman who becomes the obsessive's sexual partner.[139]

---

135 The Symbolic order as the "trans-individual socio-linguistic structures configuring the fields of inter-subjective interactions". See: Adrian Johnston: Jacques Lacan. In: Edward N. Zalta (ed.): *The Stanford Encyclopedia of Philosophy* (Winter 2016 Edition), forthcoming URL = <http://plato.stanford.edu/archives/win2016/entries/lacan/>.
136 Lionel Bailly: *Lacan*. Oxford: Oneworld publications 2009, p. 130.
137 Jacques Lacan: *Le Séminaire, livre VII, L'éthique de la psychanalyse, leçon du 6 juillet 1960*. Paris: Éditions du Seuil 1986, p. 169.
138 Kateb Yacine: *Nedjma*, p. 265 (Kateb's emphasis).
139 Bruce Fink, *A clinical Introduction to Lacanian Psychoanalysis: Theory and Technique* (Cambridge: Harvard University Press), p.119.

As Lacan states, "chez l'obsessionnel [...] il nie le désir de l'Autre en formant son fantasme à accentuer l'impossible de l'évanouissement du sujet".[140] Thus, when in *Le Cadavre encerclé*, the first play in *Le Cercle des représailles*, Lakhdar states, as part of his early amorous dispute with Nedjma, "Le point culminant du supplice me serait alors apparu. Mais je ne voulais pas atteindre ton altitude, sachant que le vide était au bout"[141] and when in *Le Polygone*, the narrator informs us that "ses voisins [...] la traitaient encore comme si son existence n'avait été qu'un vide, un trou [...]",[142] we can understand these statements as allusions to a denial of the desire of the feminine Other, while we can read subsequent continuous attempts to manage Nedjma's symbolism as efforts to deny the instability of her meaning and, by implication, of the meaning of an Algeria-to-come, as both define the subjectivities of the masculine protagonists.

In a general sense, Nedjma can be considered an anxiogenic figure of obsession for masculine protagonists which, in the structure of *Nedjma*, comes to function as a motor of desire, of continuation, sometimes within the narrative, as with Rachid's progression to the Nadhor, sometimes with metatextual resonance, as with the *Carnet de Mustapha* which proceeds with Nedjma as its primary *raison d'être*. And, the perception of Nedjma as the hollow, "desireless" bearer of the *objet petit a* is continually reinforced by the obsessional structure itself. For, as Bailly writes, "desire exists in tension with anxiety, and the ultimate object of desire and power exists in tension with the ultimate anxiety-creating lack of it".[143] In other words, it is the unattainability of the *objet petit a* and consequently the inevitable failure in mastery of the obsessional structure that refuses this failure, which is represented as propelling masculine desire to control its object. Nedjma can be seen as a container for an unattainable scintilla that the protagonists obsessively seek to circumscribe, in vain, giving the impression that, in the words of Lakhdar, she is "une femme perpétuellement en fuite".[144] The impossibility of securing the remnants of the splintered imaginary phallus is, I argue, beautifully sketched in metaphor in descriptions of her allure in the Nadhor pilgrimage section in *Nedjma*, perhaps the most oneiric section in the book and therefore the one that most readily invites a psychoanalytical reading.

After Nedjma has been abducted in order to be led to the tribal homeland, Kateb produces a scene in which she is discovered bathing by Rachid. Upon see-

---

140 Jacques Lacan: *Écrits*. Paris: Éditions du Seuil 1966, p. 824.
141 Kateb Yacine: *Le Cercle des représailles*, p. 30.
142 Kateb Yacine: *Le Polygone étoilé*, p. 148.
143 Lionel Bailly: *Lacan*, p. 133.
144 Kateb Yacine: *Nedjma*, p. 264.

ing her, he progresses through different partial objects of her body, seeking that obscure object of desire:

> Je contemplais les deux aisselles [...] les seins de Nedjma [...] [les] pudiques mouvements des bras, découvrant sous l'épaule cet inextricable, ce rare espace d'herbe en feu dont la vue suffit à troubler, dont l'odeur toujours sublimée contient tout le philtre, tout le secret [...]¹⁴⁵

However, his frustrated will to obtain this essence is manifested in desperate obsessional fantasmatic attempts to bottle her potion:

> [...] fioles, bocaux et baignoires, c'est là que doivent durer les fleurs, scintiller les écailles et les femmes s'épanouir, loin de l'air et du temps [...]¹⁴⁶

Indeed it is the "chaudron", the containing vessel, which Rachid appears to cherish the most:

> [...] car il n'est point d'attributs de ta beauté qui ne m'aient rendu l'eau cent fois plus chère; ce n'est pas la fantaisie qui me fait éprouver cette immense affection pour un chaudron. J'aime aveuglément l'objet sans mémoire où se chamaillent les derniers mânes de mes amours.¹⁴⁷

Here, one may read Rachid's denial of "la fantaisie" as perversely symptomatic of his being beholden to a fantasy of plenitude of meaning, represented by the cauldron. He wishes, as obsessional, for the symbolic containment of the *objet petit a*, just as he appreciates the physical restriction of Nedjma's essence. Furthermore, he states:

> J'ai honte d'avouer que ma plus ardente passion ne peut survivre hors du chaudron, symbole d'obtuse éprouvette dont les parois étouffent la seule humaine que mon sort me prescrit pourtant d'approcher et de circonvenir, de défendre et de protéger [...]¹⁴⁸

In these last two citations one thus notes how Rachid both appears to possess a partial, perhaps unconscious awareness of the topography of his desire and an appreciation of the ramifications for "la humaine" that is Nedjma.

However, despite this partial awareness of the fallibility of the obsessional project, the order of representation that is produced by the male protagonists

---

145 Ibid, p. 148.
146 Ibid, p. 149.
147 Ibid, p. 149.
148 Ibid, p. 149.

2.3 Masculine Perspectives on the Feminine Image: Desiring Objects — 39

equates, of course, to a negation or, at the very least, an ignorance of Nedjma's desire and therefore of her agency in the progression of the narrative. By implication, one might therefore see in the texts' articulation of the protagonists' quest to "circonvenir, de défendre et de protéger", in connection with Nedjma's treatment as a void, an addressing of the non-incorporation of women's desires, women's goals during the revolutionary period. Furthermore, Kateb's texts do also provide glimmers of their female subject's desire as it conflicts with this desire to master her. To return to the Nadhor scene, we can see a clear contradiction between Rachid's conception of her circumscription and her own. This is seen firstly in her escorting by him and Si Mokhtar, and then as she is ceded to the authoritative figure of the *nègre* in an act that one might interpret as a maintenance of control through acceptance of a need for her signifying content to be sublated, transferred to a higher social/ethnic/religious identitarian plane which nonetheless continues to define the masculine subject. Firstly, Rachid states that "Nedjma ne semblait pas mécontente de son sort, bien qu'elle eût été enlevée à sa mère adoptive et à l'époux que celle-ci lui avait donné".[149] This is then almost immediately contradicted by her reported speech as Rachid tells us that "[e]lle me pria de ne plus jouer du luth en sa présence; cela lui rappelait son époux".[150] Her anguish at her marshalling, here intimated by her wish not to be reminded of the past from which she has been snatched, is then expressed again in the context of her transfer to the *nègre* and the tribal envoys. Nedjma, upon sensing his presence, "pouss(e) un cri affreux" and is consumed with "frayeur".[151] Then, once Rachid, having meekly protested, comes to state that "[e]n désespoir de cause, j'acceptai", one notes that Nedjma is represented as very much not accepting of her fate: "Nedjma sanglotait près de son père brûlant de fièvre".[152] This reaction is revealed not so much to be a product of concern for her father's wellbeing but more the result of her justified fear of her symbolic enclosure, of her being mastered and confined by her captor:

> Elle était persuadée que le nègre la guetterait désormais, méditant quelque obscur sacrifice dont elle se croyait la victime désignée.[153]

Thus, though in *Nedjma*, as in *Le Polygone* and in Kateb's poetry, the chief female protagonist is often, perhaps mostly, mediated through male desire, her repre-

---

149 Kateb Yacine: *Nedjma*, p. 146.
150 Ibid, p. 146.
151 Ibid, p. 156.
152 Ibid, p. 159.
153 Ibid, p. 161.

sentation as such is problematised through allusions to pernicious psychic structures whilst the pitfalls of neglecting feminine desire are intimated through an occasional piercing of the narrative with her own desire. Moreover, further to these allusions, Kateb's work evokes the influence of sociological structures that may serve as another way of interpreting the desire to sequester in our historical context and in a more universal sense.

2.4 Rivalrous Relations

When reading the texts of *le Cycle de Nedjma*, the repetition of terms that describe a relationship of competition amongst male protagonists with regards to Nedjma in her various incarnations is very striking. In the section on Kateb's early poetry, we noted the foundational presence of the "voleurs amis" and one encounters throughout the texts various "piquante[s] rivalité[s]" which order the perspectives of the masculine protagonists on their interactions with Nedjma and with each other.[154] In *Nedjma* the reader of course bears witness to the conflicts staged between the four chief protagonists over Nedjma, but one also detects allusions to other rivalries both contemporary to the novel's chronology and as parts of the formative experiences of the past. Early in the text there is the conflict between Monsieur Ricard and Mourad over Suzy, concluding with the former's demise. We note thereafter "Le barbu" and his "rivaux",[155] Sidi Ahmed, Mourad's father, who lived "à Tunis chez une fameuse femme, pour laquelle il s'est battu à l'épée avec un notaire marseillais",[156] the confusion that surrounds the identity of Nedjma's father which causes Rachid to ponder: "Qui sait lequel d'entre eux donna le jour à Nedjma…",[157] Rachid's childhood rivalry with Mme Clément's husband and hints of competition with a Corsican rival for Nedjma's affection, revealed in *Le Polygone* to be Marc. *Le Polygone* also contains a textually fragmentary poem which recapitulates the essence of these structures, alluding to the cessation of conflict with the withdrawal of the "amante disputée":[158]

---

[154] Ibid, p. 108.
[155] Ibid, p. 35.
[156] Ibid, p. 85.
[157] Ibid, p. 106.
[158] Kateb Yacine: *Le Polygone étoilé*, p. 150.

> Infestés en son absence
> Nous avons pratiqué
> L'escrime
> Et renoncé à la rivalité
>
> Heureux présage que son éloignement !
> En d'autres temps
>
> Elle eût pâli[159]

However, perhaps the most apposite examples of the importance of rivalry for a study of the representation of Algerian women in Kateb's work come in his "revolutionary" theatre. Towards the end of the gendered conflicts of *Les Ancêtres redoublent de férocité,* as a development of various hints at rivalrous relations in *Le Cadavre encerclé,* seen for example in the physical spotlighting of a complex interplay of gazing,[160] the Coryphaeus states :

> Et le délire des deux amis,
> En présence de la femme,
> Va déchaîner la rivalité[161]

The reader then, following the stage directions, recognises that "la femme [sauvage]" is Nedjma whilst he/she is informed that "Oui, elle marche, mais à l'écart, et le drame se joue encore à son insu".[162] The drama of which Nedjma is unaware is exposed as the culmination of a rivalrous relation as "*Hassan et Mustapha tirent l'un sur l'autre. Hassan s'écroule. La femme sauvage, qui marchait à l'écart, n'a rien saisi de cette scène, qui s'est passée en un éclair*".[163] Finally, the chorus informs us that "Oui toute guerre est pareille à celle des Grecs pour Hélène…".[164]

It is my contention that in this progression, in these citations, we have presented to us an outline of a structure in which Nedjma is conceived of as a marker of socio-symbolic import, as an object of symbolic capital, following a Bourdieusian framework. Unaware of the struggle about to take place to win her, against the backdrop of the colonial conflict that the play depicts, Nedjma is excluded from the economy of honour at work that sees her as the symbolically valuable object sought by the two parties. As was noted in the introduction to this book, Bourdieu writes in *La Domination masculine* that "[l]e principe de l'infériorité et de l'exclusion de la femme […] n'est autre que la dissymétrie fondamentale, celle *du sujet et de l'objet, de l'agent et de l'instrument,* qui s'instaure

---

159 Ibid, p. 148.
160 Kateb Yacine: *Le Cercle des représailles,* p. 38.
161 Kateb Yacine: *Le Cercle des représailles,* p. 146–147.
162 Ibid, p. 147.
163 Ibid, p. 147–148.
164 Ibid, p. 149.

entre l'homme et la femme sur le terrain des échanges symboliques, des rapports de production et de reproduction du capital symbolique [...].[165]

To return to Kateb's text, we subsequently see how "à la vue de soldats et du vautour qui plane", with rivals present, Mustapha takes Hassan's knife and asks himself the following:[166]

> Faut-il laisser la rose aux tempêtes de sable, au baiser du vautour ? Dois-je égorger la rose ou consentir à sa profanation ?[167]

Nedjma is referred to not as an actor in the conflict, but as a rose, a marker, a prize for her competing suitors and Mustapha considers destroying this feminine marker of symbolic capital in seeing that he cannot acquire exclusive mastery of it/her.

This asymmetrical symbolic structure abounds throughout the *Cycle*. To refer back to the rivalry surrounding Nedjma's mother in *Nedjma*, for example, we see how even in death, Rachid's father acquires symbolic capital as his social milieu believes in his meriting victory in the competition for the object of his affection:

> [...] le très honoré défunt qui faisait autrefois scandale, mais dont le renom, grâce à sa mort tragique, avait acquis le sel de la légende; on en parlait comme d'un preux abattu à la fleur de l'âge par un rival de moindre envergure...[168]

Moreover, one notes, turning to *Le Vautour*, the final play in *Le Cercle des représailles*, how it is the structure of rivalry, of symbolic competition, that dictates, to a large extent, the value attribuée to the feminine object and therefore the rapacity of attempts made to secure her. Lakhdar, Nedjma's spurned lover now metamorphosed into the form of the Vautour, exclaims:

> Comment l'aurais-je découverte
> Cette inconnue
> Célèbre pour moi seul
> Si ses rivales
> Ne l'avaient rendue
> Si rare
> Comment l'aurais-je découverte

---

[165] Pierre Bourdieu: *La Domination masculine*, p. 65.
[166] Kateb Yacine: *Le Cercle des représailles*, p. 150.
[167] Ibid, p. 151.
[168] Kateb Yacine: *Nedjma*, p. 183.

> Cette inconnue célèbre
> Pour moi seul ?[169]

Here the text provides a sense of the heteronomy of male subjectivity and thus the state of interdependence at work in the symbolic/honour economy. In other words, le Vautour is shown to acquire an awareness of the desirability of Nedjma due to her appreciation by other interested parties, which generate a "big Other" that regulates value.[170] He sees her through ideologically aligned signifiers, conditioned by the state of competition at work in his social milieu, which act as imperfect conduits, facilitating desire of the *objet petit a*. Additionally, the functioning of the honour economy is seen to be complicated and elevated in significance by the special value of the symbolic capital invested in women within the late-colonial context.

As was discussed in the introduction to this book, the Algerian woman, in this epoch, came to represent an important battleground in the war for independence, subjective and worldly. As Anne McClintock writes, "the Manichean agon of decolonization is waged over the territoriality of female domestic space".[171] Indeed, one can expand McClintock's territoriality to the entirety of the symbolic content invested in women, generated before and by the conflict, and emphasise, as was done in my introduction, how Bourdieu's symbolic agon, when transposed into the colonial domain, necessitates with renewed intensity the reproduction of "le jeu et les enjeux [...] les conditions de l'accès à la reproduction sociale".[172] This is to suggest that in a profoundly unequal and antagonistic rivalry, divested of "une relation essentielle d'égalité en honneur", and with its telos a sharply identifiable assertion of identity, women acquire a symbolic capital that can provoke a singularly obsessive will to manage their being, to dominate symbolically.[173]

Furthermore, returning to the citation above which evokes the Trojan war and Helen's central role, one can certainly agree with Jane Hiddleston when she links the male protagonists' conflict with the struggle for independence, writing: "The war pits not only coloniser against colonised, but brothers against one

---

169 Kateb Yacine: *Le Cercle des représailles*, p. 164.
170 The "big Other" can be understood as the figure of the Symbolic order understood by the subject as an invisible collective institution that encapsulates socio-symbolic norms.
171 Anne McClintock: No Longer in a Future Heaven, p. 90.
172 Pierre Bourdieu: *La Domination masculine*, p. 68.
173 Ibid, p. 68.

another".¹⁷⁴ There is also an interesting ambiguity at play, however, when Hiddleston writes that "this fratricide is clearly another reference to the conflict between Algerian groups fighting for independence".¹⁷⁵ For, though I have suggested that Kateb's texts reflect a particular investment of symbolic capital in Nedjma, it remains for this chapter to form a judgment as to whether she is represented as a placeholder for Algeria itself. Is the reader encouraged to read the brothers' internecine fight for independence as a product of their ascribing to *la femme sauvage*/Nedjma a symbolic hyper-importance, a product of the aforementioned structures, or is she to stand metaphorically for the nation that they might seek to hold authority over? It is of course true that one can bear witness to a history of conflating woman with nation and vice-versa in the discursive representations of our context for study and as Taïeb Sbouaï writes, "'Nedjma l'Andalouse –, la fille de la Française qui avait opposé entre eux quatre soupirants' n'est pas sans analogie avec 'ce pays [qui] n'est pas encore venu au monde: trop de pères pour naître au grand jour, trop d'ambitieuses races déçues, mêlées, confondues, contraintes de ramper dans les ruines'".¹⁷⁶ And, Jean Déjeux, in analysing *Nedjma,* also draws a direct comparison between Nedjma and an Algeria to come and between her suitors and those who competed to take charge of the territory:

> Les quatre protagonistes de Nedjma sont ici comme des [...] 'frères ennemis' à l'image des partis politiques nationalistes d'avant 1954 qui se disputent entre eux, chacun entendant être seul à la révéler à elle-même [l'Algérie]. Pendant ce temps, Nedjma reste silencieuse comme l'Algérie colonisée de cette époque. Récupérer Nedjma c'est récupérer la patrie, le fondamental.¹⁷⁷

It would be my argument that in a continuation of Kateb's texts' staging of pernicious conceptual frameworks regarding women, she does, in the minds of masculine protagonists and on the metaphorical plane of the fiction, come to symbolise and embody a future Algeria though, as the next section will investigate, the works again problematise and play with the idea of this representation as they do with previous forms of objectification mentioned (mythical, psychic etc.). Kateb's texts, whilst staging women's reduction to symbolic content in male psychology, also encourage their reader to consider Nedjma and women's

---

174 Jane Hiddleston: *Decolonising the Intellectual: Politics, Culture and Humanism at the End of the French Empire.* Liverpool: Liverpool University Press 2014, p. 35.
175 Ibid., p. 35.
176 Taïeb Sbouaï: *La Femme sauvage de Kateb Yacine.* Paris: Editions de l'Arcantère 1985, p. 78 (citations from Kateb Yacine: *Nedjma*, p. 191 + 197.
177 Jean Déjeux: *Littérature maghrébine de langue française*, p. 241.

capacity to embody an Algerian state, to think through a problematic though potentially potent metaphorical role for Algerian women in the movement towards Algeria's independence.

2.5 National Possibilities

My section on myth, on the encoding of Nedjma, alluded to her connection with a conception of a future Algerian state, produced in revolution. Her description as star, connecting her to *L'étoile Nord-Africaine*, her links with la Kahina, the Amazigh queen, and her own narrative of chimeric identity, of mixed ethnic parentage, all point to the texts' encouraging the reader to form interpretations of her proximity to the symbolic make-up of a future Algerian nation. However, before moving to discuss the manner in which the texts invite critical interpretations of a woman/geography/nation equivalence, it will be seen to be important to investigate another myth at work within the texts, that of the Keblout tribe.

Particularly in *Nedjma*, a narrative of nation-building is generated as a result of the masculine protagonists' investment in this myth, which points to the blurred threshold between their perceiving within her symbolic content desired for its importance to a conception of a disputed Algeria and thus to their identities, and their perceiving her as a living symbol of Algeria herself. Our first exposure to the myth in *Nedjma* comes as Si Mokhtar and Rachid return from their abortive pilgrimage to Mecca. Si Mokhtar explains that "notre tribu, autant qu'on s'en souvienne, avait dû venir du Moyen-Orient, passer par l'Espagne et séjourner au Maroc, sous la conduite de Keblout".[178] He goes on to outline a complex narrative of its continuation to their time and then demonstrates his intent to assure its renaissance, inviting us to draw a parallel with the will to topple French hegemony and assert Algerian nationalism. He states:

> Nous irons vivre au Nadhor, elle et toi, mes deux enfants, moi le vieil arbre qui ne peut plus nourrir, mais vous couvrira de son ombre…Et le sang de Keblout retrouvera sa chaude, son intime épaisseur.[179]

If we then read how Nedjma's transportation to the Nadhor is later described by Mustapha, we may appreciate how Khedidja Khelladi divides the mythical natures of Keblout and Nedjma into a dichotomy between "les mythes de fonda-

---

178 Kateb Yacine: *Nedjma*, p. 134.
179 Ibid, p.140.

tion" and "les mythes d'origine", between masculine founding agency and feminine rooted passivity. Mustapha states:[180]

> Nedjma menant à bon fin son jeu de reine fugace et sans espoir jusqu'à l'apparition de l'époux, le nègre prémuni contre l'inceste social, [...] ce sera enfin l'arbre de la nation s'enracinant dans la sépulture tribale, sous le nuage enfin crevé d'un sang trop de fois écumé...[181]

As, in the words of Rachid, "mon sang et mon pays", Nedjma is shown by the texts to be dragged into a conception of nation-building in which her agency is seriously compromised by a belief in her role as eternal genetrix, as a carrier of original national symbolism.[182] She is not considered an active participant in the tilling of revolutionary soil but can be viewed, where the Keblout myth obtains, as the privileged seed from which a new Algerian state may grow. In contrast to Keblout, the founder, the historical agent, Nedjma is often depicted, in the psyches of her male suitors, as a fantasy of passivity, a backdrop formed to make sense of her position as the bearer of their symbolic and imaginary agalma. This approach is depicted as being grounded in an unproductive, atavistic and unrepresentative unconscious understanding of the conditions of possibility for national identity. It is also important to note that the chief proponent of the Keblout myth's importance and the man who would see Nedjma fulfil its ties of blood, Si Mokhtar, is depicted as a false prophet who leads Rachid on a botched Islamic pilgrimage. He is also a philanderer, a murderer, and a rapist.

Mustapha alludes to the episteme upon which Nedjma's approximation to passive nationhood is predicated when, in an earlier section of the passage cited above, he refers to his understanding of his collective identity, sited in the tribe:

> [...] notre tribu mise en échec répugne à changer de couleur; nous nous sommes toujours mariés entre nous; l'inceste est notre lien, notre principe de cohésion depuis l'exil du premier ancêtre; le même sang nous porte irrésistiblement à l'embouchure du fleuve passionnel [...][183]

---

180 Khedidja Khelladi: Archétypes et paradigmes littéraires dans l'œuvre de Kateb Yacine, p. 168–171.
181 Kateb Yacine: *Nedjma*, p. 200.
182 Ibid, p. 188.
183 Ibid, p. 200.

Immediately prior to this passage in *Nedjma* we witness the referent of Mustapha's discourse, the result of the binding of Nedjma to nationhood within his limited interpretation thereof:

> De Constantine à Bône, de Bône à Constantine voyage une femme...C'est comme si elle n'était plus; on ne la voit que dans un train ou une calèche, et ceux qui la connaissent ne la distinguent plus parmi les passantes; ce n'est plus qu'une lueur exaspérée d'automne, une citée traquée qui se ferme au désastre ; elle est voilée de noir.[184]

Nedjma exists in a state of sad sequestration, wheeled back and forth as an undead symbol. Clearly, here, Kateb's text delivers a warning against nationalism's tendency to both ignore women's contiguity with the colonised's struggle, their active roles, and to assign them a fantasmatic, metaphoric or symbolic role.[185]

However, Kateb's texts also invite the reader to consider, through Nedjma's description and function and through descriptions of geographical sites, women's role in the conceptual fabric of nationhood, alluding in so doing to a pragmatic though conceptually inventive picture of their necessary implication.

For Kateb's project assigns great importance to a consideration of the woman/nation metaphor and though Nedjma is equated to "cités vaincus"[186] and to "une rue d'Alger ou de Constantine, de Sétif ou de Guelma",[187] and is described as "mon sang et mon pays",[188] and "la nation mère",[189] these signposts serve to invite a nuanced interpretive process, welcoming an analysis of the epistemological issues involved in connecting woman to territory, to land, to nation. Charles Bonn writes that he views Nedjma as being "essentiellement perçue par ces protagonistes comme un signe qu'ils sont plus ou moins aptes à déchiffrer correctement".[190] He goes on to write of our chief protagonist :

> Symbole malgré elle où à son insu, Nedjma n'incarne pas la nation, dont elle ne parle jamais [...] Le passage de la tribu à la nation, du temps et de l'espace de la tradition à ceux de la nation et de l'histoire s'opère davantage dans le travail interprétatif qui est demandé au lecteur, que dans un signifié explicite du livre.[191]

---

[184] Ibid, p. 196.
[185] As was alluded to in the introduction to this monograph, see the works of Elleke Boehmer, in particular *Stories of Nation: Gender and Narrative in the Postcolonial Nation*. Manchester: Manchester University Press 2005 for more on this gendered division.
[186] Kateb Yacine: *Nedjma*, p. 196.
[187] Kateb Yacine: *Le Cercle des représailles*, p. 15.
[188] Kateb Yacine: *Nedjma*, p. 188.
[189] Kateb Yacine: *Le Cercle des représailles*, p. 142.
[190] Charles Bonn: *Kateb Yacine: Nedjma*, p. 44.
[191] Ibid, p. 49.

What is important to highlight in these two citations is the difference between the approach of the protagonists towards Nedjma and the formal organisation of the text to which they belong. Where the protagonists work, according to Bonn, at a deciphering of Nedjma's symbolism, at an excavation of a meaning that comes ultimately from their own psyches, *Nedjma* and *Le Polygone étoilé* in particular develop a coexistence of multiple perspectives on women's approximation to nation, such that the reader is invited to take part in a multifaceted and self-problematising interpretative debate. Whilst portraying the consequences of the desire to master Nedjma's national signification, namely her sequestration, her symbolic enclosure, Kateb's work also generates renovated understandings of women's conceptual approximation to elements of nationhood normally to be conceptualised as passive and essentialising, as abrogating the agency of the Algerian woman. What is key in this literary articulation of a possible symbolic rehabilitation of the connection between woman and geography/ nation is a rejection of passive inaction, a stirring of conceptions of female permanence that would place them in opposition to male historical agency. Indeed, if we refer back to Khedidja Khelladi's analysis of an opposition between "les mythes de fondation" and "les mythes d'origine" we can supplement her conclusion by demonstrating Kateb's texts' problematising of the former's predication on the latter.

Throughout *Le Polygone étoilé*, in particular in its richly significant opening, one notes the reprise "chaque fois les plans sont bouleversés", which first appears on page 14. Initially this phrase is used in reference to "[d]es inspirateurs, coiffés de casquettes américaines et de pataugas", to modern planners of indeterminate origin and then to "[u]n ancêtre [qui] surgit des flots", a representative of a traditionalist masculinist episteme.[192] In both instances, what Kateb's reprise seemingly refers to is a doomed epistemological stance that would see a future Algerian nation as the result of the imposition of a fixed plan by a masculine historical agent upon a passive terrain. Most importantly for this study, in the second instance one notes the implication of women within these architectural "plans" for the future as we read that "Il est à l'âge où tout inceste n'est qu'un bâton de pèlerinage" and that "Il a eu trop de femmes, trop de filles [...]".[193] He has, in his blueprints for the future, seen women as foundational blocks of symbolic capital. However, he and the other "fondateurs clandestins" are destined to fail in their attempts to determine the narratives of belonging and nation

---

192 Kateb Yacine: *Le Polygone étoilé*, p. 14 + 16.
193 Ibid, p. 17.

2.5 National Possibilities — 49

as they seek, just as the modern planners do, to impose a predetermined structure on a site of resistance.[194]

Indeed, in turning to perhaps the texts' most striking refiguring of femininity and geography/nation, one notes how resistance to the plans of others and to conceptions of immobility and passivity stands as the principle by which a rehabilitation of the equation is possible, though one might argue that such a comparison remains nevertheless potentially problematic. In *Nedjma*, we read:

> Il en est des cités comme des femmes fatales, les veuves polyandres dont le nom s'est perdu... Gloire aux cités vaincues; elles n'ont pas livré le sel des larmes, pas plus que les guerriers n'ont versé notre sang : la primeur en revient aux épouses, les veuves éruptives qui peuplent toute mort, les veuves conservatrices qui transforment en paix la défaite [...][195]

Here, women are compared with ancient cities, the two sharing a peculiar and multifaceted resistant power, simultaneously protective of and eruptive from their ruins. Elsewhere in *Nedjma*, in Rachid's description of the ruins of Cirta (Constantine) and Hippone (Bône) (Annaba) he also establishes a conception of their femininity, stating:

> "J'ai habité tour à tour les deux sites, le rocher puis la plaine où Cirta et Hippone connurent la grossesse puis le déclin dont les cités et les femmes portent le deuil sempiternel, en leur cruelle longévité de villes-mères [...]"[196]

He does so having, as Seth Graebner indicates, articulated a rejection of passivity and historical relegation with regards to the nature of ruins, affirming:

> Pas les restes des Romains. Pas ce genre de ruine où l'âme des multitudes n'a eu que le temps de se morfondre, en gravant leur adieu dans le roc, mais les ruines en filigrane de tous les temps, celles que baigne le sang dans nos veines, celles que nous portons en secret sans jamais trouver le lieu ni l'instant qui conviendrait pour les voir : les inestimables décombres du présent...[197]

These comparisons invite the reader to interrogate a certain understanding of a form of feminine resistance, of her contribution to the construction of a national territory, of her embodying an Algeria been and an Algeria to come, separate from her contemporaneous active revolutionary participation. Though Kateb's works do not entirely ignore women's role as combatants in the Algerian War

---

194 Ibid, p. 16.
195 Kateb Yacine: *Nedjma*, p. 196.
196 Ibid, p. 187.
197 Ibid, p. 187.

of Independence, as is evidenced by the characterization of *la femme sauvage* in his theatre, in the citations above it is the importance of women's non-military role that we are encouraged to view differently. The texts acknowledge the tendency, in a nationalist mind-set, for women to represent geographical elements but avoid many, if not all of the pitfalls that such a comparison might yield. Women's permanence, her ability to remain and endure, to "transform[er] en paix la défaite", is highlighted, but this conception's connection with passivity is eschewed as women are figured as bursting forth, as *veuves éruptives*, agents of history.[198] Moreover, the ruins of the *villes-mères* populate the present and reject attempts to implicate their modern sisters in conceptual frameworks of honour/symbolic capital predicated on purity or virginity. As Graebner writes:

> The novel [...] does not present colonized cities or subjects passively taking abuse; Kateb knows from looking closely at the city's structure that it results from an active, if unequal, exchange between colonized and colonizer. The violation model by itself is too simple to account for the presence of ruins in Algeria's colonial past or the construction of the monuments of the present.[199]

As has been previously acknowledged, *Nedjma* in particular depicts the danger of geographical/national metaphor as, co-opted by the *nègre*, she becomes "une lueur exaspérée d'automne, une citée traquée qui se ferme au désastre".[200] Not only does this representation closely precede Mustapha's problematic understanding of Nedjma's role in nationhood, but it also comes in the same passage as the narrator's description of "cités" being like "femmes fatales".[201] Thus the text alludes through juxtaposition to the possibility of its own reworking slipping into a problematic symbolic enclosure of women. Where one might take issue with an attempted rehabilitation of the use of geographical metaphor is with the authority with which a comparison such as the one between "cités" and "femmes fatales" is made. It would be my view that these kinds of definitive representations of women cause us to be mindful of essentialisation, in the words of Judith Butler, "to consider whether [...] femaleness is really external to the cultural norms by which it is repressed".[202] However, the texts' self-problematisation, their representation of Nedjma through the lenses of masculine perspec-

---

198 Ibid, p. 196.
199 Seth Graebner: Kateb Yacine and the Ruins of the Present. In: *SubStance* Vol. 36, No. 1, Issue 112 (2007), p. 157.
200 Kateb Yacine: *Nedjma*, p. 196.
201 Ibid, p. 196.
202 Judith Butler: *Gender Trouble, Feminism and the Subversion of Identity*. London: Routledge 2002, 118–119.

tives, their attempts to deal with some of the problematic aspects of women/geography/nation equations and their inscribing of a problematic relinquishing of control of Nedjma, which the final section will now tackle, all serve to encourage a further questioning, a rethinking of such metaphors. Perhaps Kateb's texts, on occasion, do poetically fall into essentialising epistemological traps. However, they do so whilst continually undermining epistemes, both those promulgated from a position of narrative authority and those of the actors in the texts, that might lead to symbolic oppression.

2.6 Fragile Emancipation and Pessimistic Representation

Thus far in this investigation of the representation of the Algerian woman in the works of Kateb Yacine, the texts' depiction of her functioning as object/image for mastery has been often emphasised. Taking the *Cycle* as a whole, however, and following the course of its progression, one notes an arrhythmic shifting between depictions of a masculine yearning for mastery and other articulations that render a glinting possibility of a loosening of masculinist control and of feminine emancipation. Thus this final section will focus on narrative turning points, in particular narrative conclusions, that explore the unsteady potential for a subversion of the Bourdieusian structures and Lacanian phallocentric obsessional approaches to Nedjma that mark the perceptions of her as representative of Algerian women. It will be seen again, however, that Kateb's work refuses to produce representations that would appear naïve or disingenuous in their depiction of the state of women's social and personal freedoms. Indeed, this section will indicate that Kateb's work, in deliberately avoiding the provision of panaceas for gender inequality, inaugurates a "pessimistic" literary positioning that alludes to the need for greater representativity in political and literary symbolisation. Nedjma does not stride into a revolutionary sunset nor do the texts attempt to generate fully representative (*Vertretung*) representations that might purport to stage a state of unproblematic egalitarian gender relations. This section will instead argue that a constitutive element of capital importance in the texts' evocation of the possibility of improvement in socio-symbolic representation is a form of "pessimism" regarding egalitarian development and its permanence. When one considers the institutional reduction of women's status in post-independence Algeria, despite the promises made by representative organisations such as the FLN, the texts acquire a particular resonance that speaks to the facileness of positivity without vigilance.²⁰³

Beginning with Arnaud's *L'Œuvre en fragments*, she provides us with some previously unpublished "ajouts" to *Les Ancêtres redoublent de férocité*, written between 1963 and 1967, after independence. Kateb's play is supplemented by text which serves as a contextual development, a historical unpacking of a passage previously referred to in this chapter's section on 'Rivalrous Relations', which demonstrates the perils of the moment where a symbolic agon, fought over women, reaches an impasse. In the original section, Mustapha, seeing the inevitability of *la femme sauvage*'s appropriation by other masculine agents, namely the Vautour and enemy soldiers, poses himself the following questions:

> Faut-il laisser la rose aux tempêtes de sable, au baiser du vautour ?
> Dois-je égorger la rose ou consentir à sa profanation ?²⁰⁴

In the first *ajout*, the Coryphaeus speaks to the audience about another revolutionary protagonist's decision to "égorger la rose", as he is seemingly unable to consent to another type of loss:

> En attendant, il semait la terreur. Pour un oui, pour un non, il aiguisait son couteau sous les yeux du condamné et il exécuta ainsi, au nom d'Allah, au nom de la Révolution, les premières jeunes filles qui osèrent vivre la vie libre, la vie des combattants.²⁰⁵

Both cases implicate different potential conditions of a relinquishing of masculine control and both produce solutions of extreme finality to scenarios where "le jeu et les enjeux [...] les conditions de l'accès à la reproduction sociale" are compromised.²⁰⁶ In the first, Mustapha feels he no longer has any standing in the exchanges to come and therefore is confronted with two choices from which he seemingly chooses the latter:²⁰⁷ give up all claims to *la femme sauvage* by consenting to her expropriation or maintain a level of control by killing her, sacrificing the symbolic capital invested in her. In the second, the revolutionary leader's decision is explicitly conditioned by a third possibility, that of women's

---

203 See, for example, the lack of post-revolutionary political representation, covered in my introduction, or legislation like the Code de la Famille, described in this book's concluding chapter.
204 Kateb Yacine: *Le Cercle des représailles*, p. 151.
205 Jacqueline Arnaud (ed.)/Kateb Yacine: *L'Œuvre en fragments*, p. 372.
206 Pierre Bourdieu: *La Domination masculine*, p. 68.
207 The moment of Nedjma's death is obscurely rendered in the play but must be attributed to Mustapha.

extraction from mastery, that of a burgeoning equality. He nonetheless ends the military and symbolic potential of "les premières jeunes filles qui osèrent vivre la vie libre" by slaughtering them.[208] Though both scenarios appear to preclude the possibility of a positive end to the honour economy within their context, they in so doing can be argued to invoke the radical necessity for a production of conditions that might bring about its demise. Their "pessimism" is in this sense productive and this functioning becomes clearer as one reinserts the scene back into the narrative evolution of the play. Indeed, *Les Ancêtres redoublent de férocité* most clearly establishes a "pessimistic" mode through pertinent repeated depictions of the fragility of representative structures, alluding specifically to women's potential for self-representation in emancipation and the masculinist structures that would continually resist change, redoubling in ferocity.

On page 133, one notes the following interaction upon the initial meeting between *la femme sauvage*, later revealed to be Nedjma, and the female chorus, which invokes a shift towards women's self-representation, towards their active participation in the production of their own meaning:

> La femme sauvage (*pensive*): Seules, nous l'avons toujours été.
> Mais aujourd'hui nous arrivons au bout du compte.
> C'est le moment ou jamais.
>
> Chœur: Ah ! oui, parle-nous, parle !
>
> Coryphée: Nous sommes seules, dis-nous
> Ce que te dit ta solitude.
>
> La femme sauvage: C'est le moment ou jamais, c'est la guerre, prenons nos libertés.
>
> Coryphée (*timide*): Nos libertés ?
>
> Chœur (*enthousiaste*) : Oui, oui, prenons nos libertés![209]

Emboldened and empowered by their meeting, the female chorus heads into the narrative of conflict under her auspices and upon meeting the Coryphaeus of a male chorus, the feminine Coryphaeus announces: "A l'heure du sacrifice, la nation mère // Nous a courageusement rassemblés".[210] However, once the two groups have then entered "la guerre", the terrain of colonial war which continues to be marked by gendered symbolic divisions, the audience encounters a

---

208 Jacqueline Arnaud (ed.)/Kateb Yacine: *L'Œuvre en fragments*, p. 372.
209 Kateb Yacine: *Le Cercle des représailles*, p. 133,
210 Ibid, p. 142.

character called "Le Vétéran", a figure whom one is invited to see as an established member of a revolutionary faction who torments the Vautour with the following speech:

> Que toutes les vierges se dévoilent ! Oiseau maudit, regarde ! Toutes ces beautés guerrières sont destinées à l'armée royale. Il faut bien que nos hommes soient récompensés de leur fidélité, en ces temps difficiles ! Quant à celle-ci, la plus épineuse (*Il montre la femme sauvage*), j'en fais mon affaire, j'ai dompté autrefois des juments plus rétives...[211]

The glimmer of women's potential for self-representation is quickly extinguished. In a show of symbolic capital, the chorus, the representatives of a feminine audience, are assigned to serve men's desires while their representative is to be treated as a mare to be broken. Clearly, this rapid reversion tragically frames an understanding of women's acquiring agency as fleeting, as delicate and as readily crushed by parties with a stake in masculinist structures. Nonetheless, with almost Beckettian resilience and resignation, the women continue to struggle, to bear witness and to articulate their "pessimistic" awareness of this historical tendency, just as we are encouraged to think through the rationale behind the resilience of problematic structures and seek their possible resolution. The feminine chorus are ushered off stage by the character of Hassan as the Vétéran is killed and when we next see them, in the same scene, they collapse in the desert only to be later reanimated to bear witness to another scene with strong pessimistic resonances: Nedjma's opaquely rendered demise as Mustapha's "rose".

Immediately following Mustapha's aforementioned dilemma, at the conclusion of the play, one notes further gloomy affirmations that seemingly indicate the repetitive nature of the problematic conceptual approaches to women to which this chapter has been referring. First, the Coryphaeus repeats the words of the chorus, now comprising the group of reanimated *"jeunes filles tombées au cours de la marche"*,[212] in an address to Nedjma as *la femme sauvage*, the feminine leader holding the promise of feminine emancipation who is now on the point of death:

> Il t'a pillé l'amour des hommes
> Les mêmes qui te hissaient dans leur combat
> Et dont les bras ne viendront pas te relever de ta chute ![213]

---

[211] Ibid, p. 144.
[212] Kateb Yacine: *Le Cercle des représailles*, p. 151.
[213] Ibid, p. 153.

2.6 Fragile Emancipation and Pessimistic Representation — 55

We then hear again from the Coryphaeus, whose cries: "Le vautour ! le vautour ! Le vautour et l'amant se disputent la morte", are peculiarly intriguing in their potential invitation of a blackly comic reading of the denouement.[214] Despite Nedjma, as *la femme sauvage*, being dead, these two chief competitors still cannot give up the fight for her. The resilience of rivalry, of the desire for *la femme sauvage* to be possessed, absurdly exceeds her passing, the Symbolic exceeds the worldly. Connected to this reading, one notes a tone of angry weariness in the intonations of the reanimated feminine chorus as they appear aware of the continuing reoccurrence of problematic structures of honour/symbolic capital in the continuation of Algerian history, towards and potentially beyond revolution.[215] They state, concerning Mustapha:

> Non, il ne mourra pas, il est de ceux qui passent le plus clair de leur vie
> Dans la prison ou dans l'asile
> Ce n'est pas la première fois.[216]

However, this kind of "pessimism" does not imply an abrogation of action as they go on, in their penultimate declaration of the play, to cry:

> Non, nous ne mourrons pas encore, pas cette fois !
> La femme sauvage n'est plus, mais la guerre l'incarne
> Et la guerre a besoin de nous.[217]

The play thus compels its audience to understand that a "pessimistic" awareness of a historical oscillation between emancipatory potential and a return to an agency-negating, unproductive battle over women, does not preclude continuing the struggle for improved gender relations, but rather compels progressive agents, feminine and masculine, to continue that liberatory fight. Indeed, in "pessimistically" rendering scenes of potential progress as plagued by returns and death, Kateb's texts compel their reader to commence an interpretive procedure with a view to thinking through the conditions necessary for an equitable field of symbolic exchange within a given milieu. In this way, "pessimistic" awareness can be understood to be an epistemic foundation for much of the texts' treatment of women's representation as a whole, whilst its presence clearly

---

[214] Ibid, p. 154.
[215] This awareness of women's vulnerability to the repetition of masculinist structures is also alluded to on page 141, where the Coryphaeus declares: "Nous sommes celles qui reçoivent en premier lier tous les coups, d'où qu'ils viennent".
[216] Ibid, p. 155.
[217] Ibid, p. 155.

forms an exhortation to consider the importance of future inaugurations of feminine self-representation.

Moving to Kateb's novels, in *Le Polygone étoilé*, the final work to be published in the *Cycle de Nedjma* and a work whose temporal context can be interpreted as wavering between the periods prior to and after independence, we witness how Nedjma herself displays a resigned awareness, following a repetition of the difficulty of breaking from the honour economy that does, nevertheless, provide glimmers of hope. Late on in the narrative, the narrator informs us about a sequestered Nedjma, echoing her deprivation of liberty in *Nedjma*'s Nadhor sequence:

> Depuis qu'elle voyageait au grand air, son visage obscur avait rougi, elle avait bu le sang, la poussière des champs de bataille, et ils ne pouvaient plus l'isoler dans un temple : "Allons-nous l'enterrer vivante ? Faut-il la sacrifier, ou bien *la laisser vivre* ? [...]"[218]

We then note the ebb and flow between potential liberation and concealment/management in a description of Nedjma's mythical status for a reverential populace which skilfully blends the contradictory poles, of which the former I mark in bold, the latter in italics:

> [...] quelle beauté, rose de sable, fleur de poussière, avait gardé la forme de leur dernier souffle, **allait grandir loin d'eux, sans eux, contre eux, pour rejeter un jour le voile de la pudeur** et s'offrir au dernier d'entre eux, qui *la ramènerait enfin à sa famille, dans un linceul ou dans un palanquin*, **libre** ou *morte*, **arrachée à la réclusion**, *à la profanation*, **à l'esclavage**.[219]

Even in the final three words we see a shift back and then forth from a will to see her mythical essence removed from sequestration to a will to see her avoid violation, profanation,[220] back to a more progressive desire to see her extricated from enslavement. Having, in one contradictory sentence, born witness to the shifting previously referred to, the reader does however note that Nedjma has gained a potentially productive awareness of her position in the symbolic structure:

---

218 Kateb Yacine: *Le Polygone étoilé*, p. 147 (emphasis added).
219 Ibid, p. 147–148 (emphasis added).
220 These terms are, of course, heavily implicated in the honour economy, being as they are a threat to male heteronomous identity. Bourdieu writes in *La Domination Masculine*, p. 69: "Lorsque [...] l'acquisition du capital symbolique et du capital social constitue à peu près la seule forme d'accumulation possible, les femmes sont des valeurs qu'il faut conserver à l'abri de l'offense et du soupçon [...]".

2.6 Fragile Emancipation and Pessimistic Representation — 57

> [...] n'avait-on pas toujours douté de sa venue au monde ? Avait-elle vécu ? Depuis qu'elle *prenait connaissance d'un destin trop riche, trop chargé*, elle avait l'air de balbutier au terme d'une crise d'amnésie et de déranger ses voisins [...][221]

And, if we then turn to *Nedjma*, we can see that it is not just Nedjma and certain characters in *Les Ancêtres redoublent* who, by virtue of their bearing witness to the repetition of self-perpetuating and regressive structures, acquire an awareness or a weariness that would seek an epistemological shift. For even Mustapha betrays an acknowledgement of the possibility that his understanding of identity, national and personal, might be couched in a hereditary symbolic objectification of Nedjma as he states of Mourad, who has just been involved in a contretemps with Suzy's father: "Qui sait de *quelle ardeur héréditaire* Mourad croyait s'être préservé lorsque, loin de Nedjma, en présence d'une toute autre femme, il eût ce geste de démence [...]".[222]

However, perhaps Kateb's most intriguing "pessimistic" rendering of a potential feminine emancipation, in this case through a depiction of the ephemeral possibility of men's relinquishing their stake in the symbolic agon, comes towards the end of *Nedjma* in what Woodhull refers to as the "whirling blood" scene.[223] In the scene, which Woodhull claims to represent "the last figurations of the emerging nationalist community", Lakhdar wrestles with letting go of a will to circumscribe Nedjma's activity, while the oneiric, swirling narrative flow speaks to a stirring of blood, a dismembering and disordering of fixed conceptions of nationhood, predicated on atavistic structures of symbolic capital and masculine control.[224] Again, gloomy references to the possibility of Nedjma's symbolic enclosure punctuate the narrative as Lakhdar fixates on the masculine subjects to whom Nedjma might be attached (Kamel, Mourad, himself). However, after Lakhdar has locked Nedjma in a room where he wrongly assumes Mourad to be, believing therefore that he is delivering her to a rival related to him by blood, we read:

> Le vent avait rasé le salon, proscrit toute vision, et le tourbillonnement du sang ne permettait à aucune idée de se fixer, comme si la ville, à la faveur de l'orage, était délivrée des feuilles mortes, comme si Nedjma elle-même tournoyait quelque part, brusquement balayée.[225]

---

[221] Kateb Yacine: *Le Polygone étoilé*, p. 148 (emphasis added).
[222] Kateb Yacine: *Nedjma*, p. 200 (emphasis added).
[223] Winifred Woodhull: Rereading "Nedjma", p. 56.
[224] Citation from Winifred Woodhull: *Transfigurations of the Maghreb, Feminism, Decolonization, and Literatures*. Minneapolis: University of Minnesota Press 1993, p. 35.
[225] Kateb Yacine: *Nedjma*, p. 263–264.

Here we see blood, Nedjma (woman) and the geography of the state to come (la ville) set in parallel and all cut adrift from their epistemological moorings. Then, at the end of section IV, Lakhdar, having previously been tortured by separations from and contact with Nedjma, seemingly leaves her to her own signification, accepting the impuissance of his phallocentric, potentially obsessional desire and his conceptual mastery of her ontology, having discovered that Mustapha, and not Mourad, "était seul avec Nedjma":[226]

> Quand je les ai enfermés, Mustapha n'existait pas, il était resté dans l'ombre comme l'arme secrète de la réalité ; mais, rompant les amarres, je savais qu'un vent ami rendrait le naufrage inéluctable. Ce vent était Mustapha et le naufrage me rapprochait de l'amante autant qu'il m'en éloignait ; c'est une femme perpétuellement en fuite [...] Lakhdar entendit des coups de pied dans la porte du salon; il conclut que c'était le petit pied de Nedjma. Il s'allongea de nouveau contre la porte du salon, remit la clé dans la serrure, tourna et sortit.[227]

However, what is subtly, indeed elegantly troubling about this final paragraph, are the chilling resonances generated by the "coups de pied" assigned to Nedjma and Lakhdar's "clé dans la serrure". A little prior in the text, Lakhdar states with regards to Nedjma: "*Un bijou pareil, je l'attacherais à mon lit*".[228] One thus wonders as to the deliverance of Nedjma, irrespective of Lakhdar's apparent surrender, whether he might have confused unlocking for locking just as he confused Mustapha with Mourad. Thus, at this very final point of this scene of nationalist culmination which implies the relinquishing of Nedjma as woman/symbol, a "pessimistic" warning is delivered, connecting with a signifying chain that stretches through the *Cycle* and that connotes the dangers of symbolic sequestration.

As a whole, Kateb's project, or at least its approach to the generation of socio-political meaning as regards women's representation, can perhaps be metaphorically summed up in a line of Hassan's in *Les Ancêtres redoublent*. He says to Mustapha, of war:

> Aucune importance. Notre peuple en a vu d'autres. Il sait bien, lui, qu'une guerre comme la nôtre, n'ayant jamais cessé, ne sera jamais finie.[229]

This is to say that Kateb's literary contribution to women's representation in the late-colonial period is a beautifully complex web of meaning in which a contin-

---

[226] Ibid, p. 264.
[227] Ibid, p. 264–265.
[228] Ibid, p. 257.
[229] Kateb Yacine: *Le Cercle des représailles*, p. 143.

ual and self-problematising focus on the approach to signification and its future generation is shown to be as important as meaning itself. Of course, Nedjma is a complex composite "polygone étoilé", incorporating innumerable referents and meanings. The fashion in which one approaches these meanings, however, as invited by the books' practices of literary subversion, is what determines their true contribution to notions of representation. Similarly, Kateb's depictions of his protagonists' approaches to Nedjma's potential meaning and value supplant in importance the protagonists' particular assessments of her. Through Nedjma's particular depiction, the Algerian woman's symbolic implication in the struggle for independence, in the identities and interactions of colonial protagonists, is emphasised such that our focus is drawn to their epistemological approach, one that rests upon a fixity of meaning that they generate. In contrast, the position of Kateb's texts represents a freeing up of meaning, a relinquishing of control, a continual struggle, assisted by a "pessimistic" acknowledgment of the resilience of retrograde epistemes, to invoke new significations determined by future action, future struggle, in particular the struggle of women.

3 Mohammed Dib: From one Gender to an Other

The literary authority of Mohammed Dib, his canonical status, is almost unrivaled in Algerian literature of the late-colonial period. Indeed, with perhaps the exceptions of Kateb and Assia Djebar, his name is almost invariably the first and sometimes the only to be mentioned by non-specialists in the West, if and when his nation's literature comes under discussion. Dib was born, of course, in Algérie Française and his name, as a writer, was forged in the revolutionary crucible that produced the independent state with which his writing is inexorably linked. Indeed, on the reverse cover of the Points edition of *L'Incendie*, the middle work in his *Trilogie Algérie*, a Louis Aragon quotation reads, "L'audace de Mohammed Dib, c'est d'avoir entrepris, comme si tout était résolu, l'aventure du roman national de l'Algérie". Dib's early literary creations were concerned with articulating the emergence of a new independent people and though his work would subsequently depart from focusing on a revolutionary milieu, indeed, from an Algerian context altogether, his trilogy of *La Grande maison* (1952), *L'Incendie* (1954) and *Le Métier à tisser* (1957), along with his Picassoesque depiction of the war itself in *Qui se souvient de la mer* (1962), would ensure the bond between Dib's work and an Algerian identity in formation, including, pertinently for this study, women's position therein.

Abdelkebir Khatibi affirmed in 1968 that "ce sont surtout Mohammed Dib et Kateb Yacine qui ont pu intégrer le thème de la révolution dans une littérature romanesque valable" and this belief in the singular validity of their depictions holds amongst critics and readers today.[230] When one thus considers, for example, how contemporary critics like Patrick Crowley and Ranjana Khanna have investigated the extent to which architectural monuments to the revolution continue to shape understandings of gender roles and relations in Algeria, one can begin to appreciate how Dib's textual monuments may have occupied a dominant position in the literary representation of Algerian women in the late-colonial period and beyond. Certainly, for the Western reader, his texts are a first port-of-call when wishing to access a supposedly "definitive" representation of the Algerian experience of late-colonialism, of the war of independence and, importantly for this study, of its actors.[231]

---

[230] Abdelkebir Khatibi: *Le Roman maghrébin: essai*. Rabat: Société marocaine des éditeurs réunis 1979, p. 94.
[231] The scare quotes here acknowledge the problems associated with realism's inability to fully represent, a key problematic that this chapter will address.

What this corpus of texts evinces, however, in disharmony with an anticipated "fullness" in Dib's representations, is an emphasis on representations of femininity and gender which undermine the sovereignty of masculinity, and which depict femininity as having a profound, radical impact upon masculinity, sparking social progress, "revolutionary" change. Moreover, Dib's representations of gender not only assign femininity a key role in political and social progress, but themselves also attempt to incorporate a progressive, non-masculinist formal stance as they represent women whilst avoiding a determination of their ontology or symbolism.

The notion of difference, of a feminine otherness, vocal, spatial and psychic/structural will be seen to probe and challenge a singular, phallic masculine logic in Dib's work. Indeed, this chapter will seek to articulate a tension within his texts between representations of masculinity and femininity, both in the Algerian trilogy and more clearly in the more historically liminal text of *Qui se souvient de la mer*, which suggests a maternal, feminine disruption, related in some instances to a conception of the *semiotic* as put forward by Julia Kristeva.

At the same time, this chapter will not shy from demonstrating how, following a Bourdieusian logic, aspects of the early realism of Dib's "definitive" representations perpetuate a gendered *dissymétrie fondementale* in their apportionment of symbolic capital from a *Vertretung* position that fails to represent Algerian women, that replicates and perhaps reinforces their symbolic exclusion from positions of social power. Furthermore this chapter will also discuss the dangers of hypostatisation and re-appropriation latent in the establishment of a feminine position in opposition to masculine symbolism, especially where metaphorisation is omnipresent, potentially overdetermining the feminine with a weighty symbolism that might approximate to a pernicious deification.

However, it will be the principal goal of this chapter to build perspicaciously on the work of critics such as Peter Hallward and Charles Bonn, in a focus on Dib's texts' evocation of spaces of signification, "other" spaces, geographical, psychic and sonorous, which, as sites of subjective and societal change, produce productive visions of gender difference and gender relations. I hope to describe how the women of Dib's texts are intriguingly associated with understandings of intangible otherness, contrary to the plenitude of the male position, how concordantly the texts yield an order of their *Vertretung* positioning and in so doing illuminate the possibility of and the necessity for reflection on and change in gender relations, in both literary and socio-political contexts.

A substantial section of this chapter will, for example, investigate how Dib's texts depict a particular melancholic subjective relationship with figures of maternity/femininity that, whilst not without potentially problematic ramifications, holds the potential to undermine and subvert a masculinist epistemic order. Not only this, but it is my contention that in *Qui se souvient de la mer*, a critique of a masculinist episteme is formed by the text, suggesting its unwillingness, or perhaps rather its inability, to accept a non-phallic space, represented as feminine. This critique resonates with a key epistemological coordinate in Kateb's work in its underpinning by a melancholic, "pessimistic" critical stance which depicts a quest for an understanding of femininity which is continually forestalled by the workings of masculine desire.

As with the analyses of Kateb's œuvre, the corpus of works will be dealt with as a whole (the Algerian trilogy and *Qui se souvient de la mer*), allowing for resonances and disharmonies between works to be illuminated. At the same time this chapter will perhaps maintain a greater appreciation of the texts individually and of the importance of their chronology as together they cannot be conceived as a literary *cycle* in the same way that Kateb's works could. To begin, this chapter will focus on perhaps the most readily apparent level of women's representation in Dib's work, on the "realism" of their depictions, on the way that women are constituted as historical actors in the corpus.

3.1 Realist Plenitude and the Coming Revolution

Peter Hallward, in his section on Dib's work in *Absolutely Postcolonial*, evokes, via a couple of citations from *Peau noire, masques blancs,* the Fanonian thrust of the early texts that constitute the Algerian trilogy. Hallward cites, in connection with these works, Fanon's conception of literature's "only truly pressing task, which is to move the community toward reflection and mediation" in order to transform "the subjective certainty I [Fanon] have of my own value into objective universally valid truth".[232] Additionally, David Macey, in his biography of Fanon, writes that "in terms of Fanon's schema, the most significant [of Algerian writers] is probably Dib", emphasising in particular the articulation of a people in revolt in *L'Incendie*.[233] A necessary corollary to this coincidence of revolutionary ideals is an emphasis on the importance of a specific, representative, realism that serves as a means to form an anti-colonial subjectivity.[234] Fanon, in *Les Damnés de la terre,* insists on the imperative of the writer's proximity to the

---

[232] Peter Hallward: *Absolutely Postcolonial: Writing between the Singular and the Specific.* Manchester: Manchester University Press 2001, p. 194.
[233] David Macey: *Frantz Fanon: a biography.* London: Verso 2012, p. 783.
[234] Azzedine Haddour, for example, in *Colonial Myths.* Manchester: Manchester University Press 2000, emphasizes Dib's specific realism, contrasting it with the effacement at work in the œuvre of Camus.

people, on the importance of avoiding an exoticising "stock de particularismes" by situating oneself "au centre même de la lutte de libération".²³⁵ In turn, Hallward shows us how the Mohammed Dib of the 1950s proudly claimed that "everything that is said about Omar [the chief protagonist of the Algerian trilogy] and of his environment was taken directly from reality" and that "a work is of value only to the degree that it is rooted, that it draws its sap from the country to which it belongs, that it introduces us into the world that is our own".²³⁶ What this section will principally investigate is the extent to which this project of realist specificity, an ideologically informed quest, necessarily cannot avoid missing its target, that is to say a production of an inclusive picture of the Algerian citizen, especially with regards to women.

Timothy Brennan famously states that "[n]ations [...] are imaginary constructs that depend for their existence on an apparatus of cultural fictions in which imaginative literature plays a decisive role".²³⁷ Equally, however, cultural fictions, in articulating notions of a nation and its people, depend on these "imaginary constructs", imaginary identifications with the structures resultant from the Symbolic order of a given context. Slavoj Žižek writes that "in the network of inter-subjective relations, every one of us is identified with, pinned down to, a certain fantasy place in the other's symbolic structure".²³⁸ In producing an image of society, all subjects are necessarily viewed, however enlightened the viewer might be, through an ideological prism that conditions and takes its cue from the Symbolic order of language, from the "trans-individual socio-linguistic structures configuring the fields of inter-subjective interactions".²³⁹ The object conforms, in the perception of the subject, to a fantasy place conditioned by the constitution of the Symbolic order, in representations of people differentiated as genders or "types" by societal discourses. Where a society's dominant ideology is such that women are overlooked, excluded, considered as inherently "other" to man and his activities, representations that claim to produce "reality" will inevitably struggle to produce a picture that this other might recognise. This is not to say that it is impossible to challenge the ideological interpellation produced in relation to a masculinist socio-symbolic order but rather to say that representations that act in a mode that seeks to reproduce "the way things are" really reproduce "the way things seem", the way reality is viewed through

---

235 Frantz Fanon: *Les Damnés de la terre*. Paris: Éditions La Découverte 2002, p. 212 + 222.
236 Peter Hallward: *Absolutely Postcolonial*, p. 190.
237 Timothy Brennan: The National Longing for Form. In: Bill Ashcroft/Gareth Griffiths/Helen Tiffin: *The Post-colonial Studies Reader*. London; Routledge 1995, p. 173.
238 Slavoj Žižek: *Enjoy Your Symptom!* London: Routledge 2008, p. 6.
239 Adrian Johnston: Jacques Lacan, http://plato.stanford.edu/archives/win2016/entries/lacan.

the intermediary of fantasy and the Symbolic. Thus, as one might anticipate, the language of Dib's work, where it clings to a mode of realist plenitude, where, in the words of Stephen Slemon, his texts cannot be seen to operate in a mode that acknowledges "an awareness of referential slippage", does constitute a masculine vision which is to some extent blind to a potential feminine reality, foreshadowing a central theme that this monograph will cover in its chapter on Mouloud Mammeri.[240] Simply, we can sometimes view the pictures of women generated by Dib's texts as reproducing models and stereotypes that exist as a product of masculinist ideology or as overlooking feminine existences that this ideology ignores. And, it is where Dib's texts do not allow space for the production of other meaning through a literary mode that undermines a fully realist project, where we are invited to see "the way things are", that, inevitably, one can most readily detect the potential influence of sexist "imaginary constructs", to refer to Brennan once more.

Evidently, one cannot affirm that it was Dib's intention, nor is it possible in a finite literary construct, to detail all the possibilities of women's agency; a novel, even a trilogy, is always a partial image. One might perhaps argue that Dib's texts are completely free from ideological interference and simply represent the partial picture that he wished to create. However, where representation purports, through its realist stance, to be able to speak the truth about an emergent people as part of a project of national culture, it is crucial to identify the points in representation that collude with patriarchal/masculinist economies through a form that comes to assign certain essential attributes to women, whilst failing to include aspects of historical reality. Dib's trilogy represents a politically engaged attempt to articulate a people and a nation in gestation, in revolt against colonial oppression. Where a realist mode is employed, therefore, it is of import to investigate how his depictions of the reality of this people and nation in fact represent a vision conditioned by the masculinist ideology of his era. With regards to the failure to include aspects of historical fact, again, it would be churlish to suggest that all writers should have been compelled to cover women's active engagement in the Algerian War and the insurgencies that proceeded it. Yet it remains important to point out these oversights as examples of the continuation of what Bourdieu calls "la division du travail d'entretien du capital social et du capital symbolique qui assigne aux hommes le monopole de toutes les activités officielles, publiques, de *representation*", especially when discussing the work of a figure of

---

[240] Stephen Slemon: Modernism's Last Post. In: *ARIEL* Vol. 20, No. 4 (1989), p. 12.

such authority as Dib.[241] As Bourdieu states, "les hommes sont aussi prisonniers, et sournoisement victimes, de la représentation dominante".[242]

The first novel of the Algerian trilogy, *La Grande Maison*, follows the struggles of Omar, a young boy living in Tlemcen, as he negotiates the singularly female space of Dar Sbitar, the large communal dwelling alluded to by the book's title. He lives in a small apartment with his mother, Aïni, his two sisters and, for a time, his grandmother. These four characters can be seen, to some extent, to represent three potentially problematic, ideologically informed registers that determine a realist mode which depicts the women of this text and those of the other two in the trilogy. The proximity of the characters to Omar lends them a template status that, although undermined elsewhere by Dib's exploration of the subversive potential of a notions of femininity that oppose masculine plenitude, impacts upon the reader in its plenitude, in its realist thud.

To begin with Omar's sisters, they can be seen to represent a banal, infantile idiocy that almost comes to justify Aïni's dispiriting negation of female worth when in free indirect speech we are told: "Une fille ne compte pour rien. On la nourrit".[243] Where Omar is quiet and thoughtful, Aouïche and Mériem chatter and giggle; where he is understanding of Aïni's constant fight to provide, the girls are thoughtless and plaintive; where Omar gradually begins to pose questions about his condition and the condition of his peers, they continue to complain and seemingly remain oblivious to the possibility of there being systemic reasons for their situation. Indeed we may view their representation as part of what Naget Khadda refers to as "la vision misogyne du discours social ambiant qui enferme les femmes dans une essence faite de futilité, de sottise, de propension au bavardage, et au commérage".[244] Khadda also emphasises the preponderance of verbs such as "jacasser", "piauler", "glapir", "caqueter" and "glousser" that suggest a trivialisation of women perhaps best encapsulated in a scene in which the political leader Hamid Saraj sits reading, engaging his mind in the cause of furthering his understanding and the understanding of others. In this same scene we read:

---

[241] Pierre Bourdieu: *La Domination Masculine*, p. 71 (Bourdieu's emphasis).
[242] Ibid, p. 74.
[243] Mohammed Dib: *La Grande maison*. Paris: Points 1996, p. 86.
[244] Naget Khadda: *Mohammed Dib, cette intempestive voix recluse*. Aix-en-Provence: Edisud 2003, p. 120.

> En ce temps-là, les femmes allaient souvent épier Hamid. Il était toujours en train de lire. Elles s'en retournaient en courant, avec des mouvements de volatiles effarouchés, dans un grand froissement de robes.[245]

Omar's grandmother, on the other hand, is the ultimate representation of woman as pure suffering victim. The reader is encouraged to feel great sympathy as this ancient, sore-ridden woman cries out in the night, only to be admonished and punished by her daughter for disturbing her. She is defined by her status as victim even more so than the unhappy Mama of *L'Incendie* and can be viewed as exemplary of the fate of Algerian women in poverty induced by colonialism. This exemplarity, however, despite the pathos that the texts generate, unfortunately tends towards an understanding of Algerian women as helpless, as unable to match the stance of their male counterparts in resisting the oppression of the colonial system.[246]

Finally, Aïni must perhaps also ultimately be viewed as a victim, though her victimhood is only outlined once we have been compelled to face her cruelty and her lack of motherly kindness, as an explanation thereof. She appears to represent, to some extent, a view of Algerian women as in hock to emotion, as defined by affective responses to the conditions with which they are presented. In contrast, in *La Grande Maison*, the first female character we encounter, Yamina, can be viewed as an ideal imaginary figure, since it is an absence of Yamina's characteristics, chiefly of her ungrudging provision of food and kindness, that marks Omar's relation to his mother. Indeed, immediately following an encounter with Yamina, at the very outset of the text, we are confronted with a perfect example of Aïni's reluctance to *bercer*, the verb that is so omnipresent in Dib's later work, *Qui se souvient de la mer*. Omar sees his mother peeling cardoons, and enquires as to when they will be ready. Aïni almost immediately flies into a rage, insults Omar by crying "Tu n'as pas honte, fille!" and throws her kitchen knife at him, which imbeds itself in his foot.[247] Aïni's narrative agency is often determined by descriptions of her failure in a duty of tenderness towards her children, a failure which appears to stem from her inability to deal with the strain of subsisting in the context of Dar Sbitar. This duty of tenderness is evoked by Omar's frequent reflections on protection and affection. Omar wishes for "le présence d'Aïni près de lui pour qu'elle le recouvr[e] de sa toute puissance de mère" and when he does have an encounter with feminine warmth and protec-

---

245 Mohammed Dib: *La Grande maison*, p. 61.
246 This kind of victimhood representation contrasts with the representations of feminine resistance visible, as one will see, in the works of Feraoun, for example.
247 Ibid, p. 12.

tion, his experience is framed in a kind of uncanny relationship to a primordial connection in an unattainable past, evocative of the infant-mother bond prior to castration, entry into the Symbolic order.[248] Following his sexual interaction with Zhor, a girl who also inhabits Dar Sbitar, we read the following:

> Une douceur sourde s'amassait en lui, qui finit par faire place à un sentiment de dépaysement. Brusquement il éprouva une sécurité jamais connue et qui semblait familière.[249]

It should be made clear that the registers outlined above do not, of course, entirely determine Dib's representations of women in the texts of our corpus. They do, however, persist as tags easily applied to the women of the trilogy and, particularly with regards to the first and third registers (women as infantile, women as determined by affective responses to their context), the texts produce in their marked juxtaposition of masculine and feminine subjects, an emphasis on the active productivity of the former and the relegation to triviality of the latter. In *La Grande Maison*, near the beginning of its final third, we leave the "prison" of Dar-Sbitar, to witness a recollected political gathering of men. Where Omar informs the reader prior to this recollection that in response to the question "Mais pourquoi sommes-nous pauvres ?", nobody could provide him with an answer: "Jamais sa mère, ni les autres, ne donnaient de réponse", here, Hamid Saraj, as his audience diligently listens, outlines the reasons for the suffering of the Algerian worker and the anti-colonial remedies for his condition.[250] In the penultimate passage in the section, we read that "[d]e tels hommes sont forts. Et ils sont savants et courageux : ils connaissent la vérité comme nous la connaissons, nous".[251]

With no subject directly assigned these words, the passage can be read as belonging to Omar's thoughts, or indeed to an omniscient representative, a Man recognising the power of inscription held by another. And, throughout the trilogy, notwithstanding the occasional probing and questioning of characters like Mansouria, it is male characters who ask "le pourquoi et le comment de ceux qui mangent et de ceux qui ne mangent pas".[252]

However, though one might argue that a certain essentialisation is created by the masculine/feminine dichotomy mentioned above, Dib's texts do examine, or invent, a level of explanation for the "failings" of their female characters. Aïni

---

[248] Ibid, p. 42.
[249] Ibid, p. 74.
[250] Ibid, p. 112.
[251] Ibid, p. 117.
[252] Ibid, p. 163.

is perhaps the best example of this. Though neglectful, reactive and violent, her inability to act in a maternal mode is still predicated on the difficulties she faces, generated ultimately by the colonial system. Naget Khadda writes that "Aïni (source ou œil en arabe) porte un nom de douceur et d'amour mais la misère et le surmenage l'ont acculée à une violence récriminatoire".²⁵³ Indeed, what Dib's early texts also appear to allude to is a compulsion for women to forsake the "douceur" of an ideal of motherhood, stemming from a need to occupy a more liminal position in a spectrum of gender roles, as a result of the pressures of colonial poverty. Aïni's rage can be thus interpreted as the taking on of a masculine pose, forbidding and harsh, whilst remaining an impoverished, downtrodden woman. Furthermore, in spite of her apparent neglect, implied for example where we read that "[o]n aurait étonné à sa mère si on fût avisé de lui dire qu'il n'était pas bien indiqué de laisser un enfant traîner de la sorte [in the streets]",²⁵⁴ she takes great pride in her status as provider, in work:

> Je dis que je travaille pour eux, ajouta Aïni. C'est sûr. Je me fatigue, je me tracasse, je me casse la tête... Mais c'est leur bien.²⁵⁵

Perhaps also the fact that Aïni rarely holds a maternal sobriquet and is seldom referred to as being a mother at all, in contrast to Mama of *L'Incendie*, also alludes to the acquisition, through her daily strife, of a level of self-perceived agency in the sense that she holds her own name, as actor. However, ultimately what the texts reveal, up to and including *Le Metier à tisser*, is the fruitlessness of feminine "work" in its exclusion from milieux of political import. This is not to say that the feminine, in Dib's early work, cannot participate in the overthrowing of colonial norms. Indeed it will later be argued that these early texts imbue notions of femininity with a subversive potential that opposes colonial order. Rather, it is my argument that where characters like Aïni, Mansouria and Zahra aim at work and socio-political inscription in a masculinist order whose nature is reflected in the gendered divisions present in the texts themselves, their power is extremely limited, their effect negligible. Ultimately they are victims. And, though Dib's masculine characters do not bring about tangible change in the colonial order and are also at times depicted as victims, bound as many are to a belief in the irrevocable nature of their second-class status and with seemingly little hope of improving their situation, they do engage in a specific proto-political reaction, in what, in reference to *L'Incendie*, Charles Bonn refers to as "l'af-

---

253 Naget Khadda: *Mohammed Dib, cette intempestive voix recluse*, p. 123.
254 Mohammed Dib: *La Grande maison*, p. 24.
255 Ibid, p. 56.

fleurement progressif d'une prise de conscience", as they organize, associate and debate.²⁵⁶ Aïni's striving and posturing, in a similar fashion to Mama's bravery in the face of her husband, Kara Ali's abuse, is certainly depicted with great pathos such that the reader is encouraged to feel great sympathy for her, to the point that we are to share in Omar's position of descriptive pity when we read that "[i]l restait saisi et comme étranger devant tant de faiblesse et d'abandon".²⁵⁷ My contention, however, is that when part of a realist project of historical representation, the women of Dib's texts seem not to participate in the proto-*littérature de combat*, that the trilogy represents. In a sense, one can interpret their presence as lagging behind the men, as cut off from a revolutionary present. This division is encapsulated in a description of Moul Kheir in *L'Incendie*:

> Grand-mère Moul Kheir se tient comme un roc sur ce que fut notre passé.
> [...] Cela, c'est pour le passé. Mais revenons au présent.²⁵⁸

It is of course, in this discussion of a literary exclusion of Algerian women, important to consider the historical referent, the extent to which the thrust of these representations reflect reality. Again, one cannot expect a text, or a trilogy, to fully represent the myriad realities that constitute a group's lived experience of history. Equally, if there were no engaged referent, no "real" committed women for a realist proto-*littérature de combat* to represent, one could perhaps only expect an absence in their reflection. A statement like the one that Dib himself made in 1970 that "Les romanciers sont empêchés de donner aux femmes le rôle essentiel, puisqu'elles ne l'ont pas réellement" could perhaps underpin a justifiable reluctance to lend women, in their realist representation, a role that they did not possess.²⁵⁹ It is, however, important to note that women were engaged, even as *militantes*, before Dib saw *La Grande Maison* published in 1952. In *Les Femmes algériennes dans la guerre*, Djamila Amrane-Minne rejects arguments that point to an inevitable, culturally-determined, political exclusion of women, demonstrating that though the PPA-MTLD acted such that women's participation in the organisation was limited in its scope, there were notable exceptions who succeeded in playing important political roles whilst, perhaps most importantly,

---

256 Charles Bonn: *Lecture présente de Mohammed Dib*. Algiers: Entreprise nationale du livre 1988, p. 41.
257 Mohammed Dib: *Le Métier à tisser*. Paris: Points 2001, p. 37.
258 Mohammed Dib: *L'Incendie*. Paris: Points 2002, p. 29.
259 Mohammed Dib: Interview. In: *L'Afrique littéraire et artistique* No. 18 (August 1970), p. 14.

there existed more generally a will to engage amongst Algerian women.[260] Amrane-Minne informs us that "[l]es femmes [étaient] reléguées dans une organisation féminine à activités surtout sociales; seules quelques-unes d'entre elles arrivent à s'intégrer au parti [...]".[261] She goes on to describe how Hocine Aït Ahmed, a member of the central comity of the PPA-MTLD dedicates his *Mémoires d'un combattant. L'esprit d'indépendance. 1942–1952* to "femmes algériennes, gardiennes de la culture populaire, et dont le rôle, toujours méconnu, fut essentiel dans la perpétuation de la personnalité algérienne et de la résistance, aux militants et aux *militantes*", whilst writing of notable examples such as Mamia Chentouf, highlighting the existence, if not the abundance, of women taking an active role in the early revolutionary period.[262] [263]

Of course, it should be borne in mind that the trilogy's narrative proceeds from the beginning of the Second World War and concludes with the American invasion in 1942. However, the events of its temporal setting, as has been outlined by critics like Charles Bonn and Jean Déjeux, take a post-Sétif context as their referent. Déjeux has shown how, for example, the events of *L'Incendie* are based on a strike in Aïn Taya, which Dib covered in the communist newspaper, *Alger Républicain* in 1951.[264] Indeed, though set prior to the events at Sétif, the historical moment that has been cited by so many as the catalyst for mass revolutionary participation, Dib's narrative clearly invokes the substance of a contemporary *prise de conscience* in its situatedness as "littérature de combat, littérature révolutionnaire, littérature nationale".[265] Bonn writes that "[l]e fait passé [the Second World War] et connu désigne ainsi indirectement le fait à venir, dont l'importance est bien plus grande pour le peuple algérien", continuing to write of how "*L'Incendie*, par ailleurs, a été composé explicitement dans

---

260 The 'Parti du Peuple Algérien', previously 'l'Étoile nord-africaine', became, on its dissolution, the 'Mouvement pour le Triomphe des Libertés Démocratiques', in 1946. The paramilitary wing of the MTLD, known as the 'Organisation Spéciale', was the forerunner to the FLN.
261 Djamila Amrane-Minne: *Les Femmes algériennes dans la guerre*, p. 31.
262 Djamila Amrane-Minne: *Les Femmes algériennes dans la guerre*, p. 34–35 (emphasis added).
263 Chentouf participated in the demonstrations at Sétif in May 1945 and from 1946 was responsible for the first women's clandestine cell of the PPA-MTLD in central Algiers, comprised of women of differing socio-economic backgrounds. On page 36 of *Les Femmes algériennes dans la guerre* Amrane-Minne also notes that "[d]'autres cellules de femmes se constituent sur le même modèle que les cellules d'hommes".
264 See John Déjeux: À l'origine de *L'Incendie* de Mohammed Dib. In: *Presence Francophone* No. 10, (Spring 1975), p. 3–8.
265 Frantz Fanon: *Les Damnés de la terre*, p. 211.

l'optique d'une efficacité pédagogique militante".²⁶⁶ The texts of the trilogy take the completed recent past as a context in which to situate, as an omnipresent haunting referent, a contemporary, incomplete happening. The struggles of the fellahin being referred to as *"la drôle de guerre"*, for example, indicates both the historical distance between the events and their inscription as well as the texts' invocation of a *vraie guerre*, a revolutionary war, stemming from a mass awakening that will reach a historical conclusion like that brought about by the Americans' arrival at the end of *Le Métier à tisser.* ²⁶⁷ Of course, as a depiction of events metonymic with those of Dib's time of writing, these texts do not seek to articulate an *omnipresent* blossoming of radical nationalist consciousness as this was yet to exist in either the stated temporal context of the texts or its contemporaneous referents. They are, to an extent, testimony to the need for the Algerian people to find a voice. However, they do provide the necessary foundations of a constitution of actors for any kind of progression-in-plenitude to be felt by the reader. By a "progression-in-plenitude" I understand a bodily advancement of the consciousness of the Algerian people, a physical manifestation of a growing self-assertion in the face of colonialism.

This is where I would again refer to the figure of Grand-mère Moul Kheir, as a marker of women's lagging behind participation in the template for a *prise de conscience* that the trilogy represents. Once more, it cannot be argued that literary texts are obliged or indeed fully able to incorporate a sufficient portrait of a people or a nation in progress. What is noteworthy for my work, though, is that what we read about the Algerian women of the texts does not slide into place, in a metonymic relation to Dib's contemporary moment, in the same way as that which we read about our male figures does. More simply, where we can view a group of male actors who tally with their contemporary equivalents, entering the realm of revolutionary engagement, the women of the trilogy are not represented, through a realist mode, as relating to contemporary female agents. We may note, for example, in *L'Incendie*, an equivalence formed between masculine and feminine positions of subjugation as we read, upon Omar's learning of the fate of a country worker, mangled by a colonial agricultural machine, that "[s]on esprit avait déjà saisi le rapport qui existait entre cette mort et la pauvre fatigue de sa mère, entre le sort des fellahs et la faim de Dar Sbitar[...]".²⁶⁸ But, there is a palpable difference in the texts' depiction of the potentiality of their present and

---

266 Charles Bonn: *Lecture présente de Mohammed Dib*, p. 34.
267 *la drôle de guerre* was a term coined after the event, purportedly in 1940 by *Le Figaro* newspaper, which entered common parlance in the post-Second World War period to refer to an early period in the war in which hostilities were limited between its major belligerents.
268 Mohammed Dib: *L'Incendie*, p. 78.

future action. Consequently, with regards to women's tangible, extant impact upon the narrative, in both the context of the text and that of its referent, one is almost compelled to see these historically situated situations as tallying with Comandar's understanding of gender when he states:

> La terre est femme, le même mystère de fécondité s'épanouit dans les sillons et dans le ventre maternel. La puissance qui fait jaillir d'elle des fruits et des épis est entre les mains du fellah.[269]

Indeed, what really underscores the distance between the women in the trilogy and the sorts of referential actors to which a proto-*littérature de combat* would allude, is the accent placed on gendered contemporaneous change in *Qui se souvient de la mer*'s depictions of the Algerian war. Here, Dib's work appears acutely aware of women's role as actors in revolution. For, framed in an overtly masculine vision, that of its nameless male narrator, the text functions to a large extent as a commentary on a male reluctance to incorporate women into a "masculine" social realm. In his chapter 'Sex on Fire: Mohammed Dib and the Algerian Revolution', Jarrod Hayes spells out the thrust of the social commentary that the book enacts, of its evocation not only of women's active participation in insurgency but also of the progressive impact on gender relations that such participation promised to inaugurate:

> Nafissa's newfound freedom to circulate, to come and go independently of her husband's wishes (a necessary freedom in light of her participation in the revolution) disturbs and threatens the narrator and, in short becomes his obsession. In Dib's vision, the Algerian Revolution is therefore a sexual revolution as well.[270]

Dib's text, like Kateb's work, alludes to a fear of *fitna*, the Arabic term connoting an association between socio-political disorder and feminine desire.[271] For the masculine narrator of the text, the militant "porteuses de feu" whom he encounters, in particular his wife, Nafissa, are initially the cause of much consternation and provoke fearful accusations such as: "Est-ce que Nafissa se dérobe, me trahit?".[272] Indeed, the women of *Qui se souvient* are described in a minimally real-

---

[269] Ibid, p. 27.
[270] Jarrod Hayes: *Queer Nations: Marginal Sexualities in the Maghreb*. Chicago: University of Chicago Press 2000, p. 137.
[271] *Fitna's* cognate *nushuz* is also investigated in my chapter on Feraoun.
[272] Mohammed Dib: *Qui se souvient de la mer*. Paris: Éditions de la Différence 2007, p. 55.

ist way as involving themselves in revolutionary acts and as associating in political dialogue amongst themselves, excluding our narrator, much to his dismay:[273]

> Elle [Zoulikha] s'adressait aux autres femmes.
> – De quel droit ? Nous ne sommes pas des...
> Dans l'éblouissement du soleil de midi, les mots s'envolèrent, désintégrés. J'entrai dans notre chambre [...][274]

The Algerian woman stands out in *Qui se souvient de la mer*, her presence is felt, and her representation can be seen to reflect a lived masculine experience which begins to accept a change in her role in society. Famously, our narrator, for example, poses the question:

> Qu'est-ce qui me faisait redouter une métamorphose que je pressentais devoir être inévitable et pourquoi voulais-je refuser aux choses de se révéler sous d'autres figures ?[275]

The text's depiction of women's political involvement is a crucial inclusion if Algerian literature of the revolutionary period is to allow the reader to gain access to an inclusive and "verisimilar" picture of a nation in gestation. However, what is perhaps rather more important in this text is that, in contrast to much of the realist plane of the Algerian trilogy, here we view women through a particular lens that acknowledges its inability to represent in plenitude, thus inviting us to question the parameters of narrative control. For even in the gesture of producing a minimally realist portrait of women as historical actors, a part of the oppressive gesture of a determination-in-representation that cannot accurately (re)produce her image will remain present. Indeed, in the next section it will be seen that it is where women are represented as escaping the control of realist narration, where the texts attempt to reject a potentially oppressive, determining gesture of ideologically conditioned representation, that Dib's work yields a framework rich with interpretive possibility that calls into question, undermines and exceeds representation that excludes women from the revolutionary project. This is not to say that Dib's texts' formulations of the feminine beyond realism are without problematic knots, but rather to suggest that the ontology of Algerian

---

[273] I characterise the form of their description as "minimally realist" because though their description does not break in style from the oneiric narrative, the outline of their active participation in history is clearly present.
[274] Ibid, p. 44–45.
[275] Ibid, p. 105.

women is interestingly associated with notions of radical progression which exceed her limited role as historical actor in the trilogy.

3.2 Feminine Voices, Articulating Change

Charles Bonn's study, *Lecture présente de Mohammed Dib* affirms that "l'essentiel de l'inscription historique de *L'Incendie* n'est point tant son signifié, que codifiait ma première lecture, que le signifiant lui-même".[276] To the extent that Bonn is here referring to the development of an anti-colonial "parole", I would agree with the thrust of his analysis and would argue that it is not just in *L'Incendie* that one notes a focus on manners of speech, on the productivity, or non-productivity, of differing orders of articulation. Where I would differ in my use of language when considering this idea is in the use of the word "signifiant" as, when understood within the linguistic frameworks instituted by Jacques Lacan and developed by subsequent psychoanalysts, the *signifiant* comes loaded with a masculine logic, as representative of the metonymy of desire instigated by the imposition of the name-of-the-father and the separation from the mother. What one detects throughout Dib texts, in contrast, is the insistence of a femininity, of representations of a conception of maternity, in the presence of a poetic language that, following the words of Julia Kristeva, "is coupled with crises of social institutions (state, family, religion), and more profoundly, a turning point in the relationship of man to meaning".[277] Indeed, whilst it is clear that for "revolution" to proceed, Dib's texts illuminate the necessity for action-in-plenitude which would of course equate to ordered discourse, to the linking of signifiers in the Symbolic realm, a key motor, if not the chief motor in the revolution of signifiers appears precisely as the feminine, the maternal, perhaps the Kristevan *semiotic*. Though not without important difficulties to address, Dib's representation of Algerian women through a mode that emphasises a nature different from the Symbolic but impactful upon it allows for her consideration beyond the parameters defined by the realism of the text. Her influential force and her sempiternal oppression are thus articulated, or rather presented, such that a further debate regarding gender relations and the nature and potential of the feminine and of women is invoked, outside the confines of the descriptions of the narratives.

---

276 Charles Bonn: *Lecture présente de Mohammed Dib*, p. 37.
277 Julia Kristeva: *Desire in Language: A Semiotic Approach to Literature and Art*, p. 140.

3.2 Feminine Voices, Articulating Change

Beginning with the first text of the trilogy, one notes a profound difference between the representations of gendered voices. At the level of what is articulated in discourse there is a somewhat troubling difference between the limited speech-texts that the women produce and those of their male counterparts, with Hamid Saraj's interventions making this division particularly clear. However, within descriptions of the hubbub of Dar Sbitar, "la grande maison", one notes the presence of a heterogeneity to meaning and signification that one can connect with the "rhythms, intonations, glossalalias" to which Kristeva refers in 'From One Identity to An Other' as she details the symptoms of the insistence of the semiotic, of the remnants of the relation to the mother prior to entry into the Symbolic order.[278] Perhaps the key example of this comes within the interaction between the law and the women of the internal world of Dar Sbitar, as the police arrive in search of the political leader Hamid Saraj, producing a state of commotion that is interrupted by "la voix de Menoune":[279]

> Après quelques instants d'accalmie, elle se mit à chantonner à voix basse :
> *Quand la nuit se brise*
> *Je porte ma tiédeur* [...][280]

Introduced by italicisation, a visual break with the standard prose of the preceding text, Menoune's voice, her "chant", her "cri", disrupts the narrative whilst invoking the cries of other women in the shared dwelling. As Naget Khadda writes, in a formulation very much akin to Kristeva's articulation of the presence of poetic language, "la malade délirante, déjà postée au seuil de la mort, libère par la force poétique de sa parole, l'enfoui des consciences féminines, fait retentir par-delà la communion identitaire du moment face aux intrus la dénonciation d'une autre oppression [...]".[281] The poetic vibrations of her speech are depicted, though not explicitly, as setting off a chain reaction, causing other women to join in an order of speech that the text depicts as escaping the discursive logic of the episode and as affecting the possibility of change at its conclusion. Fatima, Hamid Saraj's sister, first follows suit and we read that "[s]a plainte monta, vrillante, et Dar-Sbitar tout entière vibra, pénétrée de part en part par la malédiction qu'elle proféra".[282] Menoune then replies in kind, seemingly welcoming "the rhythm of a drive that remains forever unsatisfied":[283]

---

278 Ibid, p. 133.
279 Mohammed Dib: *La Grande maison*, p. 45.
280 Ibid, p. 44.
281 Naget Khadda: *Mohammed Dib, cette intempestive voix recluse*, p. 121.
282 Mohammed Dib: *La Grande maison*, p. 45.

> Sans se rendre certainement compte de ce qu'elle disait, elle reprit plusieurs fois:
> *Mère fraternelle,*
> *Les femmes dans leurs huttes*
> *Attendent mon cri.*[284]

Subsequently, her unconscious invocation is again responded to, as Attyka joins the clamour: "Il se forma un son aigu qui résonna sans relâche, perçant le cœur endolori des gens de la maison. Et l'air se mit à trembler".[285] The section closes with the police leaving Dar Sbitar and with Ben Sari forming a critique of the law: "Elle m'a condamné avant même que je sois né. Elle nous condamne sans avoir besoin de notre culpabilité. Cette justice est faite contre nous, parce qu'elle n'est pas celle de tous les hommes. Je ne veux pas me soumettre à elle...".[286] Seemingly, here, the very structure of the episode articulates a value, underappreciated and impossible to articulate, that obtains in a feminine cry, in a voice that is other. The text does not establish tangible discursive links between its feminine speech acts and between these speech acts and the departure of the police, nor is Ben Sari's critique linked in symbolic conversation with them. Instead, we have represented a feminine force, a drive, heterogeneous to the Symbolic that bubbles up when activated by the catalyst of a traumatic event, resulting in a progression in the narrative and its fully symbolised realisations of opposition (Ben Sari's critique). Furthermore, beyond narrative progression stemming from the irrational interconnectedness of the poetry of feminine voice, is the indication that there is a true heterogeneousness to ordered speech that is associated with the women and that perhaps, to refer back to Kristeva again, "utters incest", the pre-linguistic relationship between proto-subject and mother.[287] Kristeva uses the notion of "incest" in connection with a heterogeneity to ordered speech because, in her work, the semiotic recalls the connection to the mother in the pre-oedipal state, before the incest prohibition established by the father that also brings about entry into ordered language. Consequently, the articulation of this kind of "incestuous" heterogeneity itself alludes to a potential feminine/maternal disruption of the structures of the Symbolic order, of oppressive ordered discourse, colonial or masculinist.[288]

---

283 Julia Kristeva: *Desire in Language: A Semiotic Approach to Literature and Art*, p. 142.
284 Mohammed Dib: *La Grande maison*, p. 46.
285 Ibid, p. 47.
286 Ibid, p. 49.
287 Julia Kristeva: *Desire in Language: A Semiotic Approach to Literature and Art*, p. 137.
288 Of course, a Beauvoirian reading of this Kristevan feminine "heterogeneity" might also argue that Dib's evocation of difference replicates the practices of othering, mystification and mythologisation highlighted in *Le Deuxième sexe* and elsewhere.

Many examples present themselves in the texts of Dib's corpus where one can detect attempts to evoke a feminine order of speech that, in its representation as contrary and resistant to a fixed, symbolic logic of discourse, holds a unique potential to engender change. Khadda herself discusses the scene in *L'Incendie*, for example, where the women of the village of Bni Boublen gather to lament the departure of the young male conscripts and in so doing seemingly invoke a force that, though connected to the events depicted, stands as a unifying yet irreducible rejection of an eternal subjugation. And Bonn discusses how he interprets "la parole des femmes" which "refuse de se réduire au service d'un 'message', si progressiste soit-il" as being articulated by Zhor's body-as-voice in the chapter that immediately follows chapter XV, in which the politicisation of the fellahin's speech has taken place.[289] Consequently we can view an underdetermined feminine voice, literally "incorporated", as holding a significance that escapes the ordered discourse of the text whilst bearing a weight of resistant meaning within it. One may also point to instances where Aïni's speech is recorded in similar terms and, perhaps most poignantly, to the speech of Omar's grandmother when we read that "[l]a voix de l'aïeule ouvrait un passage à une détresse immémoriale".[290] In each case, Dib's texts hint at the potential of the feminine/maternal voice without fully determining it, instead deploying narrative signposts, incorporating incomprehensible noises ("Bouh! Bouh!") as markers of difference and, perhaps most commonly, generating descriptions that remain underdeveloped in their refusal to deploy full, ordered articulation, definitive discourse, often by situating these voices as part of Omar's necessarily limited perspective.[291] Dib's representation of a potentially Kristevan feminine voice maintains the poetic disruption that it stands for through this voice's very articulation, in the refusal to have it comply formally with the determining realist descriptions of the texts.

Moreover, though one could suggest that the return that is witnessed in each book, the lack of an improvement in the lives of Aïni or her family, can be read as speaking to the failure of a masculinist Symbolic order to truly change, it can be convincingly argued that *Qui se souvient de la mer*, by contrast, foresees a more radical symbolic and epistemic break whilst at the same time forming a critique of the potential for socio-symbolic arrangements to fail and even to become "counter-revolutionary".

---

[289] Charles Bonn: *Lecture présente de Mohammed Dib*, p. 48.
[290] Mohammed Dib: *La Grande maison*, p. 155.
[291] Ibid, p. 128.

Aside from the *mère/mer* homophony constantly at work in *Qui se souvient*, one also notes a proximity between "pierres" and "pères", a feature with whose significance the text often plays. In the early movements of the book, where we witness the first allusions to the strife of revolutionary war (the presence of the winged *iriaces*, the abduction of certain men, the desperate enquiries of their wives and children) we note how our narrator, when pushed to articulate the crisis, can only form "pierres": "Forcément, mon gosier n'était plus apte à former des sons mais exclusivement des pierres".[292] This failure of language is expressed in the same section of the book in relation to masculine characters Lkarmoni and Ismaël who are both subject to this "langue des pierres/pères" and who are both comforted, or perhaps cured, by the speech of women.[293] Indeed, in the case of Ismaël we find that the poetic force of a feminine voice is directly connected with the resolution of his fruitless speech-acts: "Ismaël [...] ne jetait la pierre à personne [...] Il avait encore une autre femme pour lui chanter l'air à faire passer la frayeur: sa femme".[294]

Here it would seem that though the text encourages its reader to face a failure in masculine articulation, the role of women remains limited to liberating men of the burden of their stones/signifiers. However, as the narrator departs from this scene with his wife, Nafissa, a more radical alternative to masculine discourse is alluded to where we read of a "bourdonnement porteur d'un chant échappant aux lois de l'harmonie [qui] s'accordait pourtant à ce qui m'entourait", which would tally more closely with the music that the narrator confuses with the revolutionary movements of the "taupe" and "les coups de boutoir de la mer".[295] From this point onwards, the narrative is punctuated with sites of "other" speech that are alluded to as accompanying radical change, but whose nature remains undetermined. One might reference the song of the star, the truth-bearing intonations of Nafissa's conversations, the sounds of the sea and, of course, "ce grondement de fin du monde" juxtaposed with the exclamation: "La mer!" just prior to the final revolution of the text where we read that "[q]uelquefois me parvient encore un brisement, un chant sourd, et je songe, je me souviens de la mer".[296]

---

[292] Mohammed Dib: *Qui se souvient de la mer*, p. 31.
[293] One sees an intertext here with Samuel Beckett's *Molloy*. Paris: Éditions de Minuit 1982 [1951], as his protagonist, compelled to continue to articulate something, finds relief analogous to speech in sucking stones.
[294] Ibid, p.33.
[295] Ibid, p. 36 + 31.
[296] Ibid, p. 211 + 216.

However, what this last citation also intimates is the potential for new configurations in consciousness to snap back into their original position, to fail, as their attempts to represent reality rest on the dominion of the Symbolic. For remembrance (of the mother/sea) implies the piecing together of something that has been lost. One notes how despite the momentous "revolutionary" changes that the text alludes to, a "retour au langage des pierres" is noted,[297] both where "un movement collectif" is concerned and, where our narrator, as representative, finishes his quest.[298] As Louis Tremaine notes, the narrator, upon entering the underground, works on "pointless, distracting, and ultimately self-centered scholarly study", overlooking the epistemological revelations that he has seemingly been privy to on his quest.[299]

Moments of epistemological revelation run the risk of being undermined and overthrown in the act of articulation/representation/embodiment by our masculine narrator within the text just as evocations of a people/nation in gestation have been shown in this chapter to be undermined by realist articulation. Indeed, on reading of the narrator's blinding to difference and cleaving to academic articulation, where he states at the conclusion of the book that "[i]l me faut étudier de près les structures de la ville du sous-sol, sans quoi je ne pourrais pas m'adapter, comme il serait souhaitable, aux nouvelles conditions de vie où me voici placé",[300] I was compelled to think of how Luce Irigaray discusses the sublimated male homosexuality of pedagogy. As Jane Gallop puts it: "There is a certain pederasty implicit in pedagogy. A greater man penetrates a lesser man with his knowledge".[301] Our narrator, despite his entry into the revolutionary space of "la ville du sous-sol", seemingly regains his will to penetrate, to determine meaning in a phallic mode through a return to a masculinist epistemological form as he ceases to be attentive to the feminine voice that has conditioned his quest. Similarly, in the trilogy, the potential radical change to which a feminine voice seemingly calls, in its political determination by masculine agents, can be argued to be subsumed, co-opted, whilst nevertheless remaining in some sense inaccessible to the text.

What is crucial to note here regarding women's representation and gender relations, is that *Qui se souvient de la mer* illuminates the dangers that lurk in

---

297 Ibid, p. 132.
298 Charles Bonn: *Lecture présente de Mohammed Dib*, p. 58.
299 Louis Tremaine: Psychic Deformity in Mohammed Dib's *Qui se souvient de la mer*. In: *Research in African Literatures* Vol. 19, No. 3 (1988), p. 298.
300 Mohammed Dib: *Qui se souvient*, p. 214.
301 Jane Gallop: *Feminism and Psychoanalysis: The Daughter's Seduction*. London: Macmillan 1984, p. 63.

an approach that acknowledges femininity while ultimately assigning it a position of supplementarity. And these dangers are reprised in the rationale behind reservations regarding the extent to which Kristeva's conception of the semiotic represents a truly radical interpretation of signification and the influence of the mother. Judith Butler, for example, writes that "Kristeva argues that this libidinal source of subversion (the semiotic) cannot be maintained within the terms of culture" and that "it is unclear that the subversive effects of such drives can serve, via the semiotic, as anything more than a temporary and futile disruption of the hegemony of the paternal law".[302] Indeed, Kristeva herself writes that "however elided, attacked, or corrupted the symbolic function might be in poetic language, due to the impact of semiotic processes, the symbolic function nonetheless maintains its presence".[303]

My argument is that like Kristeva's theoretical texts, Dib's texts seek to establish another site of language, a feminine site that purports to be "revolutionary" whilst acknowledging a degree of inevitability regarding its co-option into a masculine logic at the point of discursive articulation. Consequently, whilst producing an order of representation that allows the Algerian woman, in a disruptive manner, to step beyond her symbolic inscription of the text, to evade determining representation, Dib's texts, in particular *Qui se souvient*, display a "pessimism", similar to that found in Kateb's texts, that dissuades the reader from developing a utopian view of revolution, political and sexual. Nonetheless, *Qui se souvient de la mer* does highlight women's political engagement and, as this chapter will now investigate further, evokes, along with the trilogy, the influence of feminine structures and spaces, including a particular melancholic relation to maternal femininity, which encourages the reader to consider the relation between colonised subject and mother in a universal sense.

Dib's texts do not produce a conclusive picture of an ideal of women's representation but do represent a profound attempt to present a potentially impossible representative formal structure in their depictions of vocal otherness. *Qui se souvient* differs from the trilogy in that it does so from a narrative position that suggests more clearly the fallibility of its representation, leaving behind the sure moorings of the omniscient third person to acknowledge the necessary failure of *Vertretung* representation, even where feminine alterity, vocal and otherwise, is recognised and evoked.

---

[302] Judith Butler: *Gender Trouble*, p. 102 + 103.
[303] Julia Kristeva: *Desire in Language: A Semiotic Approach to Literature and Art*, p. 133.

3.3 Gendered Frontiers

Towards the conclusion of *L'Incendie* we read of Omar the following:

> Il n'acceptait pas l'existence qu'on lui offrait. Pour quelque raison informulable, ce qu'il pressentait au-delà lui paraissait plus important, plus essentiel. Au milieu des siens il était persuadé qu'il ne saurait y atteindre. Mais sans les siens, il refusait d'y atteindre.[304]

Here we have articulated for us, in appropriately ambiguous terms, a subjective tension predicated on the interaction between the "au-delà" and the "milieu", between conceptions of the outside and the inside, forming a link between a notion of progression, in this instance with reference to Omar's existential development, and the negotiation of physical spatial thresholds that evoke conceptual borders between genders. This tension can be seen to characterise the identifiable quests for psychic, revolutionary and gender-related forms of progress in the trilogy and *Qui se souvient*. And, just as with my investigation of a vocal femininity, though we have here evoked a progression from inside to out, from Dar-Sbitar to the outside world, which we can figure as a movement from the maternal to the paternal, we simultaneously note the perdurance of the importance of the interior ("sans les siens, il refusait d'y atteindre"), which we can link to notions of the pre-Symbolic, the maternal, a perdurance that the texts illuminate both in its own right and in its relationship with a desire to explore, to make progress. Both Omar and the narrator of *Qui se souvient* are involved in movements between physical spaces, areas that are explicitly or implicitly gendered, (usually following a feminine/maternal/interior vs. masculine/paternal/exterior schema), but Dib's texts maintain a sense of interaction, overlapping and ambiguity of function that complicates a binary understanding which might produce a representation of the maternal as an oppressive interior space of impotence. Furthermore, Dib's texts produce representations of feminine spaces that seemingly defy appropriation into their male protagonists' quests, indicating an independence in importance, historical and perhaps essential, beyond their (masculine) articulation and their use for the furthering of the texts' male protagonists. Though in the first instance one sees women associated with areas that have to be left behind, Dib's work comes to lay the conceptual groundwork for a potential feminine destination.

Initially, at the simplest level of interpretation, one detects in Dib's texts an opposition between what one might term "unproductive wombs", in contrast to the productive feminine underground discussed later, and an outside that repre-

---

[304] Mohammed Dib: *L'Incendie*, p. 167.

sents freedom and exploration, accessible only once a break occurs that, in Hayes' words, would "separate the male child from his mother's body (cutting the umbilical cord) and from the childhood world situated within women's spaces (circumcision)".[305] Thus the maternal space of Dar Sbitar, for example, is equated by Omar's narration and by a parallelism with Hamid Saraj's incarceration, with imprisonment, while the outside world is equated with Omar's freedom. However, taken even at this level, our texts appreciate a basic dialectic that engenders a will to investigate other avenues that may bring about greater fulfilment. This is encapsulated perfectly in *Qui se souvient*, where, in an early section that relates the narrator's experience of the smothering blackness of his family chateau we read:

> N'eussé-je connu que cette oppression, j'aurais sûrement gardé pour notre maison, avec son domaine, une rancune inaltérable, mais la vie familiale me rejetait vers la lumière qui ruisselait sur la campagne et par opposition intégrait toute chose dans un ordre rayonnant.[306]

From Dar Sbitar to the workshop of *Le Métier à tisser* to the maternal chateau of *Qui se souvient*, each of these primary spaces is represented as being a foundation for desire in this way. However, in exceeding the boundaries of these spaces, a profoundly disturbing severance must take place whose ramifications Dib's texts intriguingly evoke. In both *La Grande Maison* and *Qui se souvient*, a departure from maternal space is accompanied by a wound in the foot, almost evocative of an Achillean vulnerability as Achilles was, of course, dipped in the river Styx by his mother Thetis, rendering him invulnerable up to the ankle by which his mother held him. Indeed, these injuries are also evocative of an Oedipal connection, echoing the wounds that Laius dealt to his son Oedipus' ankles before arranging for his abandonment.

What is evoked in these instances, strongly echoing the Lacan's framing of the mortifying departure from the satisfying maternal space into the Symbolic, is a sense that a departure cannot be undergone without suffering. What this means for Dib's representation of gendered space is that, in the progression of its protagonist, a simple break, a valorised departure into a "masculine" space, connected with political and personal progression, is not and cannot be achieved. Indeed throughout *Qui se souvient*, we read references to an originary cataclysm that can be interpreted in many ways, not least as referring to colonisation, but that the reader is certainly encouraged to view as linked in a

---

[305] Jarrod Hayes: *Queer Nations: Marginal Sexualities in the Maghreb*, p. 252.
[306] Mohammed Dib: *Qui se souvient de la mer*, p. 51.

profound sense to quasi-Œdipal constellations, including the mortifying entry into the Symbolic:

> Un ancien et silencieux cataclysme nous ayant arrachés à nous-mêmes et au monde, seul un nouveau cataclysme pouvait nous y reprojeter.[307]

Dib's picture of femininity is further complicated, however, by the feminine/maternal functioning of the "ville du sous-sol", the underground area in *Qui se souvient* that, in its contrasting representation to that of Dar-Sbitar and the maternal chateau, one might describe as representing a "productive womb". The underground, in its connivance with the sea, its positioning in the belly of the city, its production of counterdiscursive "language" and its deep bond with the narrator's wife, comes to represent a maternal/feminine space par excellence. However, like Nafissa, it represents a productivity that, in its representation as a destination from the narrator's perspective, embodies a potential future rather than a longed for past. Indeed, one may argue that the underground which "ne connaît pas de limites", which stands as the site of a "revolutionary" future in opposition to the rigid, phallic rock of the dead city, interrupts the possibility of an easy fit with a psychoanalytical metaphorisation that would see the feminine/maternal as primary/imaginary space and the masculine/paternal as secondary/Symbolic space.[308] Indeed, what much of the figuration of the underground does, tallying with the functioning of the characterisation of Nafissa, is problematise and split the conceptualisation of space that conflates the maternal and the feminine and associates the feminine with return, backwards movement. The underground represents a site of radical agency in the text and, despite its welcoming of uterine comparisons, our narrator struggles to stage a return to the womb, to enter the underground at the end of the text.[309] The narrator understands not only that bridging the gap between the city, the space of mortal symbolism, and the underground, a limitless zone of evolution, will require more than simple recognition but also that a drive to proceed in such a way should be understood in communal terms: "Le savoir certes ne suffit pas, il faut pouvoir y entrer. Que chacun, en ce cas, y consacre ses énergies, au lieu de les gaspiller à cette vaine existence".[310] However, perhaps the most important gendered "space" in Dib's oeu-

---

307 Ibid, p. 96.
308 Ibid, p. 214.
309 For a perspective on the prominence of the *regressus ad uterum* as a feature of Maghrebian literature, see Hédi Abdel-Jaouad: "Too much in the Sun": Sons, Mothers and Impossible Alliances in Francophone Maghrebian Writing. In: *Research in African Literatures* Vol. 27, No. 3 (1996), p. 15–33.
310 Mohammed Dib: *Qui se souvient de la mer*, p. 205.

vre and the space which does the most to associate femininity with progression is the sea. What one may argue as regards this space is that, though akin to the underground in many ways, it draws our attention more closely to a particular masculine psychic relationship with a maternal figure that Dib's work evokes.

3.4 Maternal Melancholy

Like the underground, the sea, "la mer", can be read as an active feminine space, engaged in a revolutionary process that would see the colonial city undermined and washed away. From the beginning of the narrative of *Qui se souvient* until its conclusion, the sea is presented as aiding the underground in its battle against "la sournoise reptation des murs", the shifting make-up of the Symbolic city. Indeed, in the penultimate paragraph of the text we are told that:

> la ville était morte, les habitants restant dressés au milieu des ruines tels des arbres desséchés, dans l'attitude où le cataclysme les avait surpris, jusqu'à l'arrivée de la mer dont le tumulte s'entendait depuis longtemps, qui les couvrit rapidement du bercement inépuisable de ses vagues.[311]

However, even here, at what might be adjudged to represent the final victory of the feminine force that the sea represents, the text attests to the ineluctable bond between "la mer" and "la mère". While she wipes away the dusty remnants of the crumbled city and its inhabitants, she maintains her duty of care, her traditional maternal credentials. Here, as at many other points in the narrative, the reader is invited to recall the French nautical saying "La mer berce comme la mère". The sea's specific proximity to a conception of maternity within an understanding of femininity, beyond the obvious homophony, is reinforced time and again within the first-person narrative of the text through narrative descriptions, repeated subjective responses, that emphasise its soothing, nurturing qualities. Furthermore, the constant repetition of the verb "bercer" and like terms comes to substantiate a singularly strong metaphorisation, as the sea remains peculiarly underdetermined in terms of its material attributes, in contrast with other spatial zones like the underground.[312] Some critics have seen this metaphorisation

---

[311] Ibid, p. 216.
[312] The most famous citation that establishes the sea's motherly representation comes where we learn from the narrator that "[s]ans la mer, sans les femmes, nous serions restés définitivement des orphelins; elles nous couvrirent du sel de leur langue et cela, heureusement, préserva maints d'entre nous ! Il faudra le proclamer un jour publiquement" (Ibid, p. 33).

as part of a symbolisation that would draw focus on a fear concerning the revolution's foreclosure of the Algerian woman's traditional guise as mother, a fear they argue is conveyed by a plaintive reading of the text's title as a question. Miriam Cooke, for example, writes that "Dib was warning Algerians that the mother, the most honoured role for women within Algerian society was going to be forgotten".[313] Certainly we have seen how Dib's texts do concern themselves with a breakdown in a certain ideal of motherhood, in particular in their depictions of Aïni, in the *Trilogie Algérie*. It also cannot be denied that the narrator of *Qui se souvient* is greatly disturbed by what he perceives as Nafissa's abdication of a protective, maternal role that he would see as extending not just to their children but also to himself. Thus, for example, he says of her the following, indicating his expectation of her catering to his need for cradling:

> Nafissa, elle, se gardait de dire quoi que ce fût. Gagnée par la douleur de l'homme ? Non, patiente, attendant. Persuadée que son moment viendrait tôt ou tard, qu'il lui faudrait soigner, guérir, *bercer*.[314]

Nevertheless, what this section proposes is that though Dib's texts do focus heavily on the figure of the mother, making of her a somewhat oppressive figure in conceptualising femininity, *Qui se souvient* in particular provides material rich in subversive potential in its depictions of metaphorised and real maternity. It does this by engaging both with the narrator's peculiar colonial preoccupation with the mother (a bond that can be viewed in the texts as melancholic, as representing a disturbed repression of a loss) and with a contingent potential for a renewed relation to a feminine otherness.[315] This renewed relation will be shown to oppose the limiting circumscription of established feminine/maternal roles, engendering productive change and, possibly, epistemological revolution.

Moreover, it is possible to argue that the narrator's bond with the figure of the mother may stand as a template that alludes to a shared masculine experience and that the attending ramifications for his epistemological quest are relatable to a wider context. Both Judith Roumani and Louis Tremaine have noted that the psychological journey that the narrator takes can be read as inviting a representative bond between the "community and the 'self'", and Dib's monumental text does indeed invite us to consider its narrator as exemplary, as just

---

[313] Miriam Cooke: *Women and the War Story*, p. 135.
[314] Mohammed Dib: *Qui se souvient de la mer*, p. 33–34 (emphasis added).
[315] This maternal bond also recalls the importance that Kateb placed on his mother's creative influence.

one of the "orphelins" contending with colonial reality.³¹⁶ This is achieved through statements that allude to a shared male experience; through the articulation in many passages of a feminine solidarity between "porteuses de feu" and in opposition to the narrator's bewildered subjectivity; and also through the lack of description of the narrator. He, like the sea, can thus be understood as a representative figure as well as a common result of a peculiar colonial structure.

Tremaine's study produces a reading that sees the text as a depiction of arrested development amongst Algerian men. Indeed, in many ways his article sees Algerian male adulthood as a stage more intensely preoccupied with childlike concerns than childhood itself. Tremaine writes:

> It is the *adult's* world that is full of "monsters" – iriaces, spyrovirs, minotaurs, mummies, and so on – not the child's.³¹⁷

For him, the narrator is perennially beset by the psychic consequences of unsatisfied childhood needs, chief of which he cites as being "the child's need for comfort and protection" from the mother.³¹⁸ I would certainly agree that the narrator's monologue and his actions evince signs of an inescapable yearning for, indeed r*emembering* of, a maternal presence manifest in his reflections on people and spaces, from Nafissa to the sea. Where I would differ with Tremaine's conclusions, however, is in his gloomy assertions that see his narrator as ineluctably constrained by this bond, as unable to admit new, complex existential understandings into "full conscious consideration".³¹⁹ Tremaine cites, for example, a passage that, he argues, demonstrates how the narrator is "painfully aware of the arbitrariness of his perceptions"; however, he refuses to then grant him psychic development, despite this awareness.³²⁰ The passage, the beginning of which has been cited before in its connection to changes in Nafissa's role as a woman, reads as follows:

> Qu'est-ce qui me faisait redouter une métamorphose que je pressentais devoir être inévitable et pourquoi voulais-je refuser aux choses de se révéler sous d'autres figures ? (Peut-être plus vraies ; je m'arc-boutais à des significations que je savais être entre toutes les moins sûres.)³²¹

---

316 Judith Roumani: Mohammed Dib's *Qui se souvient de la mer:* Literary Technique and the Drama of Algeria. In: *Revue CELFAN* No. 2.2 (1983), p. 10.
317 Louis Tremaine: Psychic Deformity in Mohammed Dib's *Qui se souvient de la mer*, p. 286.
318 Ibid, p. 286.
319 Ibid, p. 287.
320 Ibid, p. 297.
321 Mohammed Dib: *Qui se souvient de la mer*, p. 105.

Surely what this passage precisely illuminates is the narrator's opening up to new epistemological constellations, the imperfect tense implying a past habit? At the very least the reader can determine that the narrator has been shaken in his certainty regarding the make-up of his existence and the figures that inhabit it. His affective relation with Nafissa, a figure of femininity identified with the mother in the representation of his psyche (the 1st person narrative), disturbs his epistemological foundations, pushing him in the direction of considering existence otherwise.[322] And, as one follows his quest, time and again one is compelled to view his goal as the reaching of a new configuration with a feminine Other, in a Beauvoirian sense, sometimes figured as Nafissa, sometimes in more spatio-metaphorical terms (the sea, the underground).

Indeed, many passages could be cited to support this reading of the narrator's quest as driven by a desire to modify and ameliorate his relation to a Beauvoiresque feminine Other, to form a more mutually appreciative "rapport sexuel",[323] but one that is particularly of interest, considering its yoking of the sea and Nafissa, begins with the following citation, near the "revolutionary" conclusion of the text:

> Les plus coupables sont ceux qui se défiaient de la mer, choisissaient de s'enfermer chez eux. Celle qui prodigue le plus d'elle-même ne le fait pas par contrainte ou pour donner l'exemple, mais par une poussée, une nécessité qui récusent le calcul.[324]

The narrator thus establishes the feminine presence of the sea/mother as a force of primary importance with whom a relationship must be maintained. The reader is then impelled in the next line of text to form a connection between the narrator's chastising of those who would turn their back on the feminine/maternal presence of the sea and his struggle to exist in relation to his wife:

> Marchant et réfléchissant ainsi, je découvre devant moi Nafissa dont je reconnais l'allure rapide malgré le voile qui la dérobe aux yeux.[325]

Thus Nafissa and the sea/mother are located together, juxtaposed in the text and positioned in the narrator's quest as omnipresent teloi which are sought as a

---

[322] Indeed, one might interpret the narrator's relationship to maternity/femininity as evocative of an appreciation of a Lacanian feminine "not-all" that undermines phallic meaning/order, which I evoke in my chapter on Feraoun.
[323] See Jacques Lacan: *Le Séminaire. Livre XVII. L'Envers de la psychanalyse*. Paris: Éditions du Seuil 1991 for more on a Lacanian view of the dysfunctional nature of the "rapport sexuel".
[324] Mohammed Dib: *Qui se souvient de la mer*, p. 188.
[325] Ibid, p. 188.

function of revolutionary progress. Moreover, Nafissa, as the representative of a feminine subject, is depicted as partially revealed, as having her essence veiled, implying that the narrator is incapable of mastering an understanding of her ontology but that a search for comprehension thereof is of capital importance. Finally, of the section that subsequently describes the narrator's meeting with Nafissa, Winifred Woodhull argues that the scene has her appear as "a vanguard figure who brings her husband to consciousness of social change that renders the old public/private distinctions, and this the old order of gender relations, untenable".[326] The narrator presents her with two small figurines, a man and a woman, representing a retrograde gendered configuration, which she rejects, explaining that "[t]u voulais que je leur redonne vie et les réchauffe sur mon sein, de mon souffle. Le savais-tu au moins ?".[327] Importantly, her husband, the narrator, does recognise his unconscious will to have her nurture, to have her return to a maternal determination, allowing for his subsequent understanding of the precariousness of his positioning with respect to the feminine Other, as he states: "C'était bien ça, je le reconnais".[328] [329]

Furthermore, though I would accept that the narrator does not find Nafissa herself again in the "ville du sous-sol", a point whose pertinence will later be again emphasised, it is certainly clear that his ingress therein is driven and conditioned by his focus on the feminine marker that she gives him (a rose) and by the feminine/maternal spaces with which she is so linked. With regards to his attempt to enter the underground, the text states:

> Pour cela, les nuits ne me sont pas d'un faible secours. Influentes, elles m'enseignent le chemin. Les nuits, la mer. Identiques dans leur substance. Mais il me faut aussi surveiller l'apparition ou de la rose, ou de l'étoile, avant de retourner chez Osman Samed : c'est une condition nécessaire.[330]

This kind of motivated progression must, in my view, be understood differently to the infantile complaints of the adult narrator that litter earlier sections of the

---

326 Winifred Woodhull: *Transfigurations of the Maghreb, Feminism, Decolonization, and Literatures*, p. 61.
327 Mohammed Dib: *Qui se souvient de la mer*, p. 190.
328 One might think here of de Beauvoir's affirmation that, in respect of the relationship of *l'homme* to the feminine Other, "la conversation par laquelle il atteint la véritable sagesse n'est jamais faite, il faut sans cesse la faire, elle réclame une constante tension", and how this tension is ineluctably intensified by women's embodiment of his "rêve de quiétude dans l'inquiétude". See *Le Deuxième sexe 1*, p. 240–241.
329 Mohammed Dib: *Qui se souvient de la mer*, p. 190.
330 Ibid, p. 201.

text. However, perhaps it is indeed a demand to be "bercé", an intense connection with the figure of the mother, which Tremaine associates with "psychic deformity", that alludes to a particular psychic foundation for the narrator's quest.

For it would appear that it is the manifestation in Dib's text of a melancholic incorporation of a lost connection with the mother that is precisely depicted as causing the narrator – and the Algerian male which he might represent – to enact a disturbed and disturbing relationship to the masculine Symbolic city, and to seek an otherness that might instigate profound change. Indeed, a melancholic interpretation certainly rings true with Judith Butler's investigations of formulations of melancholy first developed by Nicolas Abraham and Maria Torok, formulations which imply that the maternal body is given permanent residence in the body as a part which is "inhabited or possessed by phantasms of various kinds", echoing the subjection of the narrator in *Qui se souvient* to the mythical, possibly fantasmatic, figures of the text which disrupt and seek to overthrow the functioning of the masculine Symbolic city.[331]

Hédi Abdel-Jaouad contends that "in many respects, the Maghrebian text in French – predominantly the story of an Oedipus searching for a Laius to kill – can in fact be seen as the vindication and glorification of motherhood".[332] He cites this partiality for the mother in the context of an oppressive patriarchy and refers to Abdelwahab Bouhdiba's understanding of "le complexe du hammam", as figuring a brutal separation from the mother that engenders an intense playing out of the Freudian Oedipal schema in adulthood.[333] Exceeding this primary Freudian schema, what Dib's work perhaps further alludes to is that the colonial context itself intensifies or illuminates a connection with a maternal/feminine object lost and uneasily incorporated at the point of Symbolic castration. At the very least, one can argue that Dib's text presents the moment of decolonisation as an opportunity for the reconsideration of those repressions that condition normative masculinity and the symbolic agora of power.

Though many critics, including Tremaine, have argued that *Qui se souvient* does not explicitly reference the Algerian colonial situation, and that its narrator is seemingly unaware of, or unable to process, the specificities of the colonial relation, I would echo Peter Hallward's statement that while Dib "certainly evacuates the specif*ied*, he continues to write the *minimally specific*" and would further suggest that the text does allude to a partially aware, specific subjective re-

---

331 Judith Butler: *Gender Trouble*, p. 87.
332 Hédi Abdel-Jaouad: "Too much in the Sun", p. 18.
333 See Abdelwahab Bouhdiba's *La Sexualité en Islam*. Paris: Presses Universitaires de France 1975.

sponse to colonisation.³³⁴ ³³⁵ Certainly the reader is invited to read *Qui se souvient* within a Algerian colonial context as early on in the text s/he is presented with specific geographical coordinates: "De la Souiqua au Beylick, je coupe à travers le coeur de la Cité".³³⁶

It is my contention that in a later passage which refers to the realm of childhood, what is alluded to is the presence of colonisation as a determining force in a revalorisation of maternal otherness. In this context, the father is presented as failing in his role as a bridge to a greater Symbolic order, to its precarious constellations of exchanges which constitute the language of society, its hierarchies and divisions. The text encourages us to understand that in a colonial context in which outside space, understood by the subject as the space of men, is in some sense compromised by the coloniser, the father does not shepherd his son, the narrator, into this realm. At least, the father's attempts or non-attempts to shepherd are perceived by the narrator/subject as a failure. To put it in Butlerian melancholic terms, the "prohibitions that demand the loss of certain sexual attachments and demand as well that those losses not be avowed and not be grieved" are found lacking in their determination of the Symbolic world.³³⁷ What one might then posit in response to Dib's text, in contrast to Ahlam Mosteghanemi's claim regarding Algerian literature that "l'absence du père [...] engendre fatalement la recherche d'une paternité perdue",³³⁸ is that from this lack of introduction to the space perceived as external/masculine, a sensitivity to the structure of a melancholic bond with a lost maternal/feminine object, rejected and reincorporated as a condition of masculinity, is activated or stimulated in the narrator. It is then from this bond that the beginnings of a more subversive, progressive epistemological stance are formed towards a feminine otherness in the text. Of course, one should hesitate when situating the formation of a more progressive approach to femininity in opposition to a potential engagement in the external revolutionary sphere. Indeed, it must be emphasised that it is not non-engagement in the war that is represented by the notion of the feminine/maternal object but rather opposition to a masculine order that appears to require radical disruption for "revolutionary" change to take place.

---

334 In echoing Hallward's separation I contend that though Dib does not produce a picture wholly determined by its context, the reader is still aware of a proximity to a specific milieu.
335 Peter Hallward: *Absolutely Postcolonial*, p. 193 (Hallward's emphasis).
336 Mohammed Dib: *Qui se souvient de la mer*, p. 29.
337 Judith Butler: Melancholy Gender-Refused Identification. In: *Psychoanalytic Dialogues: The International Journal of Relational Perspectives* Vol. 5.2 (1995) p. 168.
338 Ahlam Mosteghanemi: *Algérie, femmes et écritures*, p. 47.

In the aforementioned passage referring to childhood, the narrator recounts how a mysterious figure appears, calling to him from the external space surrounding the property. We read:

> Immobile, enveloppé par la lumière, pendant que, le dos tourné au soleil, je le fixais avec saisissement, il ne semblait guère comprendre pourquoi il se trouvait ici.[339]

The figure then vanishes and our narrator is left in a position of peculiar dissatisfaction whilst an interdiction from discussing this outside zone reigns in the household: "Ma rencontre avec cet inconnu ne fit qu'aiguiser ma haine de cette existence, de cette maison, de l'atmosphère qu'on y respirait".[340] The figure is referred to as "*il*", in italics, and we are told that "son image ordonnait le monde".[341] When the narrator finally speaks of him in front of his parents, italics are again employed, signposting a heightened significance attributed to this masculine figure for the narrator. Upon speaking about "*lui*", the narrator's parents, in particular his father, act such that he understands that "je ne devais plus parler de *lui*, que je ne pouvais faire moins qu'effacer l'impression déplorable que j'avais produite.[342] Dib's character appears to achieve this desired repression, stating:

> Je me sentis, miraculeusement et sans restriction, doué de ce génie qui consiste à se réinventer à tout coup sous une autre apparence pour donner le change.[343]

Dib's text invites interpretation of the figure and the familial interplay that proceeds from the son's discovery of his presence. An initial reading, indeed, might see "*lui*" – a masculine presence that disrupts the life of the home – as the coloniser himself. Certainly, the parental injunction against speech that appears as a desire to shelter the son and themselves against the outside would support this assumption. However two small details perhaps somewhat undermine this conclusion: the narrator refers to the figure as "mon ami" and describes him as being materially impoverished: "Ses pieds étaient nus comme les miens".[344] These details notwithstanding, the figure constitutes a marker of an external, perhaps impoverished reality that one can identify as being conditioned by the colonial context. This identification is encouraged most clearly, beyond the

---

339 Ibid, p. 91.
340 Ibid, p. 93.
341 Ibid, p. 93.
342 Ibid, p. 94 (Dib's emphasis).
343 Ibid, p. 94.
344 Ibid, p. 94 + 91.

historical context of the novel, the appearance of an intriguing yet disruptive masculine figure, and the reaction of the parents, at the conclusion of the passage. Here repression fails, the narrator cannot escape facing the presence of "ces choses qui continuaient, sans rémission, à lancer leurs attaques sournoises".[345] The narrator's claim that he could have remained in ignorance of the presence of these external chimera if "ces événements, à l'origine de quoi nous ne sommes pour rien n'étaient venus tout jeter bas et créer une situation nouvelle", compels the reader to view them as products of colonialism which are to be exposed to the light and swept away by revolutionary events.[346]

Focusing on the father's failure, after having been compelled to repress the image of the figure designated as *lui*, the narrator refers to the attitude of his parents towards himself following his outburst as "dépourvue de clémence" but focuses immediately on his father without any mention, even concessive, of his mother's potential presence as being without clemency, a term whose French equivalent is used to describe the feminine figure of the sea on page 67. The father, the masculine, is framed as follows:

> Mon père, je n'avais qu'à l'observer, m'écrasait sous la vigueur de ses sens et de ses muscles, son égoïsme naturel, *l'inflexibilité* de son caractère. Ce n'était très certainement qu'un piège, très certainement, ce faisant, il visait ailleurs. Seulement, le piège m'étant tendu, il me fallait l'éviter, mais l'évitant, je devais prendre garde de tomber dans un autre.[347]

What this passage seems to allude to is twofold: First, the presence of the narrator's father is mortifying, he forms no bridge to understanding, he simply orders, stands as interdiction, providing no subjective resolution. Second, this state of psychic affairs, understood by the narrator from a position of relative maturity, in appearing to present a "piège", alludes to the sense that, in the narrator's perception, the danger of intolerable mortification posed by his father stems from his father's concern regarding another space, that of the colonial exterior as "il visait ailleurs". The narrator thus, in fearing the intervention of the paternal super-ego, does not assume a masculine psychic template that would be comfortably reconciled with the law of the father and comes to associate the unexplicated (what the figure represents of the colonial exterior) with anxiety. I pointed out that in Tremaine's reading of *Qui se souvient de la mer*, the narrator yearns for a maternal comforting deprived in childhood. It is my contention that he also

---

345 Ibid, p. 95.
346 Ibid, p. 97.
347 Ibid, p. 95 (emphasis added).

lacks in childhood the paternal guidance embodied in the text by the figure of El Hadj, for example. Because of the father's over-protection, an oppressive closing-off from access to an already traumatic colonial/external Symbolic order is staged that forges it in a forbidden, unexplicated *unheimlich* material whilst perhaps allowing the masculine and the colonial in the guise of a forbidden Law to become psychically entwined. This then provokes a particular sensitivity to and valorisation of an opposing, perhaps partially semiotic, maternal value or logic that starts the narrator on his journey towards another epistemological stance. This journey is represented in Dib's text through a kind of melancholic relation that sees the narrator project manifestations of the refused loss of the maternal/feminine sought in response to the masculine foreclosure described above, in a kind of "magical, […] psychic, form of preserving the object", displacing the worldly process of incorporation which Butler describes in works like 'Melancholy Gender-Refused Identification' onto his perception of colonial space, in the body of the text.[348][349] In this sense one can argue that the narrator is he who remembers la mer/mère.

Qui se souvient clearly gestures towards the mother as taking on a potentially "revolutionary" importance as a potent catalyst for avoiding and overthrowing a psychogeographical realm, that of the external/masculine from which our narrator has been alienated. However, the underground, the night, the sea and initially Nafissa are perhaps on one level welcoming because they represent an impossible order of "comforting" jouissance. As Judith Butler also writes, dependency on the woman is "*pursued* by the masculine subject, for the woman as reassuring sign is the displaced maternal body, the vain but persistent promise of the

---

[348] Judith Butler: Melancholy Gender-Refused Identification, p. 167.
[349] In the trilogy also, one may note allusions to an elevation of a maternal melancholic incorporation illuminated by a lack of a paternal bridge to an external colonial reality, as well as a boyhood resolution of this lack. In *La Grande Maison*, for example, one notes the invasion staged by the French troops into the home, in the absence of a paternal buffer, that provokes the text's articulation of feminine "semiotic" speech while in *L'Incendie*, where we bear witness to a greater presence of a paternal bridge as, in the words of Naget Khadda, Comandar incorporates "la médiation entre savoir ancien et aspiration révolutionnaire" (*Mohammed Dib, cette intempestive voix* recluse, p. 122–123), Omar and the narrative's focus seemingly centres more comfortably on the ordered discourse of the masculine/political. In *Le Métier à tisser*, of which Peter Hallward remarks that it "describes a situation of paralysed dispossession that could have been transcribed directly from Fanon's clinical observations" (*Absolutely Postcolonial:* p. 205), Omar remains in the womb-like workshop, surrounded by men who cannot guide him, trapped in their presence. Indeed, in itself *Le Métier à tisser* can be understood as a sign for the dysfunction of the paternal in the historical context of Dib's trilogy and concomitantly for the necessary desire for a break, for a positive disruption that was never fully lived to be inaugurated.

recovery of preindividuated *jouissance*".³⁵⁰ Crucially though, Dib's text intimates that this obsession with figuring the maternal goes beyond a simple configuration of desire which seeks to contend with the lack inherent to the displacement of desire into the Symbolic order and is borne as a kind of melancholic attachment. The narrator's narrative represents the maintenance of the maternal loss, his perspective is depicted as embodying the unresolved loss of the mother, aligning and confusing her, his wife, the sea and other feminine figures in a logic disruptive of the phallic Symbolic realm, and this leads to a quest to understand the world and its hierarchies and separations differently. In Dib's work the subject, and thus the state, are rocked: cradled *and* shaken, by an appreciation of feminine difference, instigated by a maternal focus seemingly begun in the psychic development of the child. Following on from the previous citation, Butler writes that "[man's] seemingly self-grounded autonomy attempts to conceal the repression which is both its ground and the perpetual possibility of its own ungrounding".³⁵¹ Where Butler here refers to the universal structure of man's entry into the Symbolic order and the break from a state of preindividuated *jouissance* with the mother, *Qui se souvient* delivers representations of the subversive potential of melancholic repression where sensitivity to a repressed loss is generated by a particular set of colonial gendered symbolic exchanges in which the masculine Symbolic, embodied by the father, fails in its attempts to fully represent the world and the masculine subject. In this way, the text produces depictions which echo her melancholic formulation of gender identity where she writes that "une identification mélancolique est essentielle au processus par lequel le moi assume une identité dotée d'un genre".³⁵² In *Qui se souvient* it is sensitivity to the primordial failure of an essential melancholic repression, depicted through the colouring of the masculine protagonist's world as maternal/feminine and the elevation of maternal/feminine figures to positions of subjective necessity, that is represented as benefitting the colonised subject and state, forcing the consideration of complex gendered configurations in the symbolic constitution of the nation to come.

In Dib's texts, where awareness of a melancholic subjective structure is alluded to as being activated or stimulated by paternal influences or their lack, repression is under-realised, the text, as a representation of the narrator's psyche, can and does speak the mother, constantly, involuntarily, finding her to be omnipresent in those sites of opposition to colonial space which come to define a

---

350 Judith Butler: *Gender Trouble*, p. 58 (Butler's emphasis).
351 Ibid, p. 57.
352 Judith Butler: *La vie psychique du pouvoir : l'assujettissement en théories*. Paris: L.Scheer 2002, p. 200.

geography of resistance. This does not mean, however, that Dib's texts necessarily produce subjective structures that work at an ungrounding of the colonial/masculine *for* Algerian women, and the final section of this chapter will investigate the extent to which the valorisation of the maternal can be read as holding the perilous promise of producing forms of dedication/hypostatisation that might endanger the literary and worldly representation of women's positioning as agential subjects in social relations.

3.5 For whom the Texts?

Many critics, as I have alluded to in my section on 'Feminine Voices', have concluded that Dib's revolutionary texts, though acknowledging the importance of conceptions of femininity for social and nationalist revolutionary change, assign women a supplementary role in that they facilitate change without appearing to be its beneficiaries. For example, Naget Khadda writes of Zhor in *L'Incendie* that she "prépare le rôle de médium entre le connu et l'inconnu que le personnage féminin va être appelé à jouer dans l'œuvre future de l'auteur",[353] while Winifred Woodhull affirms that "while the underground city of the future is gendered female by virtue of its figuration by Nafissa, it is far from certain that women, as well as men, will participate in spelling out all its names [the names of the new city].[354] Whilst this may be true, it is important to remember that the representations of women as mediums, as supplementary to male subjective and political revolutions, come with differing, yet readily perceptible degrees of self-awareness and do act as textual testimonies that incorporate new feminine potentialities. Furthermore, in the case of *Qui se souvient de la mer*, it seems that Nafissa and women's absence in its conclusion are key to its critical/epistemological/ethical stance.

To begin with the example cited above by Naget Khadda, *L'Incendie* does produce what might appear to be a somewhat troubling instrumentalisation of women through the confluence of two scenes that refer to a future Algerian state. Early in the book, a collection of the citizens of Bni Boublen see a horse running through the night, a symbol of longed-for liberty, past and future: "Galope, cheval du peuple, songeaient-ils dans la nuit, à la mâle heure et sous le signe mauvais, au soleil et à la lune".[355] The horse as a symbol of nation later

---

[353] Naget Khadda: *Mohammed Dib, cette intempestive voix recluse*, p. 129.
[354] Winifred Woodhull: *Transfigurations of the Maghreb, Feminism, Decolonization, and Literatures*, p. 63.
[355] Mohammed Dib: *L'Incendie*, p. 26.

returns when Omar views Zhor's naked body, making of it a kind of catalyst for his subjective development:

> L'image d'un cheval traversa brusquement son esprit à la vue du ventre nu de Zhor, un cheval somptueux, de nature mystérieuse et quelque peu funeste, mais c'était un animal qui lui permettait tous les espoirs.[356]

The idea that Zhor serves as material for Omar's fantasy is then supported by a curious addition that sees Omar take "une boule d'étoffe" from her in a kind of desperate attempt to maintain the object of his desire without granting it desire itself, recalling the obsessional mode outlined in my study of Kateb.[357] What is also quite pertinent in this scene, however, is how Zhor's gaze, initially hidden from both the reader and Omar, is revealed to have been nonchalantly present from the beginning of his spying, interrupting our yoking with Omar's perspective, causing us to take a distance from his subjective quest: "Omar, répéta-t-elle. (Elle renifla bruyamment.) Que regardes-tu ? Tu es là depuis un quart d'heure".[358]

Dib's trilogy has, as its basis, Omar's perspective. However, by incorporating a feminine voice that interrupts the plenitude of his focalised narration, the "realist" writing of the texts is subverted. While one might argue that in passages such as the one reproducing the cacophony of "le chant de Menoune", a feminine space of representation remains separate from Omar's perspective – his epistemological stance itself is left untouched – what the passage above demonstrates is that the fallibility of a masculine outlook, including therefore its ignorance of a potentially semiotic value, is highlighted in the texts. Indeed, beyond the texts' concession of Omar's socio-political ignorance, we have here an acknowledgment of the ignorance of the male gaze, of the very theatre of his episteme, again foreshadowing a focus in my later study of Mouloud Mammeri's work. We can also appreciate a tendency to undermine the perspective of the masculine narrator in *La Grande Maison*, where Dib sabotages our realist comfort in sharing Omar's perspective through the opaque writing that typifies the description of his early sexual encounter with Zhor.

In *Qui se souvient*, the supplementary position of a feminine Other, as a means of arriving at a "goal", is further problematised by an even greater degree

---

[356] Ibid, p. 98.
[357] In 'Subversion du sujet et dialectique du désir', Lacan, interestingly, refers to "le fantasme" as "proprement l' 'étoffe' de ce Je qui se trouve primordialement refoulé, de n'être indicable que dans le *fading* de l'énonciation" (Écrits, p. 816).
[358] Mohammed Dib: *L'Incendie*, p. 97.

of proximity to its male protagonist, generated through a 1ˢᵗ person perspective, in tandem with the failures of his quest. I have commented on his inability to comprehend Nafissa's change in social role and one can readily appreciate how the oneiric order of description that typifies the narrative might undermine the rectitude of his masculine stance. However, what is potentially more subtly important is the fashion in which the text presents a precarious epistemological positioning, both potentially progressive and retrograde that, with the punctuation of the narrative's conclusion, compels the reader to interrogate the danger latent in a valorised and perhaps stereotypical conceptualisation of feminine otherness.[359] The conflict between a subjective stance that appears to seek difference, that has as its goal a renewed relation to feminine otherness, and a hypostatising subjective stance that makes of "woman" a kind of deity, along with the text's conclusion (Nafissa not entering the underground), allude to a fallibility in the narrator's quest predicated on the nature of masculine psychology. Jacqueline Rose evokes this fallibility as she frames a tension between a kind of valorisation and deification thus:

> As negative to the man, woman becomes a total object of fantasy (or an object of total fantasy), elevated into the place of the Other and made to stand for its truth. Since the place of the Other is also the place of God, this is the ultimate form of mystification.[360]

She goes on to write:

> In his later work Lacan defined the objective of psychoanalysis as breaking the confusion behind this mystification, a rupture between the *object a* and the Other, whose conflation he saw as the elevation of fantasy into the order of truth.[361]

Clearly, our narrator's quest is contingent on "woman" in all her various signifying guises. While he seeks a new gender relation, her presence can be interpreted as coming to bear his *objet petit a* and as he is led along a conceptual path to a "revolutionary" future, her potentially melancholic displacement onto spaces (*la nuit, la ville du sous-sol*) along with the emphasis on her import as a maternal presence (*bercer, bercer*) may also simultaneously be interpreted as a tendency to produce a comforting hypostatised Other. A precarious epistemological approach contends with figures of femininity/maternity until a real representative

---

[359] A stereotypical conceptualisation that can be thought through within the Beauvoirian schema of the "éternel féminin" developed in *Le Deuxième sexe 1*.
[360] Juliet Mitchell/Jacqueline Rose (eds.): *Feminine Sexuality*. Basingstoke: Macmillan 1982, p. 50.
[361] Ibid, p. 50.

of woman is no longer needed. The narrator, in the underground, no longer needs or seeks to hold Nafissa's hand.

Bearing similarities to Kateb's "pessimistic" position, Dib's narratives, most noticeably *Qui se souvient*, thus refuse to produce an integrated, non-problematic subject position. Indeed, a melancholic critical posture founds their epistemological relation to "revolutionary" progress. This is to say that Dib's "revolutionary" narratives are organised around a telos whose importance is continually reinforced but whose attainment is perpetually problematised, invoking a need for continual future struggle. In *Qui se souvient* the insatiable yearning for, or psychic maintenance of, the loss of the mother that the narrator manifests exists in relation to an awareness within the text of the treacherous ground that must be crossed for a post-colonial, post-masculinist position to be reached. Melancholy for a maternal feminine value sits alongside a critical melancholy indicating an awareness of the difficulties for the male protagonist to proceed unproblematically.

Concomitantly, Ranjana Khanna, in her article 'Post-Palliative: Coloniality's Affective Dissonance', writes of an understanding of melancholia that operates as an ethical critical position within postcolonial theory that one can apply to the functioning of Dib's work. First she writes:

> The undoing of ego places the self in a different economy of subject constitution, in which normative gestures, palliatives, and alibis will always need to be critiqued. It is therefore future-oriented as much as attached to a past that cannot be forgotten or recognised within the logic of knowable memory.[362]

And then:

> Critical agency develops as the subject starts criticizing the swallowed object, and this symptom appears as self-critique. Melancholia manifests itself as an impoverishment of the ego [...][363]

Dib's textual ego and its contingent "revolutionary" literary project, particularly in *Qui se souvient*, is "undone". His texts thus function as a critical reflection of the previously mentioned melancholic relation to the mother, of its productive possibilities and possible dangers. They demonstrate that something has been swallowed and continues to make its presence felt: a relationship to the object

---

[362] Ranjana Khanna: Post-Palliative; Coloniality's Affective Dissonance. In: *Postcolonial Text* Vol. 2, No. 2 (2006), p. 4.
[363] Ibid, p. 5.

of desire that makes of its bearer an Other with whom men struggle to form a symmetrical relation.

The Dibian mode of representing Algerian women, like that of Kateb, yields aspects of representative authority which might otherwise be associated with a *Vertretung* positioning in order to produce attempts to come to terms with difference which speak for themselves, not for their object. Though we have seen that Dib does not totally avoid an omniscient narration that is ideologically interpellated and thus sometimes exclusive of women's lived experiences, he produces narratives that are inextricably bound to a male subject pole that, in addition to being represented as self-undermining, precarious and insecure, comes to allude to a melancholic relationship with a maternal/feminine value that holds the potential to begin an engagement with the Beauvoirian feminine Other, culminating in the conceptual struggle represented in *Qui se souvient de la mer*. Moreover, just as his masculine subjects show a special proximity to the maternal that implies a sensitivity to the feminine more generally, so Dib's texts call upon a semiotic presence to represent a radical feminine value that might exceed masculine realist discourse, literary and socio-political. Indeed Hayes' description of Maghrebian childhood narratives that "resurrect the past in a way that questions privilege rather than reaffirming it" can help us to appreciate how his texts reproduce something of a Kristevan feminine force that disrupts and undermines the masculine space of the text.[364] However, as a foundation to Dib's most successful probing of masculine relations to Algerian women and rendering of femininity, there lies a critical, perhaps melancholic, "pessimism" coupled with a nuanced exploration that refuses to claim ownership of a position of representation that might escape fantasy or produce a definitive image of Algerian women, on their behalf.

---

364 Jarrod Hayes: *Queer Nations: Marginal Sexualities in the Maghreb*, p. 252.

4 Mouloud Feraoun – Humility in the Representation of Women?

Debra Kelly, in her study *Autobiography and Independence: Selfhood and Creativity in North African Postcolonial Writing in French*, writes that "the publication of Mouloud Feraoun's *Le Fils du pauvre* in 1950 is generally recognized as a founding moment in the literary, cultural and political context of North African writing in French".[365] She goes on to emphasise the importance of the work, begun in 1939 and finished in 1944, as an expression of Algerian autochthonous lived experience in opposition to the Western ethnocentric, orientalist narratives that had long defined the Algerian literary domain. Moreover, the importance of Mouloud Feraoun, born 1913 in Tizi-Hibel, a small village in Upper Kabylia, as a standard-bearer for Algerian literary expression can be defended not just with reference to his status as an originator but also from the perspective of his reception in both European and, perhaps more interestingly, Algerian milieux. For studies conducted by critics such as Christiane Achour and Charles Bonn have identified Feraoun as being perceived as a peerless figurehead of Algerian literature, in particular in cultural sites under the purview of the Algerian State (schools, universities, radio etc.), in part due to a doubtless undesired martyrdom following his tragic assassination at the hands of the pro-colonial paramilitary *Organisation Armée Secrète*. Bonn writes of a survey of his students at l'Université de Constantine, conducted in 1974:

> [L]orsque dans cette enquête je demandais de citer des écrivains algériens, le nom de Feraoun revenait le plus souvent, et très souvent seul, chez des enquêtés qui n'avaient fréquemment pas lu ses textes et en tout cas trois fois plus souvent que celui de Kateb (Feraoun : 100, Dib : 82, Mammeri : 59, Kateb : 30).[366]

And Achour, in her book *Mouloud Feraoun: une voix en contrepoint*, having presented a fascinating analysis of how Feraoun's work has been manipulated and mobilised by post-colonial governments, mentions, for example, how an important section from *Le Fils du pauvre*, which this chapter will later discuss in greater detail, was repackaged as *Poterie Kabyle* and was, from 1964–1980, the first section of text studied in French in Algerian primary schools.

---

[365] Debra Kelly: *Autobiography and Independence: Selfhood and Creativity in North African Postcolonial Writing in French*. Liverpool: Liverpool University Press 2005, p. 53.
[366] Charles Bonn: De l'ambigüité tragique chez Feraoun, écrivain réputé "Ethnographique". In: *Nouvelle Revue Synergies Canada* No. 6 (2013), p. 5–6.

Unfortunately, however, this kind of State-sponsored consumption has perhaps contributed to an unjust appraisal of Feraoun's texts and in particular of *Le Fils du pauvre*, as lacking in literary innovation, as representing no more than an early attempt to voice the particularities of Kabyle existence. Indeed, Robert Elbaz and Martine Mathieu-Job boil down the dismissive tendency of some critics to the deployment of the term "scolaire" in reference to Feraoun's writing.[367] What they then go on to state though, quite astutely, is that "la confrontation de ces textes avec d'autres écrits tout à fait concomitants (comme les textes critiques, le journal et les lettres personnelles, édités de nos jours [...]) montre que cette écriture est loin de relever d'une maladresse de débutant ou d'une admiration sans distance d'un certain académisme français".[368]

This chapter will seek to demonstrate how Feraoun's novels beg close inspection both of what is related and of the literary fashion in which this information is delivered, for separately and together they incorporate a fascinating complexity which is of great pertinence for this study of the representation of Algerian women in novels of the late-colonial period. Feraoun's novels, perhaps more than those of any other male author covered in this book, devote a considerable amount of textual space to the articulation of feminine characters and their lives. This chapter will thus investigate how Feraoun's texts act as important sociological monuments of testimony both to the rule and the exception, to perceived norms of Kabyle society under colonisation and the ways in which women formed breaks in a masculinist socio-symbolic order, or at least contributed to its governance. At the same time, what is perhaps even more important in this chapter is an analysis of the inventive literary strategies that subtend Feraoun's representations of women and that consequently, to a great extent, address the problematic nature of un-representative *Vertretung* representation in its potential to symbolically determine from without.

Though Feraoun's texts clearly represent a great investment in the feminine and its embodiment in the particular context of Kabylia under French rule, this investment is matched by a richness of fragmentary, subversive and explicitly factitious narrative complexity that allows Feraoun to talk about Algerian women without claiming a full power of inscription over them. It is as though, through his often underestimated formal virtuosity, Feraoun is at pains to

---

[367] They include critics such as Abdelkebir Khatibi, Abdellatif Laâbi, Jean Déjeux and Christiane Achour.
[368] Robert Elbaz/Martine Mathieu-Job: *Mouloud Feraoun ou l'émergence d'une littérature*. Paris : Karthala 2001, p. 10.

match the humility of tone that the narrator of *La Terre et le sang* deploys, following his attempt to evoke the lives of women:

> Au demeurant, il convient de se défier de toute exagération lorsqu'on parle de la femme kabyle. On peut simplement la supposer plus près de la réalité, sa seule école, et en général plus malheureuse que ses sœurs de n'importe où. *Tout jugement définitif sur la vie des gens est figé comme un axiome. Or la vie est à l'opposé de l'immobilité.*[369]

Furthermore, like those of Mohammed Dib, Feraoun's works also experiment with the expression of a feminine presence in the masculine psyche and indeed more generally Feraoun's texts seek to convey with great emphasis how the subject which seeks to depict his/her community is greatly influenced by it, how the community therefore maintains a presence in the process of its own articulation. This incorporation of the object within the text's narrator is interesting both simply as an attempt at inclusion but also, perhaps more powerfully, as an articulation of its own impossibility. Like Kateb and Dib, Feraoun seems keen to maintain images of failure in the articulation of progress, to maintain a kind of productive "pessimism" in representation. Thus his texts are full of failed relations, of deaths which invoke the necessity for epistemological revolution.

This is not to say, however, that Feraoun does not clearly articulate much of what he does know and can say about Algerian and, more specifically, Kabyle women. As will be noted in the first sections of this chapter, the corpus of *Le Fils du pauvre* (1950), *La Terre et le sang* (1953) and *Les Chemins qui montent* (1957) does perform, whilst couched on a formal bed that decentres the narration, the task of (re)animating feminine existences, of saying important and complex things about Algerian women and the symbolic structures they were obliged to face.[370]

4.1 Masculinist Structures and Women's Participation

> Lorsque les enfants sont petits, on dort sur la même natte, l'un à côté de l'autre : le plus petit contre le maman, le papa derrière, les autres, par rang d'âge, alignés le plus loin possible des parents. Mais quand les enfants sont grands, le fils aîné déserte la maison

---

[369] Mouloud Feraoun: *La Terre et le sang*. Paris: Points 2010, p. 41 (emphasis added).
[370] I will be using the 1995 Points edition of *Le Fils du pauvre*, a reproduction of the canonical 1954 Éditions du Seuil edition, in contrast to the 1950 edition, which contained extra material, and to which Debra Kelly refers.

pendant la nuit et tôt ou tard, il a sa chambrette ; le père a ostensiblement sa place à l'écart ; la mère occupe un coin où elle se niche avec les tout-petits [...][371]

In *Queer Nations*, Jarrod Hayes writes in reference to Pierre Bourdieu's articulation of a masculinist system of honour that "in "The Sentiment of Honour in Kabyle Society" (1966) [Bourdieu] articulated the classical account of this system and it might be tempting to read Feraoun as literary evidence in support of Bourdieu's arguments".[372] Indeed, as an example among many others of the Bourdieusian echoes detectable in the œuvre of Mouloud Feraoun, the citation above, taken from his second novel, *La Terre et le sang*, directly resonates with perhaps Bourdieu's most famous formulation, that of the Kabyle house and its binary divisions which symbolise and support a conceptual and physical gender separation.[373] The passage both produces gendered positions in the sleeping arrangements and in the separation of outside (the son) and inside (the mother and the children), and is also delivered in an ethnographic tone that alludes to a potential structural permanence, as though it were conveying the universal and sempiternal symbolic principles of the Kabyle people.

Critics like Jane Hiddleston and Naget Khadda have identified varying modes of achieving "ethnography" within Feraoun's novels, indicating a depth of tone that speaks not just of structural reality but also both of fallacy, of perceptions falsely held by both the protagonists and the reader, and of the need for change within the society described.[374] Thus Hiddleston identifies how "the descriptions of the settings in Feraoun's autobiographical *Le Fils du pauvre,* as well as in his apparently ethnographic *Jours de Kabylie*, are at once realist and parodic"[375] while Naget Khadda writes:

> [C]'est dans un mouvement discrètement "militant" et comme élément d'information ethnographique à résonance de drame historique que le sort des femmes est exposé,

---

371 Mouloud Feraoun: *La Terre et le sang*, p. 30.
372 Jarrod Hayes: *Queer Nations: Marginal Sexualities in the Maghreb*, p. 266.
373 See 'La maison ou le monde renversé' in Bourdieu's *Esquisse d'une théorie de la pratique précédé de trois études d'ethnologie kabyle*. Paris: Éditions du Seuil 2000, p. 61–82.
374 I place ethnography in scare quotes to allude to the charged nature of the term owing to its implication in ethnocentrism as well as to the fact that because of the differing cultural positions of Bourdieu and Feraoun, one might be loath to consider the latter's description of the social object in which he is implicated (Kabyle society) as "ethnography".
375 Jane Hiddleston: *Decolonising the Intellectual*, p. 189.

intégré dans l'économie du discours romanesque par le présupposé de l'écriture réaliste [...].[376]

In echoing Bourdieu's binary distinctions within and outside the Kabyle house, then, Feraoun's late-colonial novels can be understood not merely as illuminating the gendered structures of Kabyle life under colonisation but also as acting as an implicit and knowing critique of these norms. This is perhaps most immediately and deliciously evident in the use of irony throughout his work, most memorably in *Le Fils du pauvre*. Here, one can detect this ironic distance as early as the first chapter of Fouroulou's journal where we read that "[l]e fellah n'a guère l'habitude de passer ses heures de repos dans sa masure au milieu des femmes et de la marmaille. La djema est un refuge sûr, toujours disponible et gratuit".[377] The opposition of "marmaille" and "refuge sûr" evokes the proud exasperation of the masculine figure in the face of domestic concerns and produces a complicity between reader and narrator that undermines the legitimacy of the gendered division.

The following sections will thus firstly investigate and hopefully shed light on Feraoun's discreet militancy in his articulation of women's roles and positions in the society that he knew and represented. It will also, however, look at the ways in which the literary can both evoke and, perhaps, engender new links or even breaks in a masculine contiguity of symbolic domination. For what Feraoun also alludes to, in relating the actions of women, is the presence of sites and moments of resistance. Firstly, his late-colonial novels invite us to understand that from within an order of subjugation women find means of symbolic expression, which the literary text can then relate and, in a sense, (re)create. Secondly, and perhaps more interestingly, however, women are also represented as incorporating a "revolutionary" traumatic kernel that one can associate with what Slavoj Žižek has identified as Lacan's third period formulation of the "death drive" or *Thanatos*. Žižek writes:

> The Symbolic order is striving for a homeostatic balance, but there is in its kernel, at its very centre, some strange, traumatic element which cannot be symbolized, integrated into the symbolic order – the Thing [...] And what, at this level, is the death drive? Exactly the opposite of the Symbolic order: the possibility of the 'second death', the radical annihilation of the symbolic texture through which the so-called reality is constituted.[378]

---

[376] Naget Khadda: L'Allégorie de la féminité: Deuil d'une civilisation et mutation d'identité dans Le Fils du pauvre de M. Feraoun. In: *Peuples méditerranéens* No. 44–45 (July–December 1988), p. 74–75.
[377] Mouloud Feraoun: *Le Fils du pauvre*. Paris: Points 1995, p. 18–19.
[378] Slavoj Žižek: *The Sublime Object of Ideology*, p. 147.

Once this chapter has established the ways in which Feraoun's novels represent women's roles, their subjugation and their ability to create, to self-inscribe from within this subjugation, it will analyse the extent to which one can detect the incorporation of a feminine "Thing" and will discuss his works' allusions to a liberating "death drive" that shares a connection with manifestations of *nushuz*, the Islamic concept of women's rebellion. This feminine embodiment, though perhaps ultimately unsuccessful in overthrowing masculinist oppression when considered within the time-frame of an immediate present, nonetheless seems to appear in Feraoun's work as a symbol of a larger need for revolution, as an expression of the intolerable nature of a contemporary socio-symbolic order, a socio-symbolic order reflective of a reigning masculinist epistemological mode in the late-colonial period. Moreover, this chapter will also illuminate Feraoun's expression of a feminine awareness of the "phallic" nature of masculinist structures which determine the socio-symbolic order depicted, and his articulation of their pernicious nature for all gendered agents in symbolic interaction.

To begin, however, with Feraoun's texts as subversive "ethnography", one can identify a number of key sites that chime with Bourdieu's gendered opposition between "l'univers proprement culturel" and "la maison, monde de la femme, vouée à la gestion de la nature et exclue de la vie publique", between *asalas alemmas* and *thigedjith*, the masculine supported beam and the feminine supporting pillar.[379] Indeed, the chapter of *Le Fils du pauvre*, Feraoun's first novel, which is narrated from the perspective of its main protagonist, Fouroulou, has as one of its principal narrative threads the dispossession of women, their exclusion from the masculine public sphere of property ownership – a prime symbolic marker of social agency, honour and power – and the text's tonal shifts amount to a powerful critique of this state of affairs.[380] Fouroulou's mother first recalls how her father had left a property to his daughters in his will:

> Ma mère s'en souvient très bien. Mais lorsque l'acte arriva, le cheikh qui le traduisit expliqua aux héritières qu'elles n'avaient droit qu'à l'usufruit.[381]

The granting of the right of usufruct as opposed to the right of ownership was not, however, the father's intention. We discover that the father had indeed hesi-

---

[379] Pierre Bourdieu: *Esquisse d'une théorie de la pratique*, p. 70.
[380] Interestingly, Al Qur'an itself condemns this kind of dispossession as a contradiction of Islamic principles for in Surah An-Nisa (The Verse of the Women), 4:7, it is explicitly stated that women are to receive a share of any inheritance while in 4:10 one reads: "Indeed, those who devour the property of orphans unjustly are only consuming into their bellies fire. And they will be burned in a Blaze".
[381] Mouloud Feraoun: *Le Fils du Pauvre*, p. 23.

tated over his decision to leave his daughters in charge of the property but had, in the end, definitively granted them ownership. Fouroulou demonstrates that a cabal of male heirs, whose perspective he textually embodies for literary effect, conspired after the patriarch's passing to take ownership themselves and he punctuates the explanation of the women's disinheritance with an ironic exclamation:

> D'abord la mauvaise volonté du vieux était évidente puisqu'il avait essayé de donner "définitivement" la maison et un champ. Le cadi avait été compréhensif. Heureusement ![382]

Then, after Fouroulou has related with great pathos over the course of the chapter his relationship with his two maternal aunts who inhabit the property, Nana and Khalti, and their tragic demise, we find that the close of the chapter and their tale is determined once more by the swarming of masculinist forces of ownership, thus emphasising the pernicious nature of their exclusion from agency in society:

> Nous, les enfants, nous comprîmes également que nous perdions quelque chose : la maisonnette de mes tantes fut vendue par mon père à un voisin qui abattit tout de suite la cloison. Nous nous désintéressâmes du champ tragique : nos cousins les Aït Moussa, le vendirent et se partagèrent l'argent.[383]

A sense of profound, indefinable loss marks the moment that underlines women's exclusion from property, from ownership, from social power.

La Terre et le sang, the Feraoun novel whose writing can be most clearly identified as utilising and subverting an ethnographic mode, also sees women expelled from ownership and left without social power. Kamouma, mother of the central protagonist, Amer, described as a woman who "a appris à supporter et à peiner",[384] sees the property that supported her existence sold off by her husband, Kaci, and "une fois Kaci enterré, il ne subsistait plus aucun lien avec la vieille. Il [the final purchaser] ne s'occupa plus d'elle".[385] Perhaps, though, the most striking evocation of a structure that relegates women to the status of *thigedjith*, of the supporting, passive, forked beam is the story of Fetta, the "mère-porteuse", to borrow a term employed by Michel Kelle in his

---

[382] Ibid, p. 24.
[383] Ibid, p. 102.
[384] Mouloud Feraoun: *La Terre et le sang*, p. 22.
[385] Ibid, p. 27.

2002 analysis of the same novel.[386] When the characters Hocine and Hemama cannot conceive a child, Hemama takes a cousin, Fetta, and has her act as surrogate whilst treating her worse than chattel:

> Le temps passa. Il n'est guère possible naturellement de relater par le menu la vie quotidienne de ce ménage à trois, la pitoyable existence de Fetta, ses renoncements, sa misère.[387]

Her mistreatment ends in her death. What is doubly disturbing about her story, however, and what also supports a reading of it as part of a historically conditioned socio-symbolic order, is the fact that other female characters, including Chabha (Amer's lover) and Hemama, appear inured to her fate and indeed see it as necessary and unavoidable.[388]

Furthermore, the machinations of the mothers of Amer and Chabha (Kamouma and Smina) to have them produce an illegitimate child, again in *La Terre et le sang*, are also predicated on an understanding that if women cannot reproduce for men, they will understandably be cast aside. Sara Poole writes of Kamouma that "she is pushed into going beyond certain bounds by the constraints of a culture in which children are seen as meal-tickets for one's old age".[389] It would be my argument that in fact Kamouma, Smina, and indeed Hemama, are presented as acting precisely *within* masculinist symbolic bounds, defined by and for men, that assign them a position of supplementarity, and that Feraoun's texts seek to shed light on the suffering that results from adherence to these symbolic parameters.

In turning to *Les Chemins qui montent*, one can also understand Feraoun's representation of Nana Melha's marital predicament regarding her daughter, Dehbia, as yet another example of the pressure exerted by social expectations based on women's notional inferiority and passivity in ideological symbolic frameworks of honour and agency:

> [E]lle savait fort bien [...] que les Aït-Slimane ne se seraient jamais abaissés à ramasser une malheureuse telle que Dehbia qui, de surcroît, était infidèle, sans famille, peut-être sans

---

386 See Kelle, Michel: Mouloud Feraoun, romancier de l'honneur, de l'amour et de la jalousie. In: *Algérie Littérature/Action* No. 57 (Jan–Feb 2002), p. 78–89.
387 Mouloud Feraoun: *La Terre et le sang*, p. 139.
388 It should also be noted here that a distinction is formed in the text between Chabha's unflustered reaction, as a member of the society, and Amer's French wife Marie/Madame's shock as an outsider.
389 Sarah Poole: Women and boundaries in the fiction of Mouloud Feraoun. In: *International Journal of Francophone Studies* Vol. 5, Issue 3 (2003), p. 162.

honneur. Une petite ordure, disaient les vieux. Elle savait, Melha, elle n'avait jamais guigné de ce côté, mais c'était plus fort qu'elle : elle détestait tous ceux qui se mariaient.[390]

Though Nana Melha is depicted as caring deeply for her daughter and as certainly not sharing the view that she is "infidèle" or "sans honneur", Feraoun's text, through a doubly removed free indirect speech which evokes both Melha and the narrator's distance from these terms, allows the reader to see how she ascribes to the big Other, the "objective spirit" of her community, views subtended by notions of feminine passivity and masculine honour. Moreover, the final sentence indicates that despite her distaste for the views of her community, her desire remains inserted in and conditioned by the same symbolic structure: she still secretly yearns for her daughter to be defined through marriage, through her passive appropriation.

Thus Feraoun's novels depict societies whose socio-symbolic coordinates are clearly based on masculinist economies whilst they allude to the need for change through depictions of suffering and through the articulation of the narrator's non-acceptance of pernicious norms. This does not mean, however, that the novels represent women's roles as fixed and unalterable and that they therefore depict Algerian women themselves as hopeless victims, in the same way, for example, that Mohammed Dib's early texts in his 'Trilogie Algérie' sometimes do. Indeed all the sections described above contain within them, to some extent, the potential for resistance, for modes of social expression in which Feraoun's texts play a role as evocations.

Perhaps the most cited arena of resistance is located in the first of the scenes referenced above. Though deprived of the ownership of their home, Fouroulou's aunts in *Le Fils du pauvre* find a powerful means of self-expression and cultural participation in the pottery, "les cruches" that they produce:

> [Les cruches] Elles sont toujours bien proportionnées, leurs lignes harmonieuses, leur col élancé, leur légèreté et la finesse de leurs ornement les font préférer par toutes les élégantes du village. *Tant il est vrai que ce que nous réalisons est toujours le miroir de ce que nous sommes.*[391]

Here it is again interesting to read the fates of Nana and Khalti alongside Bourdieu's ethnography, this time in order to highlight their feminine contribution to the socio-symbolic realm which exceeds the binary separations which the soci-

---

[390] Mouloud Feraoun: *Les Chemins qui montent*. Paris: Éditions du Seuil 1957, p. 66.
[391] Mouloud Feraoun: *Le Fils du pauvre*, p. 51 (emphasis added).

ologist sets forward when he refers to "le métier à tisser, instrument par excellence de l'activité féminine".³⁹² Bourdieu writes:

> Par opposition au travail de l'homme, accompli au-dehors, le travail de la femme est voué à rester obscur et caché ("Dieu le dissimule", dit-on): "Au-dedans, elle n'a pas de cesse, elle se débat comme une mouche dans le petit-lait; au-dehors (au-dessus), rien n'apparaît de son travail".³⁹³

He also withdraws feminine ownership of his chief example of a feminine instrument of work, as the loom, "dressé face à l'est comme la charrue, son homologue, est en même temps l'est de l'espace intérieur en sorte qu'il a, à l'intérieur du système de la maison, une valeur masculine comme symbole de protection".³⁹⁴

Of course both Nana, the highly skilled potter, and Khalti, the inventive and engaging storyteller, can be argued to act as supplements to Fouroulou's needs as, in the words of Elbaz and Mathieu-Job, "elles atténuent la morbidité existentielle de tout le village, dont l'enfant est déjà bien conscient", and as Khalti's stories can be taken as a basis for both Fouroulou's and, by extension, Feraoun's literary careers.³⁹⁵ Moreover, their work, produced in domestic space, is not seen to interrupt the masculinist economies that hold sway over the community. However, Feraoun's narrative both demonstrates the potential for women's work to represent them in a wider cultural sphere as preferred objects of the well-to-do, and itself serves to testify to the meticulousness and to the artistry of Algerian women and their "travail de création".³⁹⁶ In a sense, Fouroulou's narration acts to publicise their work, to lend it a wider circulation, to share some of its essence of precision and beauty with the notional reader.³⁹⁷

Turning to the section that details Fetta's mistreatment, one can appreciate how Feraoun's work supports the claim of *La Terre et le sang*'s narrator that "tout autant que l'homme, la femme a son existence double: privée et publique en

---

392 Pierre Bourdieu: *Esquisse d'une théorie de la pratique*, p. 72.
393 Ibid, p. 70.
394 Ibid, p. 72.
395 Robert Elbaz/Martine Mathieu-Job: *Mouloud Feraoun ou l'émergence d'une littérature*, p. 41.
396 Mouloud Feraoun: *Le Fils du pauvre*, p. 52.
397 Feraoun himself stated in a letter to Emmanuel Roblès in 1953 that the story of Nana and Khalti drew upon the lives of his real maternal Aunts, though Feraoun made up their tragic fate, most likely to support his social commentary. The letter was published in *Esprit* No. 12 (December 1962) and can be viewed at http://www.samuelhuet.com/kairos/34-doxai/517-feraoun_3.html.

quelque sorte".[398] Indeed, beyond this affirmation, time and again in Feraoun's novels one is invited to view women as political players, as agents who express themselves culturally by influencing with subtlety and subterfuge the social organisation of the village, the arrangement of power in their community. It is thus surprising that no study of Feraoun's work has seemingly touched on women's political role before, considering Feraoun's retrofitted status as a martyr of the revolution and his reluctance to involve himself in party politics, factors that critics like Jane Hiddleston have astutely highlighted.[399] One might perhaps put this oversight down to a replication in criticism of the perspective of Chabha's father, Ramdane, for whom "ces affaires de femmes ne pouvaient concerner les hommes".[400] In any event, it would seem that insufficient importance has been attributed to these "affaires de femmes" and that their impact within patriarchal/masculinist power structures and upon narrative progression in Feraoun's texts and upon narrative progression itself has been underappreciated.

First, Hemama, through her cruel manipulation of Fetta, not only secures her position as Hocine's spouse but also acquires a position of renewed consideration in the village. Her acts are depicted as being perceived as a sacrifice, and one that greatly benefits her husband, who risked yielding his land to extended relatives. Thus Slimane, in conversation with Chabha about their childlessness, talks of the misfortune that Hemama "selflessly" removes from her spouse's path:

> Et sa terre serait devenue la proie des cousins. À sa vieillesse, il risquait de se voir dépouillé comme il a dépouillé lui-même son oncle Kaci.[401]

Subsequently, Smina seeks to secure her daughter Chabha's status, through a pact with Kamouma to have Amer become the father of her child in lieu of Slimane, a pact that is explicitly articulated through a political lexicon of alliances and agreements:

---

398 Mouloud Feraoun: *La Terre et le sang*, p. 29.
399 One also notes the representation of an explicitly all-male political milieu on page 164 of *La Terre et le sang* as peculiarly disordered and unproductive: "Ces réunions absolument anarchiques avaient lieu tous les quinze jours, un vendredi [...] Tout se passait en coulisse et les assemblées générales n'avaient pratiquement pour résultat que de permettre aux fellahs des *karoubas* traditionnellement ennemis de se mesurer et de s'insulter [...]".
400 Mouloud Feraoun: *La Terre et le sang*, p. 220.
401 Ibid, p. 137.

> Smina comprend que Kamouma est son alliée, qu'elle peut compter sur son intervention discrète. Elles sont tout à fait d'accord.[402]

And, Kamouma herself has her own political projects which predate this pact but which she comes to see as achievable through it. We read early on of her anxiety that Amer, upon his return to the village after a long absence in France, conduct himself in such a way that might convince others of his social power, and thus of that of his family:

> Kamouma veut bien voir si son fils est capable d'une telle coquetterie, d'un geste ostensible qui avertit les gens, leur montre qu'on connaît les usages, qu'on tient à les respecter, qu'on est décidé à tenir son rang.[403]

She dreams of playing a privileged role, as Amer's mother and as the "maîtresse de maison ayant une bru, des alliés; ces alliés viendraient la flatter, la cajoler, elle, Kamouma. C'est là un rôle dont elle a toujours rêvé".[404] Crucially here though, the role that she envisages still exists within the socio-symbolic coordinates of the Kabyle society that she inhabits. Though she seeks power, she does so within an established patriarchal/masculinist order. She does not seek to break it.

Indeed, Ahlam Mosteghanemi delivers a representation of this type of engagement when deploying a metaphor which both resonates with the valorised notion of women's metonymic political participation put forward by Elleke Boehmer while at the same time alluding to its potential revolutionary limits, writing of the involvement of Algerian women in the revolutionary political domain:

> Ces filles trouvaient donc dans leur engagement politique la réplique adéquate à leur marginalisation par la société et aux attaques formulées contre elles. Elles devinrent donc, comme Salima dans *Les Enfants du nouveau monde*, "*un maillon de la chaine*".[405]

Kamouma, like Smina and Hemama, is shown to be driven to contribute links to the chain of the community's socio-symbolic order. The underside of this is exclusion from contribution which results in bitterness and resentment, as evidenced by Nana Melha in *Les Chemins qui montent*:

---

402 Ibid, p. 186.
403 Ibid, p. 21.
404 Ibid, p. 36.
405 Ahlam Mosteghanemi: *Algérie, femmes et écritures*. Paris: L'Harmattan 1985, p. 131 (Mosteghanemi's emphasis).

> Melha éprouve une satisfaction cruelle et se félicite d'être pauvre, de n'offrir aucun attrait aux épouseuses, d'échapper ainsi à leurs griffes et de pouvoir les dédaigner.⁴⁰⁶

Nevertheless, it might also be argued that it is precisely through depictions of a Nana Melhaesque social refusal, that is, through women's puncturing of social structures produced in relation with the Symbolic order, that Feraoun's narratives most effectively invoke the necessity for masculinist economies to change. Indeed, it is partly in their articulations of death and failure stemming from women's actions that the texts subversively and invigoratingly breathe life into their representations of Algerian women, as the next section will investigate.

4.2 Breaking the Chain

The beginning of *Le Fils du pauvre* produces an intriguing dichotomy between a peace-making, conciliatory feminine stance, and one which provokes a rupture, sewing the seeds of discord between male protagonists. The former is embodied by the matriarch, Tassadit, who works to maintain the symbolic capital, the honour value possessed by the extended family, or *karouba*. It is she who, for example, gives Fouroulou his name in order to protect him as he represents the continuation of the agnatic line:

> Comme j'étais le premier garçon né viable dans ma famille, ma grande-mère décida péremptoirement de m'appeler Fouroulou (de *effer* : cacher).⁴⁰⁷

It is also she who supports the communal ego of her *karouba*, embodying a rhetorical flexibility in a discourse aimed at maintaining power, after Fouroulou's injury at the hands of Boussad n'Amer, a member of another clan, necessitates the receipt of mediators by both parties:

> – Ils leur donneront des pois chiches, dit ma mère.
> – Certainement ! nous sommes pauvres, nous, mais, Dieu merci, de toute ma vie vos maris n'ont jamais eu à rougir lorsqu'il s'est agi de recevoir un hôte. C'est à cela qu'on reconnaît les bonnes familles.
>
> Évidemment. Mais si, par hasard, mon père n'avait pas acheté de la viande, ma grand-mère n'aurait pas été à court d'arguments et n'aurait pas cru devoir rougir en offrant, elle aussi, des pois chiches ou des fèves.⁴⁰⁸

---

406 Mouloud Feraoun: *Les Chemins qui montent*, p. 49.
407 Mouloud Feraoun: *Le Fils du pauvre*, p. 27.
408 Ibid, p. 42.

She, like the political women of the previous section of this chapter, acts as an adhesive for the social unit and so Fouroulou states:

> Il était donc bien vrai que ma grand-mère était le pilier de la communauté puisque l'une a cessé d'exister presque en même temps que l'autre.[409]

Bourdieu writes that in the Kabyle house, "L'homme est 'le crochet auquel sont suspendus les paniers', le pourvoyeur, tel le scarabée, l'araignée ou l'abeille. Ce que l'homme a apporté, la femme le range, le protège et l'épargne".[410] What the woman ultimately protects and saves is symbolic capital that depends upon social stability. Thus though it can be argued that Tassadit again enacts a process of self-inscription within the cultural life of her village, her actions can still be understood as working to maintain an established masculinist order.

Sarah Poole writes that "the complete control [Tassadit] wields can be read as 'devirilizing' the menfolk of the household – her two sons, including Fouroulou's father – and as showing her infringing upon male prerogatives".[411] Jarrod Hayes rightly counters this assertion by arguing that Tassadit's stewardship "could also be read as totally in keeping with Maghrebian patriarchal structures, since [she] has acquired this status only after producing two sons and, with Fouroulou, a grandson; these men constitute the base of her power".[412] He then goes on to argue, however, that the break-down following the removal of "le pilier de la communauté", the phrase so evocative of the *thigedjith*, constitutes a colonially determined movement towards greater patriarchy:

> The family breakup that allegorises colonial expropriation of land involves a transition from a single household headed by a woman to two households headed by men.[413]

I would argue that the text demonstrates that the split is orchestrated by and, to some extent, for the two women who then share the leadership of the separate households with their husbands after Tassadit's death. There is certainly regret expressed by Fouroulou at the familial collapse, a regret that we share with him as part of the reader and narrator's imaginary relationship of identification, but he also concedes that:

---

[409] Ibid, p. 64–65.
[410] Pierre Bourdieu: *Esquisse d'une théorie de la pratique*, p. 74.
[411] Sarah Poole: Women and boundaries in the fiction of Mouloud Feraoun, p. 160.
[412] Jarrod Hayes: *Queer Nations: Marginal Sexualities in the Maghreb*, p. 273.
[413] Ibid, p. 276.

> Je comprends très bien à présent pourquoi ma mère et ma tante Helima étaient aussi pressées l'une que l'autre de devenir maîtresses de maison. Rien n'échappait à leurs calculs.[414]

It is the two brothers, Lounis and Ramdane, who subsequently toil in separate fields and who are represented as having suffered most from the rupture in the familial structure. If anything, Helima and Fatma acquire greater control and power, albeit still within a system of gendered inside/outside separation.

My larger argument would be that at the very least one is invited to read in the actions of the two women a desire to break with the past, to kill off the old in a "selfish" search for the new. The fact that the result is not a utopian "new" socio-symbolic order that sees men and women on equal terms is perhaps, perversely, the point. For one can argue that, in depicting destruction and its aftermath, the text both alludes to a will to have done with a past configuration and to the continuing necessity for breaks that would produce a new coherent system of gender relations. Moreover, Slavoj Žižek's association of the desire to eradicate a socio-symbolic order with a personal "death drive" allows the reader to see Feraoun's novels as producing evocations of this psychological drive for continuing epistemological revolution. If one looks in all three texts at the recurrence of women characters who are driven to break with social norms, and sees their actions as more or less radical manifestations of this drive (and of a subsequent turmoil) one can begin to view these texts precisely as works which evoke and invoke "revolutionary" *Thanatos*, or "death drive". Žižek writes that "what the death drive strives to annihilate is not the biological cycle of generation and corruption, but rather the symbolic order, the order of the symbolic pact which regulates social exchange and sustains debts, honors, obligations".[415] Thus the personal death drive refuses the symbolic constraints objectified in the figure of a big Other, rejects its notional perfection and legitimacy. Glyn Daly writes concordantly that "the subject exists as an eternal dimension of resistance-excess towards all forms of subjectivation (or what Althusser would call interpellation)".[416] It is thus the resistance of the subject as incorporation of the death drive which can "selfishly" destabilise the socio-symbolic order through its own compulsion to "revolution", that can reject the call of ideology. And, the representation of forms of rebellion as producing imperfect, sometimes deeply troubling outcomes may serve to outline the many breaks and rewritings of

---

414 Mouloud Feraoun: *Le Fils du pauvre*, p. 72.
415 Slavoj Žižek: From desire to drive: Why Lacan is not Lacaniano. In: *Atlántica de Las Artes* No. 14 (1996), p. 5.
416 Glyn Daly and Slavoj Žižek: *Conversations with Žižek*. Cambridge: Blackwell 2004, p. 4.

the socio-symbolic order which must take place for gender equality to be inaugurated.

Perhaps the best example of this compulsion to reject the mastery of "the way things are" comes in *Le Fils du pauvre* with the detailing of Khalti's reaction to her sister Nana's death, a death provoked by her pregnancy by her absentee husband. From her status as enthralling storyteller, when she loses "une partie d'elle même, [l]a meilleure partie",[417] Khalti, in the words of Naget Khadda, "transforme la maisonnette de rêve en théâtre tragique, espace du saccage".[418] She rejects propriety and honour, as an embodiment of *nushuz*, the term deployed in the fourth chapter of Al Qur'an (Surah An-Nisa) to describe women's rebellion against "guarding in [the husband's] absence what Allah would have them guard".[419] The reader detects this rebellion in descriptions of Khalti that also allude to a radical awareness of the absurdity of social mores. Fouroulou relates that "elle avait l'air de nous narguer, semblait nous menacer d'une revanche comme un adversaire acharné"[420] and that "ordinairement, elle ouvrait au hasard le portail d'une maison, se tenait sur le seuil et ne disait rien. Les femmes essayaient de lui parler sans aucun résultat; lorsqu'elles lui offraient quelque chose, elle tendait la main avec indifférence, le regard toujours absent".[421] Her extended family and the village community attempt to reabsorb her distress and disconnection into their cultural sphere by assigning it palatable meaning, by associating it with a magic and a madness that cast it as supernatural, as excluded from social practice, and then by reintegrating the supernatural into the pecuniary:

> Quant aux voisines, elles prétendaient que des esprits étaient en train d'initier Khalti aux secrets des sorcières, que bientôt elle se mettrait à prédire l'avenir et qu'elle gagnerait alors de quoi nourrir largement la famille.[422]

However, in drawing Fouroulou's narration to a close, Feraoun articulates how she departs from the village, never to be seen again. He does so through a lan-

---

[417] Mouloud Feraoun: *Le Fils du pauvre*, p. 90.
[418] Naget Khadda: L'Allégorie de la féminité, p. 83.
[419] Al Qur'an 4: 34. Interpretations of the symbolic field of *nushuz*, a term related to the term *fitna* discussed in the chapter on Kateb, are varied but all understand it in some way as a break with an established propriety which would accord with the integrity of the structures of the Ummah, the Islamic community. See Fatima Mernissi: *Women's Rebellion and Islamic Memory* for analysis of its subversive and productive implications for individualist rebellion.
[420] Mouloud Feraoun: *Le Fils du pauvre*, p. 95.
[421] Ibid, p. 98.
[422] Ibid, p. 98.

guage which also sees her depart from determination in description, from reinscription into the homeostasis of narration, as the details of her leaving are absent. We are simply informed that "on ne devait jamais plus la revoir et le mystère de sa disparition restera une énigme pour toute la famille".[423]

Thus it would seem that what is evoked here is a disconnection from a society predicated on masculinist honour structures and that this break, articulated both through Khalti's behaviour and through narrative form, stems from a furious radical awareness of the precarious position of women under these structures. Though one might argue as to the significance of her "regard toujours absent"[424] and the extent to which Khalti blames her disarray on masculinist figureheads (Omar, Nana's husband, the relatives who disinherited the two aunts etc.), one can at the very least ascribe to the text itself the incorporation of a kind of textual evocation of the "death drive". This is emphasised by Feraoun's setting down of his pen, in the guise of Fouroulou, shortly after Khalti's disappearance and by his repetition of the act of inscription, in a different form, in the second section of the book, and indeed in the other novels of his late-colonial œuvre. Furthermore, Feraoun's representation of women as a force for change, as embodying *Thanatos*, need not rest upon a developed theoretical understanding of that which is to be overthrown but rather on an immediate refusal, on a selfishness that says "no" to the group and "yes" to the self, even if, as in the case of Khalti, this "yes to the self" does not yield productive results within the world of the narrative. Indeed, Feraoun's texts, through their dissemination of women's individualism in the face of a larger socio-symbolic order, evoke the importance of creating a domain in which the compulsion to change need not end in disarray, and where a certain feminine rejection of the Symbolic can be accommodated but not subsumed.

Another intriguing example of Feraoun's evocation of a certain "selfishness" comes in *Les Chemins qui montent*, in the description of Dehbia's character and story. Dehbia is raised in a Christian community, separate from Ighil-Nezman, the village where the action of her tragic love affair with Amer takes place. She is described very early in the novel in terms that emphasise her inability to fit into the ideological coordinates of her society as "Dehbia croit sincèrement qu'elle n'est pas une fille comme les autres".[425]

---

[423] Ibid, p. 100–101.
[424] I would argue that the text does indeed subtly allude to a cognizance within Khalti through her silence, her "regard" and her effrontery before male agents. Jarrod Hayes has commented on page 271 of *Queer Nations*, for example, on her combative spreading of her legs, forcing the men of the village to look away.
[425] Mouloud Feraoun: *Les Chemins qui montent*, p. 19.

Immediately afterwards we discover that Amer "sentait en Dehbia une espèce de révolte identique à la sienne mais plus profonde, plus désespérée et difficile à exprimer" and this "révolte" can precisely be traced back to her upbringing, which is staged outside of the socio-symbolic order of Ighil-Nezman and, interestingly, to her relationship with Christ:[426]

> Toute seule pour ainsi dire, elle découvrit le vrai visage du Christ et de Sa Sainte Mère, la Vierge [...] elle éprouvait une autre joie, *une espèce d'orgueil*, à constater qu'elle était exigeante, donc bonne chrétienne.[427]

This basis for her "égoïsme",[428] for what she sees as "le seul moyen de lutte dont on puisse disposer chez les pauvres", is intriguing and perhaps initially somewhat troubling, if one considers Dehbia's independence as a product of Western theology in opposition to native practice.[429] However, her fierce individualism is presented not just as stemming from her separation from the Islamic community of Ighil-Nezman, but also from the other members of her own faith as, disappointed by the conduct of those who represent the church, we read that "elle s'est mise à mépriser ces mauvais chrétiens".[430] [431] Thus I would argue that what is shown to be important about Dehbia is her opposition itself rather than the nature of her difference. Indeed, once Dehbia enters the community of Ighil-Nezman, mentions of Christianity are reserved predominantly for the othering discourse that excludes her as the "petite chrétienne".[432]

As the text continues we are presented with examples of how the ideological constellations of the village cannot incorporate the difference that the "petite chrétienne" represents. Perhaps the clearest example of this comes when we

---

[426] Ibid, p. 20.
[427] Ibid, p. 27–28 (emphasis added).
[428] Of course, I recognise that in fact the English term "selfishness" would fit more neatly with understandings of radical subjectivity and death drive as the latter is precisely opposed to the stable ego.
[429] Ibid, p. 40.
[430] Ibid, p. 27.
[431] Interestingly, Žižek has used representations of Christ precisely to speak about the "revolutionary" nature of the death drive, citing the Gospel of John (10:10): "I am come that they might have life, and that they might have it more abundantly" and referring to Christ's death as a demonstration of "subjective destitution" where, in Ola Sigurdson's words, "we recognize the horrible fact that any redemption is totally up to ourselves, [to] the excess of life", to the death drive. See Slavoj Žižek: *On Belief*. London: Routledge, 2001, p. 104, and Ola Sigurdson: Slavoj Žižek, The Death Drive, and Zombies: A Theological Account. In: *Modern Theology* 29.3 (2013), p. 370.
[432] Ibid, p. 78.

read Mokrane's father's discourse on order, immediately following a passage where Mokrane's troubling, potentially disruptive desire of Dehbia is discussed:

> – L'ordre, avait dit son père, la veille des fiançailles, alors qu'il tenait à l'informer et même à connaître son avis. L'ordre, mon fils, exige que chacun occupe sa place, se tienne à son rang. Sans cela, où seraient les Aït-Slimane, à présent ? L'ordre, c'est l'honneur, la religion, la famille.[433]

Dehbia is perceived as opposing order and thus cannot be married, cannot be accommodated as part of the body of the community. Moreover, she cannot be fully accommodated as part of the text. The first section of the book, though mostly presenting us with aspects of her perspective, flits between several agents in the text and the second section takes the form of Amer's journal. Of course, Dehbia's most impactful break with a "symbolic pact which regulates social exchange and sustains debts, honors, obligations", occurs with her partially depicted betrayal of Amer n'Amer with Mokrane.[434] This kind of breaking of a symbolic pact is presented as producing disastrous consequences, as is, for example, the adultery of Chabha with Amer-ou-Kaci, Amer n'Amer's father, in *La Terre et le sang*. Feraoun's texts thus do not produce a rose-tinted representation of women as agents of change whose compulsion to break symbolic pacts are morally unambiguous acts of freedom. Indeed, were they to do so, they would simply constitute another form of othering: deification. Nevertheless, their opposition to the status quo, manifested in more or less radical forms, is supported as an ethical act by the texts through the representation of the internecine masculinist structures that they act against.

The masculinist structures in Feraoun's novels can of course be argued to have as their foundation *nif*, male honour,[435] and it is *nif* that ultimately provides the psychological basis for Amer's self-destruction upon his discovery of Dehbia's "impure" act, in *Les Chemins qui montent:*

> Ne crois pas que je t'en veuille, que je doute de ton amour, de ton amitié, mais je n'accepte ni ton amitié ni ton amour. Trop tard, ma fille. Je me disais: si jeune ! si *pure* ! si innocente ! Que reste-t-il de mon idole ?[436]

---

433 Ibid, p. 78.
434 Slavoj Žižek: From desire to drive: Why Lacan is not Lacaniano, p. 5.
435 See Bourdieu passim, including *Esquisse d'une théorie de la pratique* for a full description of *nif* and its symbolic relationship with passive, feminine *hurma*.
436 Mouloud Feraoun: *Les Chemins qui montent*, p. 218 (emphasis added).

Amer's preparations for suicide by barbiturates are seemingly driven by an anguish conditioned by a conception of gendered purity which stems from the structures of honour present in his socio-symbolic milieu. Indeed, all the texts in our Feraounian corpus stand as testaments to pernicious socio-symbolic structures that take *nif* as their fulcrum and that are intolerable as they work to exclude women's self-expression as full agents whilst in many cases producing clearly misogynist behaviours and, ultimately, violence and/or death. To refer once more to the conclusion of Dehbia's section of *Les Chemins qui montent*, one reads therein a perfect articulation of a cyclical, unproductive symbolic relationship between male agents, whose deadly repercussions place emphasis on the ethical imperative to revolt. Ouiza is reported as telling Dehbia the following:

> – Les Aït-Hamouche, ma fille, portent malheur aux Aït-Larbi ! Un Aït-Hamouche a tué Amer, le père, pour laver son honneur ; un Aït-Slimane tue Amer, le fils, pour Ouiza n'Aït-Hamouche. C'était écrit, c'était écrit. Tu n'y peux rien, tu n'y peux rien ![437]

Moreover, though it is Ouiza who makes the above statement, it is predominantly men in Feraoun's work who are depicted as struggling with a fatalistic belief in the inevitability of symbolic debt, given their ineradicable duty to subtend honour and power in their many guises. This is certainly not to argue, however, that women are unaware of the power of symbolic economies. Indeed, it is rather to suggest that Feraoun's texts allude to a notion that whilst both men and women are, to an extent, forced to follow the "rules", a gendered division remains precisely in respect of an awareness of the pernicious and profoundly compromised nature of socio-symbolic structures. It is productive to think of this division as holding similarities with Žižek's Lacanian readings of the split between the masculine and feminine approach to the symbolic Phallus, the primordial signifier of desire that simultaneously stands as a marker of a lack inherent to socio-symbolism, and of women's determination as "not-all" in their relationship with it. He writes:

> [T]his not-all does not mean that woman is not entirely submitted to the Phallus; it rather signals that she sees through the fascinating presence of the Phallus, that she is able to discern in it the filler of the inconsistency of the Other.[438]

---

[437] Ibid, p. 98–99.
[438] Slavoj Žižek: Woman in One of the Names-of-the-Father, or How not to Misread Lacan's Formulas of Sexuation. In: *Lacanian Ink* No. 10 (1995), p. 27.

Of course, one cannot argue that all women in Feraoun's texts display an oppositional embodiment of this awareness. Some, like Tassadit of *Le Fils du pauvre*, are clearly presented as both acknowledging the rules of the perpetuation of symbolic capital and as living by them. However, on numerous occasions a productive radical feminine awareness, in contrast to a masculine posture, is indeed alluded to. In addition, for example, to depictions of Khalti's and Dehbia's wry, problematising awareness, one quite brilliant scene illustrating the honour economy, its pernicious outcomes and this split in awareness, takes place in *Les Chemins qui montent*. In this scene, Mokrane, according to custom, is to visit Ouiza on their wedding night and to consummate the marriage, if necessary, by force. As he enters the house where he is to find his new bride, Mokrane receives two final commissions: at the behest of his peers, Mokrane must assert his mastery, perpetuate masculine domination as "[c]'est à elle de [l]e craindre", and then fire off his phallic weapon, a rifle, as a proof of his masculinity, after consummation.[439] For Mokrane, this rite serves the entirety of the karouba in its production of "un homme de plus, une femme de plus".[440] Ouiza, however, recognises both the phallic function of Mokrane's visit, in particular his firing of a weapon to symbolise enjoyment, consummation, and the fact that the phallus only functions when it is veiled. This is to say that the firing of the gun could take place following any action, any form, assertive or otherwise, of consummation. Equally, of course, it could be fired with none. What matters in the rite is that the firing of the gun is believed to represent Mokrane's reassertion of masculine privilege and the honour of his family and the continuation of the socio-symbolic order of the village. Thus we witness the following dialogue, beginning with Mokrane:

> – Ce fusil m'énerve, murmura-t-il, et les autres attendent...
> – Qu'est ce qu'ils attendent ?
> – Que je tire.
> – Eh bien ! tu n'as qu'à tirer.
> L'idée lui parut lumineuse.[441]

This luminous idea, provided by Ouiza, whom Mokrane calls his "poupée", strikes Mokrane as a partial resolution to his nuptial anxiety but does not, however, bring about any true appreciation of the absurdity of masculine privilege in

---

439 Mouloud Feraoun: *Les Chemins qui montent*, p. 82.
440 Ibid., p. 86.
441 Ibid., p. 83.

his milieu. He rapes Ouiza whilst she sleeps and then immediately leaves, asserting his dominance:

> Elle ne poussa qu'un petit cri mais ne réussit pas à se délivrer. Il se leva triomphant pour sortir, lui dit d'un ton supérieur :
> – Fille d'Ahmed, tu peux pleurer. Je suis un homme, moi ![442]

Feraoun's text thus evokes a feminine awareness of the fragility, of the masquerade, at the heart of the Kabyle masculinist structure of honour and this structure's pernicious resilience in the masculine psyche. Echoing the "pessimism" of Kateb and Dib, this resilience and the need for epistemological revolution is emphasised throughout Feraoun's novels through narrative conclusions, from Ouiza's rape to Fetta's death, which demonstrate women's suffering and men and women's repetitive compliance with the coordinates of "honour".

One can see further how a tendency to maintain masculinist structures is particularly well emphasised in the texts by the prevalence of "ghosts", of masculine ancestors who function as continuing forces of influence in the lives of the male protagonists. In contrast to Naget Khadda who asserts that it is "la dégradation des pratiques ancestrales qui est fustigée", I would argue that Feraoun's texts produce a picture of ancestry and "ancestors" that emphasises their damaging allure, as well as their satisfying ability to legitimate jealousy, revenge and the continuation of practices generative of inequality.[443] For example, Sarah Poole writes of how, in *La Terre et le sang*, "it is Smina's fear that Slimane might feel it his duty to his ancestors to send his wife back to her parents [on the basis of her childlessness] that drives her to scheme with Kamouma to find a solution to the problem".[444]

Also in *La Terre et le sang*, the character of Ramdane alludes specifically to a broader scope of ancestral influence, as he walks through a graveyard with Amer:

> Le cimetière est l'ombre fidèle d'Ighil-Nezman. Mais en réalité, c'est le contraire qui est juste. Le vrai village, ce n'est pas celui qui se dresse fièrement sur la crête. C'est celui-ci: figé dans notre terre, immobile et éternel mais peu effrayant à mon avis, parce que nous le connaissons bien, nous les vivants.[445]

---

[442] Ibid, p. 86.
[443] Naget Khadda: L'Allégorie de la féminité, p. 75–76.
[444] Sarah Poole: Women and boundaries in the fiction of Mouloud Feraoun, p. 162.
[445] Mouloud Feraoun: *La Terre et le sang*, p. 117.

It is seemingly symbolic permanence and repetition itself that the above citation, and Feraoun's texts in general, connect with ancestry.[446] Just as the Amer of *Les Chemins qui montent* replaces and then joins in death the Amer of *La Terre et le sang*, thus following his destiny, so in the graveyard of Ighil-Nezman bodies join other bodies in the ground while the populace is but a living mirror of the deceased. The breaking of this undead connection through feminine puncturing is, as I have indicated, invoked time and again by Feraoun's texts. And, the power of honour as part of a masculinist ideology, supported by undead imagos, is reinforced in the novels, such that the reader becomes acutely aware of this feminine imperative to rebel. Furthermore, Feraoun's narratives place emphasis on the reproduction of honour structures as the backdrop to rebellion not just for the sake of the women who are more clearly damaged by the inequality detailed in the novels. Amer n'Amer of *Les Chemins qui montent*, in contrast to Slimane of *La Terre et le sang*, who also kills Amer's father (Amer-ou-Kaci) through honour-inflicted hatred, is a protagonist with whom the reader is encouraged to form an affective bond and is depicted as, in many respects, an enlightened individual. Yet he too is caught in the tractor-beam of ideology, succumbs to a belief in *nif* and thus meets his demise.

However, throughout this monograph I make the case that it is the masculine symbolic inscription of women itself, in our period of study, that has run the risk of concretising the mastery of women in History. Though, as I have shown, Feraoun's novels do much to elucidate in nuanced and affecting fashion both Algerian women's suffering and their potential to resist, my next section will attempt to demonstrate how, through varied and subtle manipulations of form, Feraoun's novels work to undermine the mastery of the narrator and to emphasise the importance, and perhaps ultimately the impossibility, of incorporating a community in its writing, of giving body and presence to men and women in expressions of their existence. Feraoun's formal innovation ensures that the importance of its content, of its expression of a feminine "thing" in conflict with quasi-Bourdieusian honour structures, is not undermined by a sense of misplaced power in inscription. One might argue that Feraoun's fragmentary structures work to demonstrate that, in a Lacanian sense, he cannot possess the Phallus, the ability to fill in representation fully.

---

[446] Here one might form a link with the focus on "ancêtres" and the repetition of masculinist structures in Kateb's plays.

4.3 Cacophonous Narration

In 1956 Feraoun wrote:

> Je crois que c'est surtout ce désir de faire connaître notre réalité qui m'a poussé à écrire. Et de ce point de vue, je dois vous dire que la réalité ne se laisse jamais saisir dans toute sa complexité, toutes ses nuances et qu'en définitive, ceux qui prétendent la montrer ne montrent qu'eux mêmes et ne témoignent que pour eux.[447]

Feraoun here conveys his distrust of narrative authority whilst avowing his desire to act as witness to a collective reality. His use of "notre" echoes a narrative stance enacted in his novels, in particular *La Terre et le sang*, in its implication of the self and the community. Feraoun and his texts' narrators are presented as part of the object that they describe, just as the object, the community that they evoke, is presented as conditioning their articulation. And, though he does not explicitly contrast the two, Charles Bonn evokes, in an article on Feraoun's narrative technique, the aim of a Feraounian mode in a description of its opposite, with reference to the literary theory of Henri Mitterand:

> [L]a description romanesque suppose une relation de pouvoir, entre un pôle sujet, réunissant l'auteur et son lecteur dans une communauté de valeurs à travers lesquelles l'objet de la description est mis en signification, et le pôle objet qui est l'objet décrit, paysage ou société, auquel on ne demande pas sa propre interprétation, à supposer qu'il en ait une.[448]

By splintering narrative authority, making space for a multiplicity of voices and influences, Feraoun's texts allude to an attempt to disrupt this hierarchical power relation. For as the semi-absent narrator of *Le Fils du pauvre* states, "*Tu aurais tort, Fouroulou, car tu n'es qu'un cas particulier et la leçon, ce sont ces gens-là qui la donnent*".[449] Furthermore, the invocation of multiplicity is not limited to the presence of the community, prominently including female figures, but is also generated through an intricate play with the singularity of the narrator himself. Feraoun once stated in a letter to Mme Landi-Benos, a literary critic on Radio Algiers, that "[v]ous savez bien que Fouroulou c'était à peu près moi. Un enfant tel que je le voyais il y a dix ans. Maintenant, il se peut que je le voie autrement".[450] Feraoun articulates here a shifting of subjectivity present

---

447 Ahlam Mosteghanemi: *Algérie, femmes et écritures*, p. 294.
448 Charles Bonn: De l'ambigüité tragique chez Feraoun, p. 2.
449 Mouloud Feraoun: *Le Fils du pauvre*, p. 105.
450 Mouloud Feraoun: *Lettres à ses amis*. Paris: Éditions du Seuil 1969, p. 111.

in his work, evoking the Derridean idea of the "trace", and reaffirms the importance of his work as "témoignage". With the latter value in mind, I will argue in this section that Feraoun's texts, in varied and surprising ways, work to render particularly visible the complex figure of the teller of the different stories of self and community while undermining his ability to give voice to any experience, including his own, thus deflecting our attempts to identify with a singular, unproblematic voice behind the text. Feraoun's texts produce a cacophony in narration that is both undermining of its own authority in description, allowing it's object, so often women, to evade determination, and visibly appreciative of the importance of bridging the hierarchical gap between narrator and object.

To begin with the text most often cited as formally simple, *Le Fils du pauvre* must, on the contrary, be interpreted as intriguingly complex in its form from the outset. Robert Elbaz and Martine Mathieu-Job provide a brilliant analysis of the intricacies of this work, focusing in particular on the staging of its narration and coming to the conclusion that:

> Il n'y a pas de déchirement au niveau d'identité, comme chez un Khatibi, un Memmi, ou un Chraïbi, par exemple. Il y a, en revanche, une préoccupation fondamentale d'écriture et d'installation dans l'espace de l'écriture. Pour lui, la question n'est pas : qui suis-je ? mais : comment écrire celui que je suis ?[451]

They illustrate how Feraoun, though ubiquitously stating his will to use literature as a from of témoignage, hides behind layers of deliberately confused, and therefore undermined, narrative authority. The novel is divided into four sections, two which cover the plot and two extra-diegetic prefaces.[452] The first diegetic section is narrated by Fouroulou, a name which, as we are told in the novel itself, derives from the Amazigh verb *effer*, to hide. It is preceded by a preface which is narrated by another figure who claims to have found Fouroulou's journal. Thus the first section of plot, the only part of the book that might appear to represent an attempt to directly relate the lived experience of a community, is presented as encountering a readership almost by chance, having potentially been thought of as inadequate by its notional author. Following this first diegetic section, Fouroulou's pen is yielded to the writer of the initial preface who provides the narration for a second preface and a diegetic section that follow. Thus two narrators stand in for Feraoun, one who has determined his inscription

---

[451] Robert Elbaz/Martine Mathieu-Job: *Mouloud Feraoun ou l'émergence d'une littérature*, p. 22.
[452] The original novel contained three extra sections, "Bouzaréa", "La guerre" and an epilogue, removed in the 1954 Éditions du Seuil edition, and included in the collection of texts entitled *L'Anniversaire* (1972).

of his community, including that of its central female figures, to be inadequate, and one whose separation from the action of the texts is fully inscribed.

Focusing on Fouroulou's narration, his depictions of Khalti and Nana, for example, are further undercut by a problematising, a splintering of narrative authority. The text revels in distancing the figure of Fouroulou who is described from the Fouroulou who narrates. We read for example:

> Je me revois ainsi vêtu d'une vielle gandoura décolorée par les mauvais lavages, coiffé d'une chéchia aux bords effrangés et crasseux, sans chaussures ni pantalon, parce que, dans ma mémoire, c'est toujours l'été.[453]

In another example, specifically referring to one of his key feminine influences, Fouroulou states that "[l]e caractère de Khalti convenait très bien au petit Fouroulou".[454] Thus the hidden témoignage that Feraoun enacts is built upon a temporally split self, the images of women drawn from the memories of an unreliable source who can no longer be fully accessed. As Réda Bensmaïa puts it: "The hero speaks of himself as if he had (in the meantime) become someone else".[455] Moreover, the tone of Fouroulou's adult narration is clearly defined by an irony that separates him from both the agents in the first diegetic section, including himself, and the other narrator in in the text. Sometimes this irony is barely detectable and only decipherable once one has gained a fuller impression of the adult Fouroulou's perspective as when we read that "[l]e fellah n'a guère l'habitude de passer ses heures de repos dans sa masure au milieu des femmes et de la marmaille. La djema est un refuge sûr, toujours disponible et gratuit".[456] On other occasions it is more mordant as when we read that "[j]e pouvais frapper impunément mes sœurs et quelquefois mes cousines: il fallait bien m'apprendre à donner des coups !".[457]

Turning to *La Terre et le sang*, one does not find the kind of textual narrative splitting detailed above but rather a multiplicity built on a resolute sense of implication in the community described. One notes a change in the significance of plural personal pronouns from a detached "on" in *Le Fils du pauvre:* "Ici, tout le monde plaisante : on se marie à la légère, on répudie de même, on fait des goss-

---

453 Mouloud Feraoun: *Le Fils du pauvre*, p. 81.
454 Ibid, p. 49.
455 Réda Bensmaïa: *Experimental Nations, or, The Invention of the Maghreb*. Princeton: Princeton University Press 2003, p. 153.
456 Mouloud Feraoun: *Le Fils du pauvre*, p. 18–19.
457 Ibid, p. 28.

es sans y penser [...],⁴⁵⁸ to a more implicated, inclusive "on" and "nous" in *La Terre et le sang:*

> Il semble que la femme de chez nous soit encline à la sympathie, mieux que beaucoup d'autres. Chez nous, la femme est vraiment le sexe faible ; elle le sait et se prend en pitié.⁴⁵⁹

What is particularly interesting in the above citation is that it emphasises a bind between narrator and community not just through the sharing of a pronoun but through the reproduction of a commonly held, problematic discourse on women. A page later, the narrator clarifies his position on determining the being of the Kabyle woman as he produces the maxim that I noted in the introduction to this chapter:

> Au demeurant, il convient de se défier de toute exagération lorsqu'on parle de la femme kabyle. [...] *Tout jugement définitif sur la vie des gens est figé comme un axiome. Or la vie est à l'opposé de l'immobilité.*⁴⁶⁰

Thus the text has the reader understand the fallibility of the narrator, his implication in the socio-symbolic order of his community, and the potential for him to reproduce ideologically conditioned depictions. And interestingly, even his use of "nous", as an indication of the construction of his identity within the framework of a community, is to some extent replicated by other characters in their speech, alluding to a shared epistemological position. For example, a drunk, enraged Slimane states that "[u]ne mauvaise femelle ne peut nous déshonorer. Les femelles des autres, nous les...Les nôtres, nous les supprimons".⁴⁶¹

The text thus alludes to a lived bond between narrator and community, indeed asserts a male–male identification between the teller and the men of the village of Ighil-Nezman, stating in its first line that "[l]'histoire qui va suivre a été réellement vécue dans un coin de Kabylie desservi par une route, ayant une école minuscule, une mosquée blanche [...]".⁴⁶² At the same time, it also continually implies that the narrator possesses an impossible knowledge of character normally associated with an absent, omniscient third person narrator. The spotlight of narration illuminates different protagonists, men and women, incorporating their different stories and perspectives into the picture generated. Nevertheless, in incorporating varied perspectives into the story of the village, the

---

458 Ibid, p. 53.
459 Mouloud Feraoun: *La Terre et le sang*, p. 40.
460 Ibid, p. 41 (emphasis added).
461 Ibid, p. 222.
462 Ibid, p. 11.

use of free indirect discourse conveys a proximity between narrator and object that disrupts the hierarchical relation between the two. A perfect example of this comes at the beginning of chapter III, where we learn about the suffering of Amer's mother, Kamouma, in a piece of narration that communicates great sympathy and pathos:

> Elle ne sait plus où elle en est de sa vie. Mariée toute jeune à Kaci, elle a d'abord vécu sous l'autorité d'un rude beau-père et d'une belle-mère tyrannique [...] Le jour où il ne lui resta plus que Kaci, son mari, et Amer : son plus jeune fils, la situation lui apparut très nette. C'était tout simple : *il fallait élever Amer, en faire vite un homme qui pût se charger de ses vieux parents.*[463]

Indeed, one can chronologically track an increasing will to fuse narrator and object across Feraoun's novelistic projects, particularly with reference to women, such that by the time one reaches *Les Chemins qui montent*, the subjectivity of the male narrator is explicitly coloured by a desire to conjure and inhabit the being of feminine others. One might like to think of Feraoun's growing focus on the impact of others on the self in terms of Martin Heidegger's notion of *Mitsein*. Jane Hiddleston, in her recent monograph, *Decolonising the Intellectual*, elegantly outlines Heidegger's idea as follows:

> [I]n *Being and Time*, Heidegger explains that *Dasein*, being there, is always *Mitsein*, being with. *Mitsein* means that relations with others are part of what constitutes Being, we do not come into the world and then encounter others, but are already constructed by our collective sharing of the world.[464]

Les Chemins qui montent, sharing similarities with *Le Fils du pauvre*, is divided into three separate sections narrated by different agents. The first is narrated from a third person position though, as I will later emphasise, it represents an attempt to embody the female character of Dehbia. The final section is a short newspaper cutting that alludes to the ignorance that necessarily infiltrates the treatment of others in writing, as it glosses over the ambiguity in the text as to the cause of Amer's death, preferring instead to present it as an uncomplicated suicide. To focus here on the second section which takes the guise of Amer's personal journal, however, we note almost immediately his preoccupation with his mother as a determining presence in his life, even after her death. At her burial, a friend tries to console Amer by giving him his hand. Amer imagines what this gesture is supposed to convey:

---

463 Ibid, p. 22 (emphasis added).
464 Jane Hiddleston: *Decolonising the Intellectual*, p. 90.

> "Bon, on sait que ta mère est morte. Mais tu es là. Ce n'est pas la fin du monde. N'y pense plus. Elle est en dessous et nous sommes tous au-dessus à fouler cette terre [...]"[465]

In contrast to this sentiment of severance, Amer goes on to write of and for his mother with a very different relation in mind:

> Je désire seulement écrire, tout raconter à la fois. Ma vie, la sienne. Faire comprendre qu'elle est partie et qu'en même temps elle est là, autour de moi, en moi. Que c'est elle qui vous parle, qui veut que j'écrive.[466]

Throughout the book, Amer re-animates his mother's presence. She exists, like the male ancestors described in the previous section, as a "ghost" with whom he maintains an imaginary dialogue and with whom, even as his very personal story unravels, he wishes to preserve a bond in agency:

> – Tranquillise-toi, maman. Tous deux, nous tracerons notre chemin vers la crête : il montera comme les autres mais ce sera un chemin secret, une sente minuscule que mangera la broussaille, au fur et à mesure que nous avancerons. Nous n'inviterons personne à nous suivre et à tous nous souhaiterons bonne chance.[467]

Furthermore, though in the above citation it would seem that Amer favours an exclusive subjective linkage with his mother, there are other examples that allude to a value of *Mitsein* and that therefore work further to disrupt a hierarchical relationship between the narrator and the figures that populate his narration. In one particularly striking and visceral moment in his section, Amer imagines himself physically passing into the body of a woman referred to simply as "la sœur de Rahma",[468] a woman with whose being Amer is depicted as being linked after she commits suicide and who stands, for Amer, as a symbolic representative of the community, personifying its suffering: "J'imaginais, par exemple, que cette femme personnifiait notre misérable existence".[469] We read:

> J'entrais dans sa bouche avide qui me broyait impitoyablement, descendais très vite dans son estomac qui m'aspirait comme une pieuvre [...] Puis je filais dans l'intestin où j'étais entortillé, étouffé, sucé, et je passais en elle.[470]

---

[465] Mouloud Feraoun: *Les Chemins qui montent*, p. 106.
[466] Ibid, p. 112.
[467] Ibid, p. 212.
[468] Ibid, p. 176.
[469] Ibid, p. 176.
[470] Ibid, p. 177.

Thus Amer evokes a bodily union between himself and a woman who he perceives as emblematic of the Kabyle object that he describes, of which he is himself a part. She, like his mother, is an element presented as being part of a multiplicity of influence, a group identity that contributes to an irreducible subjectivity. And, this multiplicity of influence that we are encouraged to read as constitutive of Amer's and therefore Feraoun's act of remembrance, of inscription, is not exclusively female, for characters like Saïd, who accompanies Amer in departing Ighil-Nezman for France, also determine the direction of his telling. However, it is clear, paradoxically, that despite his invoking of different figures in the telling of his tale, Amer remains ineluctably isolated, in particular from his love, Dehbia. Indeed, Feraoun's novel, like Amer, attempts to summon the subjectivities of others to assist in the construction of the image generated, but in doing so ensures that failure and factitiousness characterise shared inscription and mutual comprehension. *Les Chemins qui montent* and *La Terre et le sang* demonstrate that whilst a Feraounian mode attempts to make clear the importance of complicating and undermining a singular masterful scribe, the concern that is to be shown for the relationship between self and other must be articulated in part by representing the impossibility of truly sharing agency and truly understanding others. As the next section will investigate, Feraoun's work acknowledges that ventriloquism is not equivalent to handing over the pen, even if it does at least represent a bold attempt to fulfil the community impulse referred to above.

4.4 Ventriloquism, Factitiousness, and Failure

Debra Kelly, in *Autobiography and Independence*, provides a detailed short account of Feraoun's personal life, in which she includes the intriguing detail that in 1938 he married his cousin, whose name was Dehbia.[471] As with Kateb and *Nedjma*, then, one can interpret a personal investment in the creation of *Les Chemins qui montent*, as the first half of his tragic narrative is bookended by Dehbia's coming to terms with Amer, her lover's death. Indeed, Feraoun's animation of Dehbia can be read as a sincere, personal attempt to embody the subjectivity of a Kabyle woman, perhaps envisaged with reference to his own lover, in order to gain limited access to the lived experience of Kabyle women as a whole. Moreover, as this final section will investigate, part of this attempt, which one may view as a gesture of love, is a recognition of the very impossibil-

---

[471] Debra Kelly: *Autobiography and Independence*, p. 56.

ity of its success. As Lacan's maxim states, "l'amour c'est donner ce qu'on n'a pas".[472] An articulation of the masculine narrator's failure to offer a picture of feminine characters that might equate to their self-representation is, furthermore, not limited to *Les Chemins qui montent*. All three novels explicitly testify to a necessary implication of failure in representation and indeed allude to the grim consequences of misunderstanding, of misrecognition.

To return initially to a focus on *Les Chemins qui montent*, Amer's perspective is presented as delayed, it comes to fill in (some of) the gaps in Dehbia's understanding of him and his actions. For example, Dehbia's belief that Amer has betrayed her with Ouiza is revealed to be a product of Mokrane's paranoia. It is Dehbia's perspective that initially takes centre stage and it is with her that the reader forms an initial bond of identification, a connection that arguably might be maintained throughout the text as Amer is immediately revealed as deceased. Her perspective is animated, alive, his is relayed, dead. Amer's section is, however, unified in its perspective, taking the form of a personal journal which, we are informed, Dehbia has possession of. In contrast, the section devoted to Dehbia displays an awareness, from its very inception, of its factitious nature, of the staged quality of its attempt to represent the "other side" of the story. The first chapter is split between narration, focused on Dehbia, that is delivered from an absent, third person perspective, as in the first line of the text: "Dehbia prit le journal d'Amer et le posa devant elle",[473] and narration, presented in chevron speech-marks, which conveys Dehbia's thoughts from a first person perspective: "'J'ai fait un héritage. Amer n'Amer, tous tes papiers sont là [...]'".[474] The two forms of narration, similar in length, seem initially to compete for precedence and evoke a desire to have Dehbia speak, leading the reader to believe that a ventriloquist stance will define the rest of the text. However, the inclusion of chevron speech-marks serves as an indication that her speech will not be maintained, that its status as a ploy, a lie, is to be known by writer and reader alike. Following chapter one, though her perspective is evoked by the third person narrator, her speech is not included in the same fashion; the text acknowledges its own destiny of failure.

Jacques-Alain Miller, in an interview with Hanna Waar, stated that "aimer, c'est reconnaître son manque, et le donner à l'autre, le placer dans l'autre".[475]

---

472 Jacques Lacan: *Écrits*, p. 618.
473 Mouloud Feraoun: *Les Chemins qui montent*, p. 11.
474 Ibid, p. 12–14.
475 Jacques-Alain Miller: Interview with Hanna Waar. In: *Psychologies Magazine* No. 278 (2008), p. 4.

With this in mind, one can therefore see *Les Chemins qui montent* as expressing love for its female object, including a recognition of a lack, of an inability to fully represent. Or perhaps one might describe Feraoun's narrative stance regarding women as "meta-love", as love itself, for Lacan, is presented, as Dylan Evans describes it, as "an illusory fantasy of fusion with the beloved".[476] It is the accentuated literary artifice that allows for this fantasy to be laid bare.

Similarly, in *Le Fils du pauvre*, Fouroulou's attempts to represent Khalti and Nana are presented as part of "un chef-d'œuvre *avorté*".[477] Where the narration of *Les Chemins qui montent* ceases its attempts to ventriloquise, underlining its inability to speak *for* women, *Le Fils du pauvre* abdicates the narrator-come-author's position of directly speaking *about* women, as though acknowledging that the task of evoking the gendered sempiternal oppression culminating in Khalti and Nana's deaths is insurmountable. Moreover, the cacophonous narration that characterises the text as a whole foregrounds further the factitiousness of the project, the artificial nature of its treatment of its object and thus the failure inscribed within its very articulation. In both cases one can perceive a link between a failure in communication and a tragic feminine fate within the plot. Thus while a Feraounian mode deliberately emphasises its inability to represent women's lived experience, it simultaneously advocates for increased dialogue, for another space, beyond the text, where women and men might talk and listen to each other, echoing the productively "pessimistic" stances of Kateb and Dib. *Les Chemins qui montent* presents the clearest example of this as the gulf that separates the two perspectives, textually represented by the physical divisions in the text, eventually brings about the death of its central masculine character and the desolation of its central feminine character.

La Terre et le sang is also particularly useful as a demonstration of how Feraoun's texts incorporate lacunae in perspective, how the panoptic gaze of the masculine third person narrator is continuously compromised, and how this works to achieve a similar abdication of authority as is enacted by the grander formal gestures indicated above. One can ascribe these lacunae both to the loss of a clear image due to the passage of time but also, seemingly, to a reluctance to perform on behalf of women the task of discussing particular, potentially traumatic sites of oppression. In *La Terre et le sang*, Feraoun writes the following:

> Il peut dérouler ainsi toute une série d'images, de scènes, de péripéties. Voilà de quoi est fait son passé. Il faudrait, peut-être, pour comprendre, imaginer une immense toile aux

---

[476] Dylan Evans: *An Introductory Dictionary of Lacanian Psychoanalysis*. Hove: Routledge 1996, p. 103.
[477] Robert Elbaz/Martine Mathieu-Job: *Mouloud Feraoun ou l'émergence d'une littérature*, p. 17.

> dessins ternis, un rouleau gigantesque qui enferme plusieurs années et peint par un maître avec de mauvais crayons : l'ensemble est flou, estompé. Par-ci, par-là apparaît une touche insolite ayant gardé toute sa fraîcheur – un trait noir et net comme une cicatrice récente [...]⁴⁷⁸

This passage firstly articulates the interference of time in the production of an image of the past, its pollution of a picture which consequently becomes blurry, faded. Contained even within this affirmation of doubt, however, is an undermining hesitancy which can be seen to temper depictions of women, and men, in much of Feraoun's writing. The uncertain "peut-être" which breaks the flow of the passage is mirrored with unusual frequency in the novels of our corpus, in particular within *La Terre et le sang*. Its inclusion, again, may pertain to forgetfulness, to admission that the narrator cannot summon a clear ensemble of images from the past. Thus, for example, we read as follows:

> Voilà quinze ans qu'il est parti. Mon Dieu, oui ! comme tous les autres. C'était un matin de printemps, au mois de mars, peut-être.⁴⁷⁹ ⁴⁸⁰

Equally, however, the use of "peut-être" often alludes rather to a lack of access to the subjectivities that populate the text, in particular to its central women protagonists. So we read, for example, that "il [Amer] revit Chabha telle qu'elle était : indécise, tourmentée, apeurée peut-être".⁴⁸¹ If one then looks again at the citation above, taken from pages 54–55 of *La Terre et le sang*, one can link this usage of an adverb of doubt to an inability to symbolise traumatic *cicatrices* in women's lived experiences. Feraoun here in fact uses the metaphor of scarring in a way that suggests a raised protrusion, somewhat evocative of Barthes' notion of the photographic *punctum*. However, if one thinks through the notion of scarring within the context of our corpus and looking back on the personal poetry of Kateb, its metaphorical resonance as a traumatic point that evades direct symbolisation is, for me, more productive. For, as was briefly alluded to in the section on Khalti's disappearance in 'Breaking the Chain', Feraoun's texts refuse to determine women's experiences of trauma, declining to fully articulate the "real" of women's suffering which would, as is evidenced by the psychoanalytical notion of repression, present great difficulties even to the women agents themselves. One finds this to be the case for the evocations of the familial figure

---

478 Mouloud Feraoun: *La Terre et le sang*, p. 54–55.
479 Ibid, p. 20.
480 Also interesting here is the fact that the last two sentences are in free indirect discourse, implying a shared forgetfulness between the narrator and the agents in the text.
481 Ibid, p. 193.

of Khalti in *Le Fils du pauvre,* the Western figure of Marie in *La Terre et le sang,* and, perhaps most strikingly, for the romantic figures of Dehbia and Ouiza in *Les Chemins qui montent.* In Marie's case it is her harsh daily life prior to her departure with Amer that is left hinted at, but not determined. A reference to a "protecteur"[482] and other glimpses of a possible life of prostitution or abuse act as markers that lead the reader to envisage the possibility of a harrowing tale that might be told by Marie herself; the narrator will not provide it.[483]

Les Chemins qui montent, however, takes precise key scenes of distressing sexual encounters and removes the textual content that might touch the moment of contact and women's subjective responses to it. I referred above to the scene of Mokrane's consummation of his wedding to Ouiza. After the charade of the gun-firing, a lengthy period of terse conversation between the two, and a description of Mokrane's internal anguish, the moment of rape is curiously under-determined. We read simply that:

> Il était furieux et se sentait fort, prêt à cogner. Il se jeta rageusement sur Ouiza qui dormait. Et avant qu'elle revînt de son sommeil, l'affaire était réglée.[484]

The business-like terminology deployed at the close of the second sentence is, in its black irony, indicative of a repression staged both in the text and potentially by both the physical and psychic authors of the trauma within the narrative, Mokrane and Ouiza. Concordantly, Dehbia's moment of anguish, the sexual liaison with Mokrane whose consequences bubble up throughout the text, is staged in such a way that, again, both the text and the agent with whose perspective the reader is engaged, repress, cannot recall the image of the event:

> Après, tout devient confus dans sa mémoire. L'a-t-il prise par la main pour l'entraîner vers le gourbi ? L'a-t-elle suivi sans résistance ? Sont-ils restés muets, ou bien ont-ils échangé des propos ? Elle ne saurait le dire.[485]

Feraoun's text, as has been previously evidenced, is keen to discuss women's suffering, engendered by the masculinist structures that subtend the actions of the village's protagonists. However, it is also keen that its representation of this suffering not be commensurate with an ideal of fixity. As I stated in the in-

---

[482] Ibid, p. 76.
[483] We read, for example, of how Marie is housed by her "amant" with a "hôtelier qui était un 'ami' [et qui] les reçut sans histoires et n'inscrivit que l'homme avec lequel il avait déjà 'travaillé'". Ibid, p. 101.
[484] Mouloud Feraoun: *Les Chemins qui montent*, p. 85–86.
[485] Ibid. p. 96–97.

troduction to this chapter, for Feraoun's narrator, "la vie est à l'opposé de l'immobilité", it cannot be fully depicted.[486] Indeed, the depiction of Dehbia's moment of disarray above is, in many respects, representative of the aspects of Feraoun's novelistic project that this chapter as a whole has attempted to evoke. Firstly, though, as an act of symbolic revenge against a rival (Amer), it represents the culmination of Mokrane's interpellation into an ideology of "honour", it simultaneously represents Dehbia's breaking with her symbolic pact with Amer, her enacting of an opposition to community. Or does it? For what is also important and representative in the above citation is its very ambiguity. The narrator cannot tell us definitively what Dehbia's thoughts were nor what exactly took place, his authority is revealed as false, his project of representation destined for failure. At the same time, one notes how, via the use of free indirect discourse, the separation between narrator and object is blurred, staging the animation of a feminine discourse which poses itself questions about the disturbing event. This formal decision acts once more to undermine the authority of the narrator, and of Feraoun himself, as a unified, singular agent capable of a regular omniscience that cannot be influenced, and is thus evocative of a value of *Mitsein*. It does simultaneously, however, invoke the need for women to represent themselves. Feraoun's novelistic projects are initially of interest precisely because of the importance they place on talking about women and the way women engage in the sociological reality of late-colonial Kabylia. What must be remembered, however, is that underpinning this content is a literary stance that, to some extent, perversely tallies with the unfair criticism of "humility", of a lack of literary "adventure", that some have levelled at his work. For though, of course, Feraoun's novels prove to be unusually complex and innovative in their form, they expose their literary scaffolding, the mechanics of representation. In so doing, they refuse to simply and arrogantly claim *Vertretung* mastery over their feminine object. Consequently, what Feraoun's texts reveal are holes in the témoignage of their socio-historical milieu that remain to be filled, perhaps by Algerian women themselves.

---

486 Mouloud Feraoun: *La Terre et le sang*, p. 41.

5 Mouloud Mammeri – A Dissenting Masculine Perspective

Mouloud Mammeri, Amazigh novelist, poet, anthropologist, and linguist, was born on 28th December 1917 in Taourirt-Mimoun, Grande Kabylie, into a family of both considerable traditional standing and economic means. While having referred to his father, the amin of his village, in an article in *Révolution Africaine* in 1965 as "la tradition faite homme", Mammeri's attendance at French educational institutions in Morocco and France, culminating in university professorships and honorary degrees, begins to indicate why fraught questions of class, wealth, and representativity have dogged his work from the beginning of his literary career and have, to some extent, come to define its reception, in particular with respect to his first novel, *La Colline oubliée* (1952).[487] Moreover, like the early novels of Djebar, as the next chapter will investigate in greater depth, Mammeri's early novels met on publication with accusations by nationalist critics, including Mostefa Lacheraf, of assimilation and of an ignorance of the Algerian national cause. It will thus be one of the aims of this chapter to address conceptions of Mammeri's socio-political disengagement in part by demonstrating how Mammeri's texts, much like those of Feraoun, are themselves often concerned precisely with the gap between the writer, the masculine representer, and his object. Indeed, this chapter argues that Mammeri's novels, from *La Colline oubliée*, to *Le Sommeil du juste* (1955), to *L'Opium et le bâton* (1965), deploy an array of fallible narrators who fail to engage productively with their social milieu, just as they work to differing degrees with many other subversive formal techniques of representation present in the works of this book's corpus and produce sustained meditations on the objectification of women in the masculine psyche.

When considering Mammeri's texts as sites of productive conceptualisations of women and gender relations, one aspect that renders Mammeri's modes of representation particularly interesting is the weight that he himself often lent to the communication of ideas through literary means. In an interview conducted in 1985 for a special edition of *Dérives*, for example, Mammeri stated: "Personnellement, je considère que la littérature est un moyen de communication. Il n'est pas vrai que vous écriviez pour personne. Vous écrivez pour des gens qui vous lisent. Et si les gens vous lisent, c'est que vous avez quelque chose à

---

[487] Mouloud Mammeri: Ce sont les témoignages qu'il faudrait consigner. In: *Révolution africaine* No. 128 (10 July 1965), p. 24.

leur communiquer".[488] Mammeri's insistence on the communicative capacity of literature compels one to consider both the messages that his novels work to deliver as symbolic interventions and the purpose of their varying narrative forms. Inviting comparisons with Mohammed Dib and again with Djebar, Mammeri's novelistic style undergoes a marked evolution across the three novels, in his case heading away from a more intimate form of narration which generates a proximity between the reader and the text's representations of Kabyle gendered social and psychic norms, to a more grandiose, operatic mode where questions about the postcolonial nation take precedence over issues of structural sexism. This movement towards what Mammeri himself has referred to as "une espèce de symphonie, de composition musicale" will be followed across the three novels which lead up to and indeed exceed the historical moment of independence.[489] It is stated in my introduction that this book seeks to deal with literary symbolic contributions created on the temporal path leading up to the establishment of the Algerian state. The reasons for incorporating *L'Opium et le bâton* (1965) are, however, threefold: Firstly, much of its content is drawn from pre-revolutionary experience, from "témoignages qu'il faudrait consigner" about the Algerian war of independence; secondly, the narrative describes actions taking place in the late-colonial period, most pertinently actions performed by or concerning Algerian women; thirdly, the novel impresses upon the reader the status of the period as in flux, as uncertain to produce socio-political advancement for all. Indeed, the novel reads as representative of the uncertainty and "pessimism" that marks many of the texts produced leading up to independence and it should not be ignored that the book was published barely a month prior to the coup d'état staged by Houari Boumédiène and his military supporters, thus at a particularly dubious time for the Algerian polity. Consequently, it is my belief that one should consider the novel an important and appropriate text in my corpus.

Ouarda Himeur argues that "Mouloud Mammeri, comparé à Mouloud Feraoun, n'était pas un homme de la scène publique".[490] Despite this affirmation, what is interesting is that perhaps more than any other author in my corpus, Mammeri produces representations that are marked by clearly identifiable historical moments or events, complying with a journalistic imperative. It is partly because of this that this chapter will approach the novels chronologically as their

---

488 Pierre Monette (ed.): *No. 49: Mouloud Mammeri: langues et langages d'Algérie*. Montréal: Dérives 1985, p. 113.
489 Mildred Mortimer: *Mouloud Mammeri, écrivain algérien*. Sherbrooke: Naâman 1982, p. 38.
490 Ouarda Himeur: Le permis et l'interdit chez Mouloud Feraoun et Mouloud Mammeri. In Tassadit Yacine (ed.): *Le Genre dans les littératures postcoloniales. Feraoun, Mammeri, Belamri*. Paris: Éditions de la Maison des Sciences de L'Homme 2008, p. 37.

context directs the form and content within which women's representation takes place. Nevertheless, one can identify key trends that are identifiable in all three novels and in assessing the what and the how of the texts' messages regarding women, this chapter will be seen to focus particularly on an ethnographic/sociological posture and the symbolic institution of marriage, on masculine perspective and narrative form, making use of the discussions on the male gaze and viewer participation rendered in Laura Mulvey's seminal filmic essay 'Visual Pleasure and Narrative Cinema', and upon socio-political uncertainty/pessimism. Some critics, like Miriam Cooke in *Women and the War Story*, have been less than complimentary when addressing Mammeri's contribution to women's representation. Cooke writes, for example, that in *L'Opium et le bâton*, "[c]haracters are reduced to stereotypes who act out highly determined roles" and that "women fighters are no longer frightening" but rather "dumb and innocuous".[491] It will be the central argument of this chapter that though the women of his texts do not always fulfil ideals of positive, liberatory agency, acting on occasion as potentially problematic supplements to a masculine narrative thread, the texts themselves are, to differing extents, like so many of the other texts of my corpus, self-problematising, self-critical, productively invested in a discussion about the representation of a feminine Other and the dangers of her literary determination, and dissenting of the representative/social status-quo.

5.1 Kabyle Sociology, Masculinist Structures, and Women's Suffering

As Charles Bonn's work on ethnography and Algerian literature has often demonstrated, Mammeri's depictions of a Kabyle social milieu have seen his work compared to that of Feraoun and the early Dib in its establishment by critics like Jean Déjeux and Abdelkebir Khatibi as part of "'le courant ethnographique' des débuts de la littérature algérienne de langue française".[492] Moreover, Bonn diplomatically states that at the time of *La Colline oubliée*'s publication "cette description de la société Algérienne (plus particulièrement kabyle) traditionnelle a suscité parmi les nationalistes algériens des réactions mitigées".[493] A number of scathing articles were published including Lacheraf's '*La Colline*

---

491 Miriam Cooke: *Women and the War Story*, p. 162.
492 Charles Bonn: De l'ambigüité tragique chez Feraoun, p. 1.
493 Ibid, p. 1.

oubliée ou les consciences anachroniques' (1953) and Mohammed Cherif Sahli's *'La Colline oubliée* ou la colline du reniement' (1953) in which the critic caracterises the book as a failure because "[u]ne œuvre signée d'un Algérien ne peut [...] nous intéresser que d'un seul point de vue: quelle cause sert-elle ? Quelle est sa position dans la lutte qui oppose le mouvement national au colonialisme ?".[494] He concludes by stating that Mammeri's text is "digne de l'oubli et du mépris de tout un peuple vaillant et fier".[495] [496] Indeed Zineb Ali-Benali reveals that the novel's winning of the literary 'Prix de la Ville d'Alger' produced such a critical response that "[o]n alla jusqu'à soupçonner Mouloud Mammeri de n'être qu'un prête-nom", that one suspected Mammeri's text of being the product of a French imposter.[497]

Pinpointing exactly what made Mammeri's novel so unpalatable for nationalist critics is somewhat difficult though there are numerous suppositions that other critics have made and that one can continue to put forward. Firstly, of course, there is the lack of detailed investigation regarding the struggle between a coherent "nation" and the colonial system, a lack later addressed in *L'Opium et le bâton*. Secondly, there is the unusual focus on Algerian characters of a comfortable socio-economic background. As Ouarda Himeur puts it, "[l]a mise en scène de la 'petite bourgeoisie' rurale kabyle était en soi un acte iconoclaste, du point de vue de ceux qui faisaient de la misère des colonisés le cheval de bataille des revendications nationalistes".[498] Thirdly, there is Himeur's other suggestion that the character of "le Barbu", the maquis leader, appeared as insuffisciently sympathetic. Finally, it would be my argument that the strong self-critical stance that the novel adopts, including its focus on women, was seen as less than helpful for the stabilisation of a notion of Algerian righteousness in the face of colonial oppression.[499] Indeed, depictions of women's status and of

---

[494] Mohammed Cherif Sahli: La Colline oubliée ou la colline du reniement. In: *Le jeune musulman* No. 15 (1953), p. 2.
[495] Ibid, p. 2.
[496] Two summations of the political tensions surrounding the novel's publication can be found: Mohammed Salah Dembri's Querelles autour de *La Colline oubliée*. In: *Revue algérienne des lettres et des sciences humaines* No.1 (1969), p. 171–173 and Jean Déjeux's *La Colline oubliée* de Mouloud Mammeri. Un prix littéraire, une polémique politique. In : *Œuvres et Critiques* No. 4: 2 (1979), p. 69–80.
[497] Zineb Ali-Benali: 'La fiancée du soir' : un appel de femme dans 'La Colline oubliée'. In Tassadit Yacine (ed.): *Le Genre dans les littératures postcoloniale's. Feraoun, Mammeri, Belamri*. Paris: Éditions de la Maison des Sciences de L'Homme 2008, p. 77.
[498] Ouarda Himeur: Le permis et l'interdit chez Mouloud Feraoun et Mouloud Mammeri, p. 38.
[499] One might argue that Mammeri's critical stance serves to undermine the processes of the second stage of nationalist invention, as conceived of by Clifford Geertz in *The Interpretation*

their treatment by men in the novel are neither insignificant in number nor flattering of the gendered social fictions associated with forms of Islamic practice and Amazigh tradition. Consequently, one can justifiably see women's representation in Mammeri's first novel as a particular thorn in the side of those who would wish national ideology to remain unproblematised, unchallenged.

Though initially published in 1952, *La Colline oubliée* is the product of writings carried out in the 1940s and its narrative reflects the upheavals instigated by the Second World War. Mammeri stated in an interview in 1952: "Je me disais alors que mes expériences et celles de mes proches camarades kabyles valaient la peine d'être mises noir sur blanc. Mais j'écrivais pour moi seul. C'est longtemps après, en 1946, que j'ai eu l'idée de transformer mes notes en roman".[500] Here, in Mammeri's own words, one perceives the combination of a rationale for a lack of a specific focus on colonial conflict (the detailing of events taking place prior to the uprisings in Sétif and Guelma) and an acknowledgement of a movement from writing for oneself to writing for others, generating an intervention in public discourse on the society depicted.

The novel recounts social structures and events in the lives of the inhabitants of the village of Tasga, Kabylia, focusing in particular on the tragic relationship shared by the young woman Aazi and the chief male protagonist, Mokrane, through whose journal we are initially invited to take our perspective as readers. And, as has often been noted by critics, the text foregrounds this relationship, the institution of marriage, and women's symbolic burden, on the very first page of the narrative. Thus we read the following:

> Le printemps, chez nous, ne dure pas. Au sortir des jours froids de l'hiver où il a venté rageusement sur les tuiles, où la neige a fait se terrer les hommes et les bêtes, quand le tiède printemps revient, il a à peine le temps de barbouiller de vert les champs que déjà le soleil fait se faner les fleurs, puis jaunir les moissons. Le printemps des jeunes filles non plus ne dure pas. J'avais laissé en partant Aazi de Taasast, la fiancée du soir, et c'est Tamazouzt, fille de Lathmas, jeune fille à marier, que je retrouvais.[501]

Immediately, then, women's status is linked to particular matrimonial structures which, we are told, are themselves linked with an inevitable loss in vernal vitality. As we are initially unaware of the significance of "la fiancée du soir", a significance to which this chapter will later return, the appellation appears as specific to the culture of the people described, as to a lesser extent does the naming

---

of Cultures. New York: Basic Books 1973, wherein nationalist movements attempt to solidify mass enthusiasm for a nation to come by fixing a collective identity as opposing that of the coloniser.
500 Jean Déjeux: *Littérature maghrébine de langue française*, p. 153.
501 Mouloud Mammeri: *La Colline oubliée.* Paris: Gallimard 1992 [1952], p. 13.

of Tamazouzt (Aazi) by reference to her father. The first twenty-five pages of the book continue to highlight a peculiar gendered separation in devoting a majority of their narration to descriptions of women's poverty, sickness, and symbolic oppression. The cause of the increased visibility of women's suffering, the unstated driving force behind the narrator's will to cover the events that he notionally witnesses, appears initially as indirectly linked then more precisely connected to economic deprivations engendered by colonialism.

First we read the general statement that "[d]epuis longtemps en effet, notre cité souffrait d'une maladie étrange, insaisissable".[502] This "maladie" is immediately gendered as we are told that "[i]l naissait toujours autant d'enfants, mais c'étaient surtout des filles ; il y avait aussi beaucoup de morts, mais c'étaient plutôt des garçons qui mouraient. Un vent maléfique soufflait sur Tasga".[503] Thus women's status is defined as supplementary, as of a secondary, supporting significance to masculinity, within the narrator's ideological perspective. There is a gendered *dissymétrie fondementale*, to refer back to the Bourdieu quote used in my introduction, that seemingly defines the socio-symbolic framework of Tasga. Nevertheless, despite the primordial gendered narrative that colours the narrator's perspective, we also note an appreciation of the hardships of women and an unconscious reference to the structural permanency of oppression in the use of the word "éternité":

> Mais le plus grave n'était pas là, le plus grave, c'était cette tristesse qui suintait des murs; [...] ces femmes chargées semblaient s'acquitter sans joie d'une corvée insipide qu'ils avaient tout le temps de finir: il semblait qu'ils avaient devant eux l'éternité, alors ils ne se pressaient pas [...][504]

Furthermore, where the narration deliberately betrays an interpellation to socio-religious superstition and a castrationesque anxiety about the presence or the abundance of women, the reader is encouraged to perceive the presence of the author behind Mokrane, the narrator, winking ironically:

> D'ailleurs il y avait trop de jeunes filles, il y en avait tant que cela devenait inquiétant. On n'en avait jamais tant vu à Tasga, car les jeunes gens ne se mariaient plus. Ils disaient comme les Iroumien qu'il leur fallait d'abord gagner assez d'argent pour deux ; ils croyaient, les impies, que c'est du travail de leurs bras que sortirait la nourriture de leurs enfants ; ils ignoraient que c'est Dieu qui comble et Dieu qui appauvrit. Nos aïeux étaient sages qui se mariaient d'abord, sachant bien que c'est une nécessité naturelle et un devoir

---

502 Ibid, p. 31.
503 Ibid, p. 32.
504 Ibid, p. 32.

5.1 Kabyle Sociology, Masculinist Structures, and Women's Suffering — 141

> envers Dieu et la loi du prophète et qui ensuite tâchaient de pourvoir aux besoins de la maison, car Dieu est clément et miséricordieux.[505]

God's clemency and pity having seemingly been lacking in previous descriptions, one is compelled to question the narrator's perspective both on the necessity of marriage and regarding the state of anxiety that women's increased visibility provokes. Indeed, both concerns recall Simone de Beauvoir's descriptions of men's approach to the feminine Other in that they evoke the problematic Hegelian desire to maintain the Other as distinct from both nature (man desires recognition thus potential brides are necessary) and from oneself (man desires mastery over this recognition and thus too many potential brides upset him).[506] Furthermore, the pernicious nature of the symbolic structures that discount women's agency by establishing marriage as a necessity for the maintenance of honour as a part of symbolic capital is reinforced throughout the narrative, in particular in the detailing of Aazi's struggles to satisfy the desires of her parents-in-law. It can also be interpreted as explicitly related to the sociology of the colonised interior, in opposition to the structures at work in the coloniser's world, framed as the exterior. This point will be clarified in a later discussion of *Le Sommeil du juste*.

To focus on Aazi's oppression, the text presents enjoyment of the structure of marriage as contrary to its purpose, as taboo, and demonstrates that any small enjoyment subversively acquired is short-lived:

> Sous prétexte de veiller à ce que le ramassage et le séchage fussent vite achevés avant que les grosses pluies d'hiver reviennent cette fois peut-être pour longtemps, je descendais presque chaque soir avec coutume: un mari ne sort pas ainsi avec sa jeune femme dès les premiers temps de leur mariage, mais cette guerre excusait tout.[507]

Shortly after this brief honeymoon period, Mokrane has to leave on military service and Aazi is compelled to live in the house of her parents-in-law. Unable to fulfil the unspoken marriage contract which stipulates the provision of a child, she immediately becomes the object of their displeasure. She is subject to both verbal and physical abuse and upon Mokrane's return, though he is clearly represented as emotionally affected by the events, there is no real analysis or questioning of the absurdity of the underlying ideological coordinates that have motivated the abuse (honour, marriage and its role in the acquisition

---

505 Ibid, p. 33–34.
506 See again Section 3 "Mythes" in De Beauvoir's *Le Deuxième sexe 1*.
507 Mouloud Mammeri: *La Colline oubliée*, p. 45.

of symbolic capital through the expansion of the family). Instead, the narrator's perspective sees Aazi as a child to be protected within the familial structure, not an agent in her own right who might desire a break with its imperatives:

> J'eus beaucoup de peine à calmer son agitation. Je la pris dans mes bras et la berçai comme on berce un petit enfant, puis je vis ses paupières lentement se baisser; mais je ne pus fermer l'œil de la nuit.[508]

Aazi's situation deteriorates as the novel continues. Religious rites and traditional magic are employed unsuccessfully in attempts to have her give birth, until she is repudiated by Mokrane's family whereupon she finally becomes pregnant, giving birth after Mokrane's death. Mokrane's interventions in his wife's fate are limited to a compliance with Tasga's socio-symbolic structures (caring for her in the family setting, allowing for the "aumônes symboliques" of feminine magical figures like Na Ghné, agreeing to a pilgrimage to the tomb of a local saint etc.), and these structures then persist after Mokrane's death and their son's birth, like the structures of rivalry in Kateb's *Les Ancêtres redoublent*. At the discovery of the birth we read of Mokrane's father, Ramdane:

> C'était un garçon. Quoiqu'il eût lui-même répudié sa bru, Ramdane vint chez elle avec Melha. Lathmas, par déférence, lui demanda de donner lui-même un nom au nouveau-né. Il l'appela Mokrane comme son fils, leva le bébé dans ses bras et récita une prière, demandant à Dieu pour lui une vie longue et heureuse :
> – Qu'il vive croyant et meure musulman ![509]

Aazi's suffering, her wishes, her name, are not mentioned or considered. The scene thus produces a clear representation of the function of women as inactive placeholders in a social structure which serves to accrue familial honour through masculine capital, here the birth of a boy. This subjugation of women is then linked explicitly to Islamic tradition through Ramdane's exclamation.

The novel also encourages the reader to consider the plight of the three other most important women characters: Daadi, Davda, and Kamouma, as a function of their exclusion from agency in decision-making regarding the parameters of social interaction and symbolic capital. Daadi is a victim of domestic violence which stems from her husband Ouali's belief that "toutes les femmes sont des prostituées",[510] a belief couched in the language of honour and *nushuz*.[511]

---

[508] Ibid, p. 69.
[509] Ibid, p. 173–174.
[510] Ibid, p. 129.
[511] See my chapter on Feraoun for an investigation of the notion of *nushuz*.

Davda is manipulated and compelled to undergo the same symbolic magical procedures as Aazi, as she too is unable to conceive a child. Kamouma, finally, is an example par excellence of the poverty and suffering that exists as a result of women's lack of a decision in sex and childbirth, continually pregnant with ever diminishing means.

5.2 Lévi-Strauss, Matrimonial Strife, and Positive Change

In *Le Sommeil du juste*, Mammeri moves to evoke the systematic exclusion of women from agency in decisions over symbolic capital and indeed expresses an intensification of a *dissymétrie fondementale* through both the form and content of the narrative whilst linking manifestations of this pernicious division to social structures influenced by Algerian, Amazigh and Islamic cultural practices. Though the book is divided into four chapters which highlight the separations between protagonists, one can also conceive of it as divided into three movements, with the second and third chapters constituting the second movement. The initial movement centres largely upon the conflict between Arezki, the marker of modernity, and his father, the representative of tradition, in particular the tradition of atavistic rivalry between two "çofs": the descendants of Azouaou and the descendants of Hand. The second movement sees both Arezki and his brother Slimane enter the wider colonial domain. Slimane goes to find work away from their village of Ighzer, whilst Arezki is conscripted, fighting for the Allies in France and Italy, and on the Franco-German border. The third movement sees Arezki return to Ighzer, to the site of the colonised/traditional, and the conclusion of both the atavistic rivalry alluded to in the first movement and the colonial conflict alluded to in the second. What is noteworthy with regards to women and symbolic structures is the establishment and return of marriage as a marker of symbolic domination in the first and third movements respectively.

Claude Lévi-Strauss writes of primordial social interactions in *Les Structures élémentaires de la parenté*, stating that "l'échange, phénomène total, est d'abord un échange total, comprenant de la nourriture, des objets fabriqués, et cette catégorie de biens les plus précieux, les femmes".[512] He also writes:

> Les biens ne sont pas seulement des commodités économiques, mais des véhicules et des instruments de réalités d'un autre ordre: puissance, pouvoir, sympathie, statut, émotion ; et le jeu savant des échanges [...] consiste en un ensemble complexe de manœuvres, con-

---

[512] Claude Lévi-Strauss: *Les Structures élémentaires de la parenté*. Berlin: Walter de Gruyter 2002, p. 71.

scientes ou inconscientes, pour gagner des assurances et se prémunir contre des risques, sur le double terrain des alliances et des rivalités.[513]

From its beginning, Mammeri's text also establishes women as being conceived of as goods for exchange serving as instruments for the acquisition of status and the provision of protection from risk in rivalry. This is perceptible in particular in the matrimonial plans of Arezki's father, known throughout as "le père", emphasising his patriarchal status.[514] Furthermore, as the text progresses, it is emphasised that the identity, or at least certainly the character of the prospective brides, is irrelevant. What is relevant to le père is the resolution of the symbolic problems that he believes his family to face through his word. Thus when Sliman, le père's youngest son, has his cousin Toudert, le père's chief antagonist, ask the amin of the village for his daughter Yakout's hand in marriage without le père's knowledge, le père is dismayed that the phallic patriarchal order is interrupted, that his symbolic plan has been contravened: "Le monde pour le père commença de s'effriter ce soir-là. Jusque-là les valeurs et les choses avaient eu pour lui une rigidité de métal".[515] With Sliman's offer via Toudert having been rejected however, he resolves the problem and takes back control of his plan of social exchange by finding Sliman another bride, indeed, another Yakout: "Parce que, dit le père, je t'ai marié...autant que ce soit moi qui te le dise... Oui...je t'ai marié...à Yakout".[516] Upon reading Yakout here for the first time, the reader is placed in a state of confusion which is then resolved when le père specifies the Yakout that he means: "Oui, à Yakout, la fille du bon cousin Toudert [...]".[517] This confusion serves to highlight the Lévi-Straussian/Maussian idea that women when exchanged as goods are not necessarily seen as holding inherent worth but rather produce a kind of surplus value as instruments for "un autre ordre" of exchange, the Symbolic order.[518] Indeed, whereas in an egalitarian system "value" might be produced in the individual woman by that woman for that woman, here she is alienated from the labour of self-actualisation in her exchange by others. Her value becomes determined by the web of previous exchanges of women and by other symbolic exchanges setting the parameters of honour. It is later revealed that le père consciously sees the woman-good as a

---

513 Ibid, p. 63–64.
514 He plans initially to have Arezki marry the wife of his older brother Mohand after his anticipated death from tuberculosis, and to have the third brother, Sliman, also marry.
515 Mouloud Mammeri: *Le Sommeil du juste*. Paris: Plon 1955, p. 31–32.
516 Ibid, p. 82.
517 Ibid, p. 82.
518 Claude Lévi-Strauss, *Les Structures élémentaires de la parenté*, p. 63.

5.2 Lévi-Strauss, Matrimonial Strife, and Positive Change — 145

bargaining chip, a symbolic tool of and for domination, in his exchanges with his rival Toudert, now the amin:

> Il faut l'endormir, il faut que mon fils Sliman épouse sa fille Yakout, et elle est laide, Yakout, je le sais, et Toudert, son père, est un chien...mais avec tout cela, la main que tu ne peux mordre embrasse-la.[519]

Once we enter the second movement of the book and Arezki leaves to war in Europe, these intense socio-symbolic concerns are forgotten, Arezki's interactions with women largely follow the tropes of Western love stories. Upon returning to Ighzer, however, at the very beginning of the chapter entitled 'Tous au vert paradis', it is noted how Arezki "crut avoir débarqué dans une planète inconnue" as matrimonial plans take centre stage once more.[520] In spite or because of Mohand's impending death, it is decided whilst he is in earshot that "[l]es enfants de Mohand, cela voulait dire aussi sa femme, [...] selon la coutume, doi[vent] revenir à un des frères du défunt".[521] Moreover, soon after this discussion, Yakout, the Yakout that Sliman had originally intended to marry, is presented as a figure crushed by the manipulations that she has undergone at the behest of a masculinist system of exchange. She has been repudiated having been married outside of the village to another man, by Toudert:

> Yakout dit : bonsoir, puis sa voix se brisa et elle pressa le pas...
> [...]
> – Yakout n'est pas chez son mari ? demanda Arezki.
> – Elle est revenue au bout d'un mois, dit Sliman.
> – Répudiée ?
> – Oui.
> – Pourquoi?
> – Je ne sais pas, dit Sliman.[522]

Thus the clear geographical divisions highlighted by the narrative structuring in Mammeri's work serve to underline the prevalence of masculinist social structures, in particular marriage as exchange, in the domain of the interior/colonised. This is not to argue that the domain of the coloniser is represented as a paradise for women's agency. Indeed, Arezki's lover there, Elfriede, is the victim of being reduced, somewhat like Yakout, to the status of a signifier for exchange by the German occupancy (she is forced to change her name from Germaine to

---

[519] Mouloud Mammeri: *Le Sommeil du juste*, p. 84.
[520] Ibid, p. 210.
[521] Ibid, p. 210.
[522] Ibid, p. 211.

Elfriede as Germaine is seen as insufficiently German) and her maternal guardians ensure that she does not continue a love affair with Arezki for another factor ultimately linked to symbolic capital in a Western milieu: race. Nonetheless, the formal divisions in the book do serve to emphasise a particular structure of masculinist oppression connected to the specific culture of the Algerian milieu that Mammeri depicts.

However, somewhat in contrast with the early work of Mohammed Dib and its representations of feminine suffering, Mammeri's first two novels do evoke women's capacity to break out of the status of sempiternal victims, and allude to the possibility of other, less assymetrical, inter-gender relations. In the case of *La Colline oubliée*, the presence of an ideal space in the form of Taasast, "La Garde", "notre donjon [...] debout contre le ciel et dominant les maisons basses du village comme un berger au milieu du troupeau",[523] provides an alternative configuration of gender relations whose presence repeats throughout the text, in reflections and flashbacks, in contrast to the oppressive structures detailed above. Mildred Mortimer writes of this childhood hideaway that "[l]oin de la société dominée par les vieux, ces jeunes [Mokrane, Menach, Aazi, Sekoura and others] retrouvent une certaine liberté d'expression. Là-haut, ils créent une ambiance idéale de rêves, de chants et de danses. *Taasast* reste un leitmotiv, symbole du bonheur inaccessible et de l'unité à refaire".[524] Interestingly, Anne Roche argues that though Taasast constitutes the appearance of a new social structure in the traditional milieu, "dans la mesure où des filles y étaient admises et où le système d'alliances familiales de la tradition y était partiellement contesté [...] ce n'était nullement un germe de subversion, au contraire: le groupe tend à rejeter ou à déprécier ceux qui défendent les idées nouvelles, tel Meddour, le normalien "progressiste", personnage odieux et burlesque [...]".[525] It would be my view that Taasast indeed can't be claimed to allow for truly subversive adult acts or interventions within the world of the novel, especially when one considers that its period of activity is confined to childhood and that "la bande de Taasast" represents a socio-economically privileged group in Tasga. However, one may certainly argue that it does represent a seed of subversion to the extent that, through a form typical of the corpus of this monograph, it invokes future possibility whilst both guarding against wide-eyed optimism and refusing to determine the precise parameters of a more productive social relation for women.

---

[523] Mouloud Mammeri: *La Colline oubliée*, p. 27–28.
[524] Mildred Mortimer: Le Monde traditionnel: *La Colline oubliée*. In: *CELFAN [Special Issue on Mouloud Mammeri]* Vol. 3, No. 2 (1984), p. 24.
[525] Anne Roche: Tradition et subversion dans l'œuvre de Mouloud Mammeri. In: *Revue de L'Occident musulman et de la Méditerranée* Vol. 22, No. 1 (1976), p. 101.

The close of the novel perfectly encapsulates this tentative expression of hope continually confronted with structurally defined obstacles of which the principal marker is Mokrane's death, as Menach speaks to his grave:

> Adieu jusqu'au jour prochain où, à coup sûr, mon âme retrouvera la tienne et celle d'Aazi, d'Idir, de Kou pour refaire ensemble Taasast dans un monde où la souffrance ni l'obstacle ne seront plus.[526]

Furthermore, in terms of the representation of individual women, Taasast represents the site for the expression of "la fiancée du soir", signifier of vernal vitality and, to some extent, feminine subversion in her interruption of masculinist socio-symbolic structures, in particular marriage. In a flashback to the central protagonists' youth shared in the upstairs room of Mokrane's house, Aazi is depicted in this guise, stating the following in the course of a kind of impromptu performance of make-believe:

> Je suis la fiancée du soir, et un jour je descendrai à la rivière, quand la lune sera déjà depuis longtemps levée. Je montrerai le cours de l'eau vers la montagne, et partout où la rivière sera étale, je m'arrêterai, et j'appellerai mes compagnes, toutes les autres fiancées du soir. Je les appellerai comme cela.[527]

Her call for the formation of a sorority untied through matrimony to a human masculine agent is then reinforced as twice she rejects Idir's offers to enter into her imaginings, to defend her from the enemies of darkness she invents:

- Ne me touche pas, je suis la fiancée du soir; nul n'a le droit de me toucher.[528]
- Ne me touche pas, je suis la fiancée du soir et le soir est jaloux, il mange les fiancées qui ne lui sont pas fidèles, et en remontant la rivière, la nuit, on voit surgir de l'eau les fantômes en deuil de celles-là qu'il a déjà mangées.[529]

In the case of the latter, however, one is compelled to question the break from masculinist structures that the embodying of "la fiancée du soir" might entail, as one notes that her establishment of a new status for women is still couched in the language of a jealous "il" who would seek to punish an unfaithful lover. This continued dependence can be interpreted as the reproduction of a masculinist language as a function of ideology, as was commented on in my discussion

---

526 Mouloud Mammeri: *La Colline oubliée*, p. 220.
527 Ibid, p. 153.
528 Ibid, p. 155.
529 Ibid, p. 156.

of Dib's early novels. "La fiancée" serves to reproduce, through a language of rebellion which acts merely as a displacement coherent with the demand of the superego, the coordinates of the primordial narrative of women's subservience to the will of the male dominated society depicted. One might also argue that "la fiancée" represents a kind of mythical *femme fatale* figure, whose power, unlike that of Kateb's Nedjma, is contained and circumscribed within the realm of magic and whose agency is therefore mastered in its removal from the "standard" symbolic agora. It would be my argument that through the representation of "la fiancée", Mammeri's text alludes to the resilience of masculinist structures to individual interventions, and potentially invokes the necessity for communal action, communal change. The conclusion that Mammeri deploys a figure whose characteristics play into the hands of masculinist economies in order to comment upon these economies and to suggest a need for change is supported by his articulation of fallible masculine perspectives and the pernicious nature of ideology, as will be covered in the next section of this chapter.

Focusing on *Le Sommeil du juste*, one also notes numerous indications of a call for communal change, for alterations to fundamental symbolic structures to be activated in concert. Firstly, to return once more to marriage, there are many allusions to the necessity for the Lévi-Straussian state of affairs, where women are goods whose exchange is mastered with feverish intensity, to cease. Beyond Arezki's incredulity upon his return and the depictions of women's suffering, Sliman, upon his return to Ighzer, forms an articulation of a dawning realisation, tied to communal/nationalist concerns, that "ils étaient tous des Algériens",[530] and that therefore new future inter-gender configurations should be permitted:

> "[...]c'était à Sliman d'épouser Yakout, qu'il ne fallait pas refuser à Arezki le droit de se marier avec une chrétienne [...]"[531]

It is in the final section of the novel, however, that the reader is invited to view the clearest articulation of a mass prise de conscience implied, through a "pessimistic" tone typical for our corpus, by the arrival of colonial forces and the assembly of a number of figures, including Arezki, in prison on charges of insurgency. What is interesting in particular for the representation of women here is that within this depiction of a microcosm of national struggle, one notes the development of the figure of the proto-maquisarde represented, despite her repudiation and humiliation, by Yakout. Whilst those whom Toudert, the figure of the

---

530 Mouloud Mammeri: *Le Sommeil du juste*, p. 109.
531 Ibid, p. 109.

traitor, has identified as harbouring anti-French sentiments are being rounded up by colonial forces, she is the only figure who attempts repeatedly to intervene, having acquired information on the raid by means invisible to the reader and Arezki. She repeatedly tells Sliman not to go to the meeting where the round-up is taking place, finally stating to him that "toi aussi, si tu ne te caches pas, tu seras ramassé. L'amin vous a tous vendus".[532]

What is also interesting about Yakout's status as an anti colonial messenger is the manner in which it is digested with great difficulty by Arezki, the protagonist whom the reader follows with the greatest proximity in the narrative. Initially he dismisses her warnings and even when confronted with the reality of the situation we read the following:

> Un voile couvrit les yeux ouverts d'Arezki : sur quoi se fondait Yakout pour dire que c'était Toudert qui avait vendu les frères ?[533]

This potentially pernicious determination of a woman and her actions/capacities through a masculine perspective represents an example of an effective trend in Mammeri's work which seeks to perform representation within a formal and content-based acknowledgment of an inability to represent without partially disfiguring the object of representation, and without acting as an illegitimate *Vertretung* representative. Following Kateb, Dib, and Feraoun, as the next section will elucidate, Mammeri produces images of women that highlight their status as constructed images, whilst performing an implicit commentary on the disfiguring veil-like lenses of ideology that frame them.

5.3 Masculine Blindness, Perspective and Scopophilia

Charles Bonn writes of the early texts of Feraoun and Mammeri the following:

> Anthropologiques, ces premiers textes le sont peut-être, mais au sens de Claude Lévi-Strauss dans *Tristes Tropiques* : décrire une société traditionnelle pour la faire connaître, et vivre dans cette reconnaissance, n'est possible qu'en perdant l'objet de cette description au moment même ou on le met à jour, et dans cet acte même.[534]

---

532 Ibid, p. 220.
533 Ibid, p. 220–221.
534 Charles Bonn: Mes inattendus dans ma découverte de la littérature algérienne. In: Elena Chiti/Touriya Fili-Tullon/Blandine Valford (eds.): *Écrire l'inattendu : Les 'printemps arabes' entre fictions et histoire*. Paris: L'Harmattan 2015, p. 25–26.

Throughout *La Colline oubliée* and *Le Sommeil du juste*, the representation of women is contingent on masculine perspectives that are partially blind to their object. These perspectives are established as particular to their socio-symbolic contexts and as such they somewhat stymy reader-narrator identification, they encourage the reader to view their representations of women as partial depictions stemming from a particular socio-psychic makeup. Furthermore, in *La Colline oubliée*, like in Feraoun's *Le Fils du pauvre*, the emphasis on representations as representations, as artificial renderings necessarily lacking in the analytical tools requisite for insight, without true knowledge or mandate, is heightened by the narrative devices of an interruption of the 1st person narrator and a revelation that what we have been reading is the reconstruction of a found document, Mokrane's journal. The fact that this revelation comes as a surprise is heightened by numerous moments of impossible omniscience contained within Mokrane's journal (detailed intimate confrontations, recall of precise conversations etc.) and the reader's thinking through of this surprise generated by the revelation causes representation to be further undermined. Moreover, contained within this revelation is a specific comic allusion to an incapacity of the journal's author's work to represent:

> Ici s'arrête le carnet de Mokrane. Les trente dernières pages de gros papier lisse sont restées blanches. *Seulement au revers de la couverture est dessinée au crayon un profil maladif de femme; en dessous un mot en lettres berbères que peu savent déchiffrer, sans doute le nom de la femme.*[535]

The name of womanhood remains indecipherable to the secondary author, the master of the text, as we move from a fallible narrator in what Anne Roche terms a "brutal passage à un récitatif impersonnel".[536] *Le Sommeil du juste* is also riddled with markers of factitiousness, from letters sent to and by Arezki, including one sent to his former master at the École Normale at the conclusion of the novel which recapitulates much of what the master has seen and heard for himself at the trial, emphasising its fabricated role as a part of narrative exposition.

Interesting also in the organisation of *La Colline oubliée* is the dramatis personae included at the beginning of the book whose form nods to a Western textual practice whilst simultaneously beginning to comment on the partial visibility of women when viewed through a linguistic literary code and, by extension, a socio-symbolic order. For, with the exceptions of Sekoura, the faithful and im-

---

[535] Mouloud Mammeri: *La Colline oubliée*, p. 158 (emphasis added).
[536] Anne Roche: Tradition et subversion dans l'œuvre de Mouloud Mammeri, p. 102.

5.3 Masculine Blindness, Perspective and Scopophilia — 151

poverished figure of motherhood, and Na Ghné, the chief magical woman protagonist, none of the important women of the book are given their own place on the list. Instead they are referred to through the highlighting of masculine protagonists e.g. MOKRANE, mari de Tamazouzt; AKLI, mari de Davda; OUALI, mari de Daadi,[537] just as the women of the text are evoked through a masculine perspective (that of Mokrane, that of the secondary narrator, and that of the writer) and come to be understood by its masculine protagonists through ideological parameters established in part through patriarchal structures which serve to marginalise women and occasion disaster.

Once we then turn to the content of the narrative related through Mokrane's perspective, one notes a sustained emphasis on this invisibility of the signifiers of women, on an inability or lack of will to decipher their letters, literal and psychic, which again encourages the reader to question the conditions for representation, literary and social, and their consequences.[538] When Aazi tries to inform Mokrane of the difficulties that she is facing at home, writing him a letter whilst he is away on military service, Mokrane's lack of a communicative bond with his wife, his inability to read her, ensures that he doesn't intervene:

> À l'écriture régulière et très appliquée je reconnus qu'Aazi avait elle-même écrit la lettre. Le sens en était très obscur et ce ne fut que longtemps après l'avoir lue et par morceaux que je finis par comprendre ce que ma femme voulait dire [...][539]

This same lack of a communicative bond, coupled with a blindness inaugurated by an interpellation into masculinist ideology in which men hold the answers and women are outside of reason, ensures that when he receives the deceptive message from his father that Aazi has happily agreed to her repudiation, he accepts his fallacious version of events. It is only once Mokrane reads and rereads Aazi's words in a second letter which, she admits, she was reluctant to write, no longer holding the meagre symbolic authority accorded by marriage, that he begins to acknowledge his blindness to the woman who had been his wife:

> Je crains soudain d'avoir commis une faute qui, dans la situation où je suis, risque d'être irréparable, car *plus je relis* les mots et plus resurgit devant moi une image d'Aazi que j'ai depuis longtemps oubliée, l'image de "la fiancée du soir".[540]

---

[537] Mouloud Mammeri: *La Colline oubliée*, p. 9–10.
[538] Indeed, in this emphasis on invisibility there are resonances of Lacan's analysis of Poe's *La lettre volée* in the *Écrits*.
[539] Ibid, p. 63.
[540] Ibid, p. 153 (emphasis added).

And, the reader rereads this ideal of rereading in a very similar paragraph a few pages thence:

> Longtemps, nous appelâmes Aazi "la fiancée du soir". Depuis, les scènes de ma mère, les silences de mon père, les discours du cheikh m'ont imposé d'elle une autre image, *mais en relisant cette lettre*, les fantômes d'antan en moi resurgissent et j'ai envie, comme jadis Idir, de crier:
> – Fiancée du soir, où es-tu ?[541]

The re-reading, the paying of close attention to Aazi's letter, compels Mokrane to break with the pernicious socio-symbolic constraints that bind him, as he embodies, like a number of Feraoun's feminine protagonists, the activation of a notion of radically undetermined subjectivity, of Thanatos, death drive, a factor to which the final section of this chapter shall return. Furthermore, if we compare Mokrane's receipt of a letter from Aazi to Arezki's receipt of a letter from Elfriede, at the conclusion of *Le Sommeil du juste*, the importance that Mammeri's novels assign to an appreciation of feminine subjectivity and its expression is again made clear. Having thought that Elfriede had decided to stand him up upon his departure from Paris, he receives a letter in prison from her which explains that she had been deceived by her matriarchal guardians as to a change in his time of departure. Arezki, however, decides not to read the letter, instead giving it bitterly to his guard to read, which the guard then does, whilst sat on the toilet.

Though Elfriede is clearly not a representative of Algerian women, Arezki can be understood, like Mokrane, to be representative of a certain generation of Algerian men, struggling with an interstitial social status and a developing epistemological bearing. *La Colline oubliée* and *Le Sommeil du juste*, through these protagonists' failures to read and represent women, allude therefore to the necessity for a particular amelioration in gender relations which would involve women's self-expression and inclusion in the definition of the evolving socio-symbolic parameters of Algerian culture.

However, what these novels also produce is an invitation to all readers to consider their own blindness, their own reliance on the frameworks, ideological and representational, through which they perceive feminine others. This is the case with Arezki's being stood up by Elfriede, for example, as we are unaware as he is of her having being deceived, but is best rendered in *La Colline oubliée* through the characterisation of Davda, the figure who, through Mokrane's journal, is presented for the most part as another *femme fatale* figure who torments Menach with her beauty. Towards the close of the novel, having left Mokrane's

---

[541] Ibid, p. 156–157 (emphasis added).

journal behind, the reader is on occasion invited to comprehend another perspective of Davda, as s/he reads of her sincere love for him. The manner in which reader and central protagonists alike have hitherto conceived of her is overturned:

> "J'ai visité Sidi-Yousef et Chivou, j'ai imploré d'eux ta guérison. Moi qui n'attends rien des saints, j'ai envoyé des offrandes à tous ceux que je connaissais. J'ai pleuré sur tes souffrances, moi qui ignorais les larmes. J'aurais mendié pour toi."[542]

Nevertheless, though here we share in Menach's discovery of the fallibility of perspectives generated throughout the narrative, Mammeri's texts mostly work to interrupt and play with identification with masculine characters and this allows for an inferred commentary on the male gaze.

Intriguingly, in producing such a commentary, they interact with the voyeuristic and fetishistic mechanisms upon which Laura Mulvey comments in her seminal essay 'Visual Pleasure and Narrative Cinema'. In the essay Mulvey describes the two types of cinematic viewer mechanism thus: "The first, scopophilic, arises from pleasure in using another person as an object of sexual stimulation through sight. The second, developed through narcissism and the constitution of the ego, comes from identification with the image seen".[543] She argues that in general, and particularly in the case of cinema, "woman as representation signifies castration, inducing voyeuristic or fetishistic mechanisms to circumvent her threat" but that "[n]one of these interacting layers is intrinsic to film".[544] To recapitulate, Mulvey contends that the voyeuristic mechanism is instituted through identification with a masculine figure of mastery on screen whereas fetishism satisfies the scopophilic drive by reducing the viewed subject, the woman, to inanimate/desubjectivised concepts or, as is more often the case, body parts. Moreover, castration anxiety and the mechanisms for its circumvention can be applied to fictitious protagonists themselves, interacting with representations within their notional worlds, producing a *mise en abyme* effect.

Concordantly, we can detect in Mammeri's work a fear of women imputed to masculine protagonists, where women's visibility exceeds mastery. As mentioned before, Mokrane comments in his narration that "il y avait trop de jeunes filles, il y en avait tant que cela devenait inquiétant. *On n'en avait jamais tant vu* à Tasga, car les jeunes gens ne se mariaient plus".[545] Women are anxiogenic here because

---

[542] Ibid, p. 204.
[543] Laura Mulvey: Visual Pleasure and Narrative Cinema. In: *Screen* Vol. 6, Issue 3 (1975), p. 10.
[544] Ibid, p. 17.
[545] Mouloud Mammeri: *La Colline oubliée*, p. 33 (emphasis added).

their number exceeds Mokrane's field of vision and the potential for them to look back, to turn the scopophilic tables, is increased. And indeed, when we consider castration, as Lacan does, as the subjective anxiety brought about by entry into a Symbolic order which one does not own or control and which one therefore cannot master, one begins to understand the blindness previously commented on and the concomitant reliance on paternal guidance as a part of identification. Mokrane identifies with his father's word and not Aazi's word, quelling the castration anxiety that the structure of the socio-symbolic is out of control (beyond control and inherently unstable, undermined by the shifting of signifiers, by the lack at its heart), just as the viewer of a *film noir* identifies with the private investigator who can deal with the beautiful damsel in distress or *femme fatale* for him, permitting an outsourcing that reduces the necessity to engage with the feminine object. Furthermore, what is also particularly interesting in Mammeri's work is how images of women's beauty are generated which represent the scopophilic tendencies of masculine protagonists with whom the reader can only form an uneasy identification. And, where identification *is* partially staged, the notional scopophilia of the reader is ironically undermined by a lack of representation.

Starting with *La Colline oubliée*, one notes a good example of a scopophilic drive and its tendency towards reducing, neutralising and mastering women's self-expression, their potential disruption of a masculinist socio-symbolic structure, as Mokrane's narration focuses on Aazi's beauty at a time where the women of Tasga are lamenting the departure of men to war:

> Aazi n'avait pas eu le temps de s'habiller : elle était venue dans sa robe toute simple à pois blancs, attachée à la ceinture; ses cheveux étaient défaits et malgré la tristesse que répandaient les lamentations des femmes qui s'éloignaient peu à peu, je ne pus m'empêcher d'admirer combien elle était belle ainsi.[546]

Mokrane enjoys Aazi's beauty here and elsewhere, ignoring the voices of women, while Menach attempts to devour Davda with his gaze throughout the narrative but is haunted when he is unable to master and enjoy her:

> Les traits de Davda revenaient ce soir devant ses yeux avec une netteté particulière et une obsédante insistance. La nouvelle méthode [of ridding himself of anxiety] était-elle inefficace ?[547]

---

546 Ibid, p. 41–42.
547 Ibid, p. 50.

5.3 Masculine Blindness, Perspective and Scopophilia — 155

The blindness towards women of these two male protagonists has already been commented on and it is principally this fallibility that undermines the procedure of scopic identification that Mulvey details as follows:

> As the spectator identifies with the main male protagonist, he projects his look on to that of his like, his screen surrogate, so that the power of the male protagonist as he controls events coincides with the active power of the erotic look, both giving a satisfying sense of omnipotence.[548]

Moreover, Arezki and the unscrupulous Tayeb, in *Le Sommeil du juste* and *L'Opium et le bâton* respectively, are also implicated in scopophilic practices from which a notional reader with a sexual proclivity for the signifiers of the feminine is alienated, because of their lack of mastery, their failure to support the reader's enjoyment of the feminine image through their characterisation: they are neither powerful, commanding, nor in control. Nonetheless, it must be ceded that the reader is on occasion invited to interact with the enjoyment of the feminine image but that, perhaps, this is in order that s/he might consider both his/her own enjoyment and the enjoyment of the protagonists, just as s/he was invited to consider the blindness inherent to perspectives of Davda's character. *La Colline oubliée* allows us to make this argument best by reference to two scenes which echo each other whilst also generating meaning through their differences.

Starting with the latter of the two, we should consider the scene in which Raveh and Ouali camp out in order to spy on Kelsouma. Raveh wishes to have Ouali covet her in order that he will consent to murdering her husband whom Raveh has been tasked with eliminating over an honour feud. The reader closely follows Ouali's gaze and appreciates with him the beauty of the image of Kelsouma through Mammeri's words:

> Dès que Raveh lui montra devant une vieille toute ridée cette grande femme droite, comme hiératique, légèrement vêtue d'une robe de couleur, dès qu'il eut vu le bras blanc au galbe impeccable qui ne semblait être que l'anse prolongée de la cruche, quand il eut entendu le son de la voix chaude, il ne dit plus rien. Il fixait des yeux cette apparition irréelle d'un matin frais de printemps comme si c'était une vision qu'il risquait de voir s'évanouir.[549]

Here then, though we as readers are aware of the framing of the scene, to wit the plan to steal Kelsouma as though she were property, we remain concealed voyeurs enjoying the beauty of "le bras blanc au galbe impeccable". Even here, though, one begins to note the frustration that Mammeri embeds in his represen-

---

[548] Laura Mulvey: Visual Pleasure and Narrative Cinema, p. 12.
[549] Mouloud Mammeri: *La Colline oubliée*, p. 131.

tations of the gaze, as it is "le son de la voix chaude" that truly captivates Ouali, a sound that we cannot hear or appreciate. When we then turn to this scene's twin, in which Menach and Mokrane spy together on the Kabyle women's tradition of the Ourar dance, we note firstly how the text prepares us for an intimate collusion with the two men, in particular with Mokrane:

> [...] il me mena dans une espèce de niche, où nous nous étendîmes tous les deux à plat ventre. Un peu plus bas, dans un cercle de terre battue que les ronces et les ormes entouraient de tout part, les femmes préparaient l'ourar.[550]

What then follows, however, is a passage that continuously and playfully undercuts both identification with the gazing male protagonists and the possibility of enjoying the fetishized feminine image. To begin, Menach and Mokrane are immediately divided in their gazes, to the point that they seemingly occupy different planes of consciousness, unsettling their complicity whilst inviting the reader into an increased intimacy with Mokrane:

> Davda effectivement se levait, mais Menach, qui fixait un regard ardent sur elle, ne pouvait pas savoir à quel point j'étais loin de l'ourar et de lui.[551]

We then read that "[d]evant mes yeux ouvertes toutes les images se brouillaient. Je suis incapable aujourd'hui de dire ce qui s'est passé par la suite, mais après tant de mois je vois encore très exactement chacun des gestes qu'Aazi fit".[552] Here then the text teases the reader, initially implying that no recreation of arousing details will take place before appearing to foreshadow a depiction of the exact bodily gestures of Aazi. What follows is an amusing, skilful, and beautiful act of representation which appears to provide the details that had been promised but in fact can be argued to work to maintain them as underdeveloped or as notionally exclusive to Mokrane's mind, cutting the reader off from enjoyment of the gaze and mastery of the feminine object, through Mokrane:

> J'entends son clair rire, je vois **ses doigts battre le tambourin et ses bracelets d'or s'entrechoquer au rythme de la danse, je la vois tournoyer et faire bouffer sa robe blanche**, *je peux répéter tous ses mots, redire tous les ordres.* L'ourar n'était plus pour moi qu'un bruit confus *mais tout ce que touchait à elle se gravait en moi avec une lancinante*

---

550 Ibid, p. 84.
551 Ibid, p. 84.
552 Ibid, p. 84.

précision. Tout tourner, tout tintait autour de moi. Pour échapper à l'envoûtement je me levai brusquement.[553]

First, I mark in bold those parts of the description that are underdeveloped, that are details with little detail. There is no description of the fingers, of the bracelets, of her or her dress beyond the two markers of colour. Mokrane "la voi[t]" but our vision of her is limited. Second, I mark in italics the parts of the description that are not description at all, but rather indications to the reader that the narrator could, if he so chose, recreate the details of the scene, every movement, every tactile collision. Then finally, before the reader has gained any real sense of the spectacle to which s/he has been seductively and teasingly led, one notes that Mokrane gets up "brusquement" to avoid a bewitchment of which the reader has barely been a part.

This scene, especially when it is considered alongside its twin, encourages the reader to consider his/her participation in the male gaze and the unequal representational gender relation established where it shapes the fictional narrative and its worldly referent. Seeing is related to blindness in Mammeri's work where viewpoints establish women as the object, the viewed, and work, in so doing, against a feminine self-representation that might broaden masculine perspectives, allowing masculine figures like Slimane and Arezki in *Le Sommeil du juste*, for example, to understand Yakout's suffering or Elfriede's message. Nevertheless, it remains to be discussed whether the problematisation of the reader's viewing the world through masculine eyes is enough to counteract the potentially unhelpful staging of women's narrative marginalisation. In all three novels, it is a masculine perspective that is predominantly followed and despite repeated evocations of its blindness to women, one should still ask whether the reader is also left blind to Algerian women's lives and experiences.

5.4 Supplements, Activity, and Pessimistic Uncertainty

It is certainly possible to argue that when one compares *La Colline oubliée* with *Le Sommeil du juste* and *L'Opium and le bâton* there is simply less textual space dedicated to the representation of Algerian women in the two later novels. Though *Le Sommeil du juste* does illuminate masculine blindness and though *L'Opium and le bâton* invites criticism of the patriarchal/masculinist social structures and misogynist characters depicted, their evocation of women themselves

---

[553] Ibid, p. 84.

is more limited, in part precisely as a result of their attempts to articulate problematic masculinist epistemes. Mildred Mortimer writes that "[d]ans ses premiers romans, Mammeri expose l'affaiblissement de la société patriarcale. Soumise à des pressions multiples, cette société traditionnelle perd son équilibre. *L'Opium et le bâton* décrit sa chute".[554] In the midst of the dismantling in *La Colline oubliée*, there are Algerian women protagonists whose centrality to the narrative enhances the reader's engagement with a critique of masculinist socio-symbolic structures and the male gaze. In *Le Sommeil du juste* and *L'Opium et le bâton*, by contrast, Algerian women mostly remain peripheral to the narrative and the reader shares a less intimate connection with them. Indeed, in these works one can cite a more overt focus, somewhat peculiar to the works of Mammeri though present in those of Feraoun, on "foreign" women.[555] It is consequently certainly the case that the works tread a fine line between a literary treatment of Algerian women that avoids determination and the problems associated with speaking *for*, and a construction of narratives that leave women marginalised, reducing the pathos or empathy they might generate. One can, however, also explain a diminishment in the number of Algerian women depicted by reference to the journalistic or historical impulse that I alluded to in the introduction to this chapter. That is to say that in *Le Sommeil du juste* and *L'Opium et le bâton*, the events of the Second World War and the Algerian War, which have historically been treated within a masculine focus, themselves invite another treatment from the perspective of men. This is certainly not to deny women's involvement in either but rather to suggest that in a narrative that focuses on a departure to war it is perhaps unsurprising that men dominate the narrative. Furthermore, it would be my argument that Mammeri's own conception of *L'Opium et le bâton* as "une espèce de symphonie", as opposed to the more intimate form of his first two novels, reads as a kind of "tableauisation" of *all* its characters and settings, with the exception of its central protagonist, Bachir. This is also almost certainly part of the reason why Miriam Cooke rejects the novel as a text in which "[c]haracters are reduced to stereotypes who act out highly determined roles".[556]

To return to Mildred Mortimer's comments, however, she does remind us that "*L'Opium et le bâton* présente toute une gamme de personnages féminins : femmes jeunes, vieilles, traditionnelles, émancipées".[557] Indeed, though *L'Opium*

---

554 Mildred Mortimer: *Mouloud Mammeri, écrivain algérien*, p. 35.
555 I place the term foreign between scare quotes here because it is important to note that the central character Itto, in *L'Opium et le bâton* is of a different kind of foreignness to Claude, for example and this difference needs to be addressed.
556 Miriam Cooke: *Women and the War Story*, p. 162.
557 Mildred Mortimer: *Mouloud Mammeri, écrivain algérien*, p. 40.

5.4 Supplements, Activity, and Pessimistic Uncertainty — 159

et le bâton appears to focus largely on the experiences of its central character, Bachir, and though important women characters like Itto can appear as *jalons* in the course of his movement through the tableau of the Algerian war, the text does also make room for important representations of Algerian women and their actions that relate to the historical context. Moreover, one can argue that an articulation of women's historical agency develops and is enriched as the text progresses, through the evocation of these figures.

Following the beginning of the text's depiction of the unstable relationship shared between the central protagonist Bachir and his French partner Claude, the next women we meet are Smina and Farroudja, Bachir's mother and sister, who are depicted as desperately dedicated to Ali, Smina's son, who has recently joined the maquis. Smina reveals to Farroudja the suffering she has endured in looking after her children before the two are permitted to make brief contact with Ali, causing them to weep at the pain of losing him again. Their supplementary dedication to the maquis is initially derided: "Bientôt Farroudja les entendit rire au loin".[558] A similar level of dedication, however, is also ascribed to another pair of women, Titi and Tasadit, the mother and wife of Omar, another young maquis member. This dedication is not derided but rather is framed as part of the insurgency, as Tasadit, for example, dresses in rags to pass unperturbed by colonial forces and delivers food to the rebels. And, as the text progresses, we read an increasing number of hints at Farroudja's revolutionary participation: "À la sortie de Tala, Farroudja qu'ils avaient envoyée en éclaireur n'était pas revenue [...]".[559] Next, when Bachir leaves to Morocco, having been injured in fighting against the French, the reader encounters Itto, his Amazigh lover. It should be said firstly of Itto that Mammeri's text appears to allude through her depiction to an expanded sense of national belonging relating to a pan-Amazigh sentiment. Hence we read from Bachir during his stay with Itto and her family that "[i]l est vrai que nous sommes frères et que nous parlons la même langue".[560] And, it is also through her depiction that Mammeri appears to expand his articulation of women's oppression as a function of socio-symbolic structures, in particular marriage, demonstrating the capacity for women's symbolic subjugation to cross borders whilst evoking a feminine rebellion in Itto's characterisation. Though she eventually resigns herself to the fate of arranged marriage, her liberated enjoyment of the time left to her before her wedding and her apparent awareness of her symbolic predicament, echoing Ouiza's phallic mockery in Fer-

---
558 Mouloud Mammeri: *L'Opium et le bâton*. Paris: Éditions La Découverte 1992 [1965], p. 49.
559 Ibid, p. 106.
560 Ibid, p. 205.

aoun's *Les Chemins qui montent*, lends a greater degree of potential, of inferred agency, to the character.[561] For the remainder of the text we then witness women's revolutionary involvement in both an urban context, in the passage where Bachir witnesses a mass demonstration in Algiers, and in the rural context of the village of Tala, where Farroudja and Tasadit are involved in hiding weaponry, in the passage of information, and in resistance to colonial aggression. Farroudja is even tortured by French troops.

Now, alongside this development of a somewhat peripheral feminine agency and in particular as the narrative draws to a close, one can cite four agents that are framed as masculine and that are directly linked or indirectly associated with deleterious outcomes: the colonial forces, the forces of tradition in the village of Tala and in the streets of Algiers, postcolonial politics and Tayeb, the traitor. Furthermore, these four agents of destruction are represented, in varying degrees, as oppositional to the feminine figures referred to above. Thus, for example, Farroudja and Tasadit's colonial resistance is triangulated as a gendered conflict through the details of their solidarity, through the nature of Tayeb's actions and through the explanation behind his violence and the betrayal of his community. Farroudja and Tasadit come together to resist the pressure exerted by Tayeb as he targets their motherhood directly, taking Tasadit's baby from her in order to compel her to inform on her revolutionary brothers. His abuse of his wife further indicates a misogynist episteme. And, concordantly, Tayeb's becoming a traitor is posited as a consequence of his exclusion from honour in a masculinist socio-symbolic order. So, for example, after it has been established that Tayeb had always been the butt of the joke in the village, lacking in symbolic capital, he riles against his compatriots as he forces them to cut down their olive groves at the behest of the colonial forces:

> – Vous êtes fiers de vos oliviers. Vous me méprisiez parce que je n'en avais pas. [...] Maintenant c'est vous qui allez crever de faim. Chacun son tour ! Ce sont vos enfants qui vont apprendre à se coucher le soir sans manger.[562]

Furthermore, when we consider the figures of tradition in the village who oppose the colonial presence, the apocalyptic tone employed to describe the possibility of the French assault that closes the narrative implicitly acts as a critique of an

---

[561] When Bachir argues that Itto shouldn't leave her family home with him after her marriage has been agreed, she states, for example "Eh bien ! sois tranquille, soyez tous tranquilles ! Je ne veux pas l'abandonner; dans un mois, non ! dans vingt-neuf jours je lui reviendrai. Il en aura pour toute sa vie...ou pour toute la mienne. Et qu'est-ce que vingt-neuf jours au prix de toute la vie ?" Ibid, p. 187.
[562] Ibid, p. 213.

understanding of colonial oppression filtered through the lens of masculinist tradition. For this tone that refuses compromise, refuses not just the compromise of partial surrender proposed by the revolutionary agent Belaïd, but also the compromise of traditional structures, of "the way things have always been" and this is perhaps best exemplified in the Amin's final discourse before the village:

> Peut-être est-il temps maintenant que le soir vienne et que nous vivions dans la paix. Mais si le soir pour nous n'est pas celui du repos mais de la mort, si l'aile de votre protection ne peut plus s'étendre sur ces hommes assemblés où s'assemblaient leurs pères, sur les femmes assises dans leur angoisse derrière ce mur, s'il est écrit enfin que nous devons finir, faites que ce soit dans la dignité que nous mourions et qu'il ne soit pas dit plus tard que c'est dans l'opprobre que nous avons péri.[563]

The Amin almost expresses a degree of contented resignation to the destruction of the village, with the proviso that things pass in a "dignified", honourable fashion. Meanwhile, from behind their wall, feminine voices express dissent:

> – Et bien quoi ? C'est là l'assemblée de Tala ? Les vieillards vont mourir et aller au pardon de Dieu, mais les enfants sont là, et ce sont les enfants qui deviennent des hommes, et dans les reins de nos jeunes femmes, il y a d'autres enfants encore.[564]

Echoing their rural cousins, the masculine forces of tradition in the city, here religious tradition in the service of nationalism, also express this will for death, a problematic sacrifice that does not appear productive of a new progressive nation. In the mass demonstration that Bachir witnesses, women act to protect the fallen while the men repeatedly cry out: "Qui veut mourir dans la voie de Dieu?".[565] And, closely connected to the foreshadowing achieved through this articulation of a problematic ideological justification for violence, is the depiction of postcolonial politics in Morocco and the allusion to Algeria's possible political fate rendered in the conversation between Itto and Bachir, in response to the trial and condemnation of the Amazigh revolutionary, Addi-Ou-Bihi:

> – Après l'opium du journal, le bâton du juge. Ce sera comme ça dans ton pays ?
> – Comment veux-tu que je le sache ? Notre pays n'est pas encore à nous.[566]

This embedding of problematic masculine figures in the narrative development of a novel published in 1965 and describing the birth of an Algerian nation, in-

---

563 Ibid, p. 275.
564 Ibid, p. 277.
565 Ibid, p. 259.
566 Ibid, p. 198.

cluding the participation of women, begins to colour its representation with a particular productive "pessimism" that can be seen to pervade the writings of all the authors of our corpus, a "pessimism" linked to the resilience of masculinist ideologies and their attendant epistemes/psychic frameworks. "Pessimism", as has been outlined in other chapters, perhaps most notably in the chapter on Kateb, can be conceived of as productive in that it forms a constant melancholic imperative to focus on progressive change in rights and freedoms, insuring against the complacency embodied, for example, by right-wing postfeminists today who would claim that in Western neo-liberal capitalist states gender equality already exists and no longer needs to be fought for.

And, "pessimism" is given narrative prominence and greater resonance for conceptualising postcolonial Algeria through its conditioning of Mammeri's novel's conclusions. In focusing firstly on *L'Opium et le bâton*, one can form a parallel between its ending and the conclusion of Dib's *Qui se souvient de la mer*, in which a return to a phallic epistemological approach is staged as the narrator is separated from his wife, inspecting and detailing the structures of the underground alone. In the conclusion of *L'Opium et le bâton* there is a similar allusion to the potential persistence of an ideological influence that excludes feminine difference, as one notes, in the words of Anne Roche, the "survivance de l'attitude des hommes de *La Colline oubliée* devant la rivière tueuse".[567] The attitude that she refers to relates to the tradition described in Mammeri's first novel of crossing the dangerous river that separates the community from its olive trees. Religious/patriarchal authority forbids the changing of "le jeu et les enjeux [...] les conditions de l'accès à la reproduction sociale", to once more cite Bourdieu.[568] Consequently, tradition cannot be altered, its socio-symbolic parameters are marshaled and forbidden to expand; a bridge will not be built. At the end of *L'Opium et le bâton* also, "[l]a tradition gagne: et Tala sera détruit sous les bombes des Français, tandis que Tasadit, étreignant le cadavre d'Ali, lamente la fin de son univers".[569] Thus, just as Algeria is in transition away from colonial rule, patriarchal authority holds an undead control over the village. The village dies in part through patriarchal stubbornness and Tasadit dies with it. Here also we can perhaps again raise concerns about women's supplementarity to the narrative in that Tasadit's passing, as the epitome of Algerian women's agency, is exceeded by Bachir's narration, which concludes the novel. It is masculine agents in all three novels, indeed, who accompany the reader as they conclude,

---

567 Anne Roche: Tradition et subversion dans l'œuvre de Mouloud Mammeri, p. 106.
568 Pierre Bourdieu: *La Domination masculine*, p. 68.
569 Anne Roche: Tradition et subversion dans l'œuvre de Mouloud Mammeri, p. 106.

leaving the reader to problematically consider women characters as barometers for change in masculine experience. However, contained within this closing entry is a final abortive attempt to make contact with a feminine other, Itto, that evokes a humility in representation that, I would argue, tips the scales in favour of a conception of Mammeri's work as a self-reflexive, tentative project that is wary of speaking *for* women whilst it treats Algeria's future "pessimistically". Bachir concludes a letter to Itto by writing, in a somewhat cryptic evocation of the manner in which the Algerian subject should face transitional and postcolonial politics and socio-symbolic structures, the following:

> "Je n'ai pas trouvé le remède, mais je suis monté sur la tour et j'appelle. J'appelle pour que vienne le guérisseur. Je sais déjà le distinguer du sorcier, et, si je ne guéris pas du bon remède, du moins suis-je sûr que je ne mourrai pas du mauvais".[570]

Here Bachir suggests, whilst thinking of Itto as his audience, that though he doesn't have the answers, he shouldn't cease to call for others to seek to supply them, evoking metatextually the nature of Mammeri's literature and its relationship with the reader. The attempt to make contact is abortive in that Bachir decides to destroy the letter, not wanting Itto to receive its information through the medium of "l'écrivain publique":

> Je n'aime pas les profanations gratuites. C'est en berbère que j'eusse aimé lui dire cela et d'autres choses encore. Mais, Itto, tu ne sais pas lire. J'ai déchiré la lettre. Et c'est mieux ainsi.[571]

Moreover, the disruptive imposition of a medium – language, in its essence – is reaffirmed in the final line where Bachir states with regards to the newspapers that he reads that "[l]a réalité dépassait les phrases de si loin...".[572]

Thus Mammeri's productively "pessimistic" conclusion incorporates a will to engage with a feminine Other and an acceptance of the limits both of language and of the authorship of a singular masculine subject in the representation of future difficulties, so often linked to gendered socio-symbolic structures, that an Algerian nation would seek to address and overcome. *Le Sommeil du juste*'s conclusion also rests on a conception of the impotence of letters, there the exchange of actual missives, in still bleaker terms. Elfriede's letter has no effect because Arezki doesn't read it. Arezki's journal has a limited effect on the judge who reads it though it does not effect his will to impose a harsh sentence.

---

[570] Mouloud Mammeri: *L'Opium et le bâton*, p. 313.
[571] Ibid, p. 313.
[572] Ibid, p. 313.

And finally, the last section of the book itself, which is framed as a letter to Arezki's former master at the École Normale, is organised as a failure, destined never to reach its destination as Arezki simply finishes it with the two inauspicious sentences: "Le convoi part dans un instant" and "C'est tout, je crois".[573] Nevertheless, the reader is encouraged to organise these letters, to form answers through them and to understand the potential for postcolonial and inter-gender relations to generate and perpetuate unproductive misreadings. To refer one final time to the work of Anne Roche, she conceives of the prison at the end of *Le Sommeil du juste* as a site "qui recrée la solidarité familiale devant le châtiment, comme [...] un retour à l'espace maternel" which acts as a "chant à deux portées", borrowing from the terminology of Marie Bonaparte.[574] Can we not also conceive of Arezki's letter to his master/no-one as a maternal assembly bearing two orders of possibility, just as the imaginary order of psychoanalysis can also be the bearer of semiotic disruption? And is this not the very nature of productive "pessimism": to evoke the worst of future possibilities (unproductivity/condemnation/imprisonment/death) whilst simultaneously maintaining an imperative to seek change in opposition to these possibilities?

Finally, we can see in Mammeri's first novel, at its conclusion where Mokrane fails in his desperate attempt to make his way through the snow back to his ex-wife, Aazi, the seed of a "pessimistic" form that resonates throughout the corpus of this monograph. Though not in sight of a postcolonial future in the same way as *L'Opium et le bâton* or *Le Sommeil du juste*, this form brings to bear on the simultaneous evocation of the ambiguous future possibilities of failure and success, of positive change and its lack in socio-symbolic representation, in the organisation of gender conceptualisations and relations, as subjects read and engage with their symbolic world. The conclusion of *La Colline oubliée* initially displays Mokrane's rejection of the validity of the norms, of the socio-symbolic constellations that have conditioned his treatment/neglect of Aazi:

> À mesure que j'y réfléchis, mon aberration devient évidente et énorme à mes yeux, car enfin, que puis-je reprocher exactement à ma femme ? La coutume ? Les dires ? Les plaintes de ma mère ? Ah ! pourquoi y a-t-il des pentes qu'on ne remonte plus ?...[575]

Then, as we pass into the third person narration that closes the novel, the first two moments of Mokrane's reported speech uncannily evoke both the suspension of the Other through a Thanatos drive, and Lacan's maxim that one should "ne

---

573 Mouloud Mammeri: *Le Sommeil du juste*, p. 254.
574 Anne Roche: Tradition et subversion dans l'œuvre de Mouloud Mammeri, p. 103–104.
575 Mouloud Mammeri: *La Colline oubliée*, p. 157.

pas céder sur son désir",[576] that one should not compromise on one's desire as it pertains to what Žižek terms "active subjectivisation", socio-political agency. Žižek states in his work *Lacan: The Silent Partners* that this agency is "possible only in the intersubjective Symbolic after we have temporarily suspended it and 'reshaped' it through the imposition of a new Master-Signifier and the emergence of a new (partly subjectivized) *jouissance* connected to it".[577] In other words, Lacan's maxim encourages the subject to break from the ideological coordinates of the Other (la coutume, les dires, les plaints de la mère), to not allow these to compromise desire, but also acknowledges the necessity of re-entering the Symbolic to experience and articulate change. This, I argue, is what leaves the door open to regression, and what highlights the importance of an imperative to continuously question "pessimistically" the order of symbolic interactions.

Returning to the text, at first we read Mokrane state to his companions that "[p]artir, [...] c'est mourir un peu",[578] conjuring the notion of a symbolic "death", of a break with discursive mastery, and then we read him address them thus:

> – Mes camarades, disait-il, vous êtes très aimables. Vous croyez que je cours à la mort et vous voulez m'en éloigner parce que vous m'aimez – mais je vous dis que vous vous trompez, je peinerai beaucoup, je le sais, mais j'arriverai où je dois arriver.[579]

Mokrane underlines here his rejection of compromise, his refusal to go back on what he must do, following his desire to return to Aazi. Tragically, however, he does not succeed, and dies on the mountainside. Moreover, Mokrane's final moments play with the notion of falling back into Eros, into a state of comfort that opposes a textual disruption which relates to the Kristevan notions of the semiotic and feminine voice investigated in my chapter on Dib. Whilst he attempts to reform a bond with Aazi, he begins to hear her voice on the wind and in imagining a contrasting domestic warmth in his bewilderment he wishes "d'être lui aussi docilement parqué dans un coin, avec le reste du troupeau, pour ne plus sentir ce corps qui maintenant le tiraillait de toutes parts, lui faisait mal partout, *surtout pour ne plus entendre cette voix qui sifflait dans le vent*, pleurait dans le creux des rochers, grondait dans le tonnerre ou s'estompait au bruit de ses pas sur la neige : 'Je suis ta femme.'".[580] Subsequently and finally, we are presented

---

[576] Jacques Lacan: *Le Séminaire, livre VII, L'Éthique de la psychanalyse, leçon du 6 juillet 1960*. Paris: Éditions du Seuil 1986, p. 368.
[577] Slavoj Žižek: *The Silent Partners*. London: Verso 2006, p. 347.
[578] Mouloud Mammeri: *La Colline oubliée*, p. 160.
[579] Ibid, p. 160.
[580] Ibid, p. 169 (emphasis added).

with an image that beautifully encapsulates both the potential for desire to act as a displacement rather than a tool of radical agency and the need for a continual renewal of focus on this factor as a part of an attempt to narrow the discursive gap between genders, to allow for a level symbolic playing field, even if the nature of subjectivity blocks off the possibility of a true *relation sexuelle:*

> Il marchait comme un automate, les yeux fixés sur Aazi toujours immobile et souriante. Il était plongé dans une béatitude délicieuse. Plus rien n'existait autour de lui, la neige ni le froid : dans un espace vide où rien n'était, la tempête ni la voix, ils étaient deux : Aazi et lui. Il n'aurait même pas pu dire où il était ni s'il était loin ou près de Tasga. Il était heureux, voilà tout. Mais pourquoi Aazi ne voulait-elle pas avancer ?[581]

Mammeri's work seeks to have the feminine figure advance into the frame of public discourse whilst acknowledging the limits of his literature to achieve this. Though this approach sometimes leaves Algerian women underrepresented in terms of an equality of textual space, it continuously challenges the reader to begin a careful procedure of critically reading the ways in which meaning is generated in the social world. Symbolic institutions and ideological parameters that condition perceptions must be challenged and the reader should be prepared to dissent and to anticipate the necessity for dissent. By reading the world "pessimistically", by guarding against the demise of agents of change and the potential for these agents to compromise on their desire, one may seek to bring about a field of social representation, to seek representative structures, symbolic and worldly that allow women an equal footing in the game, an equal stake in the determination of a socio-symbolic framework.

---

[581] Ibid, p. 170.

6 Assia Djebar – Movements Towards Self-reflexive Representation

Born Fatima-Zohra Imalayene in 1936 to an Arab Algerian father and an Amazigh mother, Assia Djebar, who passed away in February 2015, went on to become the first Muslim North African woman to become an "immortelle" as part of l'Académie française and was frequently tipped to receive the Nobel prize for literature. Though perhaps no other Algerian writer has received the level of international critical approbation that Djebar enjoyed, her œuvre has certainly not received uniform praise across her publications and her early works have long been associated with an image of the author that jars with later ideals of the celebrated Algerian. Indeed, when considering Djebar's writings, I was put in mind of Michel Foucault's thoughts on the relationship between the imaginary constructs of l'œuvre and its author. In a famous paper given in 1969 at the Collège de France, Foucault alludes to the fact that a readership will often sever notional ties between a work, the writer and l'œuvre where a connection would undermine an ideal image of the writer. The works to be studied in this chapter, written by Djebar at the beginning of her literary career, have been subject to precisely this kind of severance.

In the aforementioned paper, Foucault amusingly draws a comparison between "la manière dont la critique littéraire a, pendant longtemps, défini l'auteur – ou plutôt construit la forme-auteur à partir des textes et des discours existants" and "la manière dont la tradition chrétienne a authentifié (ou au contraire rejeté) les textes dont elle disposait".[582] He then provides the decision criteria for validating texts supplied by Saint Jerome in *De viris illustribus*, initially emphasising two important factors:

> [S]i, parmi plusieurs livres attribués à un auteur, l'un est inférieur aux autres de la liste de ses œuvres, il faut le retirer de la liste de ses œuvres (l'auteur est alors défini comme un certain niveau constant de valeur); de même, si certains textes sont en contradiction de doctrine avec les autres œuvres d'un auteur (l'auteur est alors défini comme un certain champ de cohérence conceptuelle ou théorique) [...][583]

As though following Saint Jerome's instructions, critics often divide Djebar's career into two stages, the stage prior to her literary hiatus begun in the late 1960s

---

[582] Michel Foucault: Qu'est-ce qu'un auteur? [1969]. In: *Dits et écrits*. Paris: Gallimard 2001, p. 829.
[583] Ibid, p. 829.

and the stage after the publication of *Femmes d'Alger dans leur appartement* in 1980. They also perform a further division, excluding her earliest works, *La Soif* (1957) and *Les Impatients* (1958) from Djebar's "proper" corpus. The latter separation has been occasioned mostly on the basis of a belief that the "true", mature, Djebar was an author who understood her country's identity as marked by coloniality and then postcoloniality. Because these concerns are not particularly in evidence in Djebar's first two novels it is thus claimed that they demonstrate her younger self to be disengaged, to be lacking in the critical "doctrine", to reference Saint Jerome, that has been ascribed to the ideal of her as author. However, in a keynote presentation given in October 2015 at a workshop staged in honour of the life and works of Assia Djebar, Catherine Brun began her paper by mounting a defence of the young Djebar against the sometimes savage criticism that she faced as a result of her early publications.[584] Furthermore, responding to the assertion made by Amin Zaoui in *Liberté* that Djebar suffered from "un complexe baptisé 'Mostefa Lacheraf'",[585] that, following his attacks on Mammeri's work, it was Lacheraf's criticism that caused her to turn her attention towards political engagement in her literature and her life more generally, Brun emphasised the fact that the criticisms of a lack of engagement leveled at Djebar were not just unmerited, but indeed had little effect on Djebar's political orientation.[586] Brun focused on an interview conducted in 1958 and cited by Daniel Lançon in which Djebar displays her appreciation of the nationalist cause in stating her wish to be viewed as an Algerian writer, by other Algerians, in the context of a nascent Algerian cultural field. Djebar's precocious political interest is also illuminated, as an example amongst many, by the fact that, as she revealed in an interview with *Jeune Afrique* in 2008, her first novel which was not published but which was written prior to *La Soif*, was produced "en fantasmant sur la vie des maquisards algériens".[587]

---

[584] Catherine Brun gave her paper entitled "Assia Djebar: jalons pour l'itinéraire d'un 'je-nous'" at La Maison Française d'Oxford, 9 October, 2015. This paper subsequently became the article Assia Djebar: jalons pour l'itinéraire d'un "je-nous". In: *Revue d'histoire littéraire de la France* Vol. 116 (2016), p. 915–934.

[585] Amin Zaoui: Pourquoi le prix Nobel de littérature est raté? In: *Liberté* (19th October 2013): https://www.facebook.com/notes/amin-zaoui/assia-djebar-pourquoi-le-prix-nobel-de-litt%C3%A9rature-est-rat%C3%A9-/476184062479346.

[586] Lacheraf accused Djebar and Malek Haddad, in a now infamous critique, of knowing little of the lives of ordinary Algerians, stating that "[Malek Haddad et Assia Djebar sont] de tous les écrivains algériens, […] ceux qui connaissent le moins leur pays". Mostefa Lacheraf: L'Avenir de la culture algérienne. In: *Les temps modernes* No. 209 (October 1963), p. 733.

[587] See Hamid Barrada/Tirthankar Chanda: Assia Djebar Interview. In: *Jeune Afrique* (30 March 2008) (http://www.jeuneafrique.com/57084/archives-thematique/assia-djebar/). Here Djebar

6 Assia Djebar – Movements Towards Self-reflexive Representation

This chapter will not simply seek to continue the debate over Djebar's fulfilment of a revolutionary function in representation, over her anti-colonial political engagement, though of course this will remain an important aspect of the analyses. It will, however, attempt to leave behind a received understanding of "l'auteur" in a consideration of her texts, seeking rather to investigate the aspects of her novels published between 1957 and 1962 which illuminate Djebar's negotiation of a feminine reflexive representation. This is not to suggest that one should ignore the colonial or revolutionary context in considering Djebar's representation of women. Indeed this chapter will demonstrate that Djebar's first two published novels, *La Soif* and *Les Impatients*, are peculiar in their glossing over of the political upheavals of the revolutionary period, especially when compared with those of the other authors in our corpus. Moreover, my interest in the novels to be analysed in this chapter stems precisely from the fact that they were published in the period leading up to Algerian independence.[588]

However, it remains important to consider that these texts represent literary constructions that are not necessarily to be taken as mirrors for the entirety of Djebar's own preoccupations, nor as media that constitute paragons of representativity. As this chapter will go on to describe in greater detail, one notes an evolving investigation from *La Soif* to *Les Impatients* to *Les Enfants du nouveau monde* (1962) that centres precisely on the dangers of imaginary self-obsession, of remaining perpetually stuck in a mirror-stage that ignores the outside, the socio-symbolic Other. And, though one might consider the influence of the colonial system to be a factor that should not be ignored for any attempt of representation undertaken by the young Djebar to contribute meaningfully to discourse on women, it should also be considered that Djebar's early novels represent the bold first attempts of a pioneer and that Djebar's own womanhood necessitates a doubly complex negotiation of the representation of femininity. Moreover, imperfection or underdevelopment present in this negotiation is to be anticipated when one considers its historical context. Though women achieved greater freedom and historical agency over the period, and though official doctrines promised much in the way of gender equality, competing discourses on women and uneven, somewhat inchoate engagement in revolutionary politics mean that a degree of incoherence and unpredictability in women's literature can be understood as representative and, indeed, important to evoke in my study.

---

also mentions how *La Soif*'s writing was facilitated by her adherence to the strike in solidarity with the FLN begun by L'Union générale des étudiants musulmans d'Afrique in 1957.
588 I have elected not to focus on *Les alouettes naïves* (1967) precisely because Djebar began writing the book in 1963, after Algeria had acquired independence.

Florence Stratton has written convincingly on colonial/postcolonial women's marginal positioning regarding national politics and "the public life of their nations" and asserts that it is no surprise that "the experience of marginality is reflected in the thematic preoccupations of African women's literature, while men's literature tends to be full of ideological valorizations of the status quo of male domination".[589] [590] Djebar's marginality is demonstrated in her positioning in this very book, being as she is the only woman who has come to be understood as canonical to the late-colonial period.[591] The fact that her early novels do indeed attempt to come to terms with Algerian women's positioning relative to community and national belonging can therefore be understood as representative of a prevalent social positionality amongst women at the time, despite her colonial French education and relative privilege, and as echoing her struggle to break into public discourse. Moreover, in analysing Djebar's early novels, this chapter will seek to follow Stratton's lead in concerning itself "less with the incorporation of works by women into the established canon than with canon reconstruction through alternative modes of reading".[592] Where my own canon, this book's corpus, has focused on male writers' negotiation of the articulation of the feminine Other, this chapter will thus initially seek to change focus by assessing how the literary act of representation of femininity is explored by a writer aware both of the intensity of discourse centered on women at the time of her writing, and of her own belonging to this gendered community.

Because of Djebar's being a woman, one can consider her early texts, as a counterpoint to those of Dib, Kateb, Feraoun, and Mammeri, as forming a special representative relation with her in two important ways: First, because of paratextual identification, because Djebar's name is on the front of the book, the text represents her as a proxy, then as now. One might argue that this is also the case for the other writers under discussion. The difference lies in the fact that during the revolutionary period "Algerian women" represented an object of discourse that came under particular scrutiny, a fact of which Djebar herself would have been aware. Consequently, her early novels which focus on women were written in the knowledge that they would be understood as particular representatives of a "woman's" perspective on "women". Secondly, just as Stratton de-

---

[589] Florence Stratton: *Contemporary African literature and the Politics of Gender.* London: Routledge 1994, p. 10.
[590] Ibid, p. 15.
[591] Another study might find space to explore the works of Taos Amrouche, Djamila Debèche and Aïcha Lemsine, three lesser-known Algerian women writers who wrote between 1947 and 1980.
[592] Ibid, p. 13.

scribes the process whereby political marginality is represented in the texts of colonial and postcolonial African women, Djebar's understanding of her own subjective and sociological status, and of that of fellow women, comes to be present in her texts. Though Djebar does not directly perform self-representation, the politics of which this chapter will later discuss, she does produce narratives that focus very closely on women of a particular time and place, a community to which Djebar belongs and which her early novels attempt to articulate. This chapter will demonstrate that it is the literary working-through of the problematic of this kind of reflexive representation, where the self is a part of the feminine community represented, in texts that can be understood as markers of a woman's entry into discourse on "women", that constitutes the prime contribution that Djebar's first three novels make to an understanding of the representation of women in my era of study.

Moreover, while it is a development of reflexive representation across the three texts that might represent a foundation for my study of her work, just as in my studies of Dib and Mammeri I focused on the evolution of their representational modes across their œuvres, it is perhaps equally important to note that Djebar's early texts explore differing forms of non-literary feminine development or emancipatory learning, individually and as a corpus, that interact to differing degrees with conceptualisations of her early literary development. This chapter will divide this nucleus of non-literary development into three interrelated aspects that the works evoke: historical/sociological progression, psychic/subjective progression and ideological/political progression. At the same time, Djebar's texts will also be seen to undermine what Gordon Bigelow refers to as a "Weberian discourse of modernization" that would track a teleological Western schema of progression from the primitive to the developed.[593] Though Djebar's early novels work to represent evolutions in the self-mastery and agency of Algerian women, understood within the conceptual parameters of a future nation to come, they maintain in varied evocations, as in the rest of my corpus, the possibility of failure, the potential for "les enfants du nouveau monde" to fail in adulthood, to undo a logic of feminine development and emancipation. And this is, of course, particularly important when one considers the discord between the monumentalisation of the revolution, as has been explored by writers like Ranjana Khanna, and the backwards steps taken with regards to gender equality in post-independence Algeria.

---

[593] Gordon Bigelow: Revolution and Modernity: Assia Djebar's "Les Enfants du nouveau monde". In: *Research in African Literatures* Vol. 34, No. 2 (Summer 2003), p. 13.

6.1 A Representative Scribe?

In his exceptional work on Djebar, Nicholas Harrison has often emphasised how readers and critics have grown accustomed to seeing the author as "une sorte de porte-parole des femmes algériennes, rôle avec lequel elle semble entretenir un rapport équivoque".[594] At the beginning of his chapter on Djebar's works in *Postcolonial Criticism*, he recounts the story of Djebar's giving a paper in 1995 on Albert Camus' autobiographical *Le Premier Homme* at the University of California, Berkeley. Harrison demonstrates how her "awareness of and discomfort with the demands of 'representativity' placed upon her" were illuminated by the distinction drawn between her and Camus with regards to the politics of identity.[595] Where Camus had written in his notes to *Le Premier Homme* that "[c]e qu'ils n'aimaient pas en lui, c'était l'Algérien" Djebar stated of herself at the conference the following:[596]

> Justement, je souris à cet Algérien-là, moi qu'on accueille de si loin et dans une université prestigieuse parce qu'écrivain, parce que femme et parce qu'algérienne : je note à mon tour, en contrepoint à Camus, "ce qu'ils reconnaissent en moi, c'est l'Algérienne". "Ce qu'ils reconnaissent" ? Rectifions : "Ce qu'ils espèrent de moi, c'est l'Algérie-femme."[597]

Clearly, as Djebar's literary career continued, she came to develop an acute awareness of a kind of ego-ideal that would, in many cases, precede her and determine her positive reception around the world. This ideal, based on the trinity of writer, woman, and Algeria, is understood by Djebar as generating an expectation of representativity that she clearly attempts to eschew despite acknowledging the impossibility of its avoidance. Indeed, if we think of the ideal of Djebar as a *Vertretung* representative and consider her material disconnection from many of her compatriots, one can further understand a recalcitrance to claim experience and representativity of colonial and post-colonial poverty and oppression. In another section of *Ces voix qui m'assiègent*, the collection of essays that contains the speech given at Berkeley, Djebar writes, for example, in dialogue with herself:

---

[594] Nicholas Harrison: Le Voile littéraire: la politique d'Assia Djebar. In: Jean Bessière (ed.): *Littératures francophones et politiques*. Paris : Karthala 2009, p. 150.
[595] Nicholas Harrison: *Postcolonial Criticism: History, Theory and The Work of Fiction*. Cambridge: Polity Press 2003, p. 113.
[596] Albert Camus: *Le Premier homme*. Paris: Gallimard 1994, p. 318.
[597] Assia Djebar: *Ces voix qui m'assiègent*. Paris: A. Michel 1999, p. 224.

> Que non, vous ne direz pas "nous", vous ne vous cacherez pas, vous femme singulière, derrière la "Femme" ; vous ne serez jamais, ni au début ni à la fin, "porte-parole" [...]⁵⁹⁸

Nevertheless, it is clear that Djebar's œuvre as a whole often concerns itself specifically with the problematic location of self-identity amongst the lost and recovered voices of an Algerian sorority. And, though of course one should avoid the temptation of identifying Djebar through her protagonists and her narrators, though one should initially separate her fictional posture from that of an autobiographical project, one may still argue that from the very beginning of her publication history her work has been determined by a quest to articulate the ontology and phenomenology of a community or grouping of which she is a part: Algerian women. Furthermore, this literary quest, even at its tentative inception, can be understood as part of an attempt to excavate a historically determined truth.

Djebar stated, for example, in an interview with Hédi Djebnoun in 1987 that "[l]a *Soif* c'était un air de flûte qui continue à être entendu, et qui continue à être juste", thus alluding playfully to the book's capacity, however inchoate, to reflect an experiential reality.⁵⁹⁹ Clearly, as we shall see in analysing *La Soif*, *Les Impatients* and *Les Enfants du nouveau monde*, Djebar's work seeks to produce realist portraits of femininity that reflect truths that the author wishes to convey, that apportion to her and, by implication, to a historical feminine *prise de parole*, a symbolic authority that allows for entry into the competition between discourses on women that was so prevalent in the late-colonial period. It is in this sense, then, that Djebar's early works can be understood as reflexive representation, as texts which stand in for her as proxies and begin to evoke a historical feminine community of which she is a part, through narrative constructions and fictional avatars. Indeed Jeanne-Marie Clerc goes so far as to write:

> Il y a donc, dès ce premier roman, une timide émergence du sujet, s'affirmant contre le silence et la claustration [...] Le masque n'est donc pas aussi total que veut l'affirmer l'auteur [...]"⁶⁰⁰

For her, then, Djebar's generation of depictions of Algerian women approximates to a veritable self-representation.

Nevertheless, what is immediately striking about Djebar's first two publications, in particular in the case of *La Soif*, is the extent to which they generate

---

598 Ibid., p. 263.
599 Hédi Djebnoun: Naissance d'un "air de flûte". In: *Arabies* No. 2 (February 1987), p. 83–84.
600 Jeanne Marie Clerc: *Assia Djebar: écrire, transgresser, résister*. Paris: L'Harmattan 1997, p. 55.

feminine protagonists whose tumultuous concerns with the self often and to a large extent dissuade the reader from forming an emotional identification with them. Consequently, somewhat irrespective of one's knowledge of the political interests or character of the young Djebar, one forms a strong separation between the notional author and her protagonists. This production of protagonists with whom the reader is dissuaded from identifying and from whose actions the notional author is consequently morally disentangled, was not widely appreciated during the period of Djebar's early publications, however. In explanation of this, Daniel Lançon writes about Émile Henriot, a critic of the period of publication whose stance he sees as representative of a larger trend, that "[s]i le critique confond le personnage de Dalila avec l'auteur, c'est qu'il estime le haut degré de réalisme d'une fiction donnée pour autobiographique", reproducing Henriot's declaration that *Les Impatients* reproduces a "vie féminine musulmane, intime et bourgeoise, où l'auteur a très certainement vécu".[601] Indeed, these texts' realism, along with their first-person narratives, are really the only factors that might cause one to conflate author and protagonist, for the constructions of character and plot at work in the novels make clear that what the reader is being presented with are anti-heroic scenarios, similar to those deployed in Mammeri's work, that invite symptomatic readings.

Debra Kelly provides in *Autobiography and Independence* a section of an interview conducted with Djebar in *L'Action* in 1958. Djebar affirms:

> J'ai toujours voulu éviter de donner à mes romans un caractère autobiographique par peur de l'indécence et par horreur d'un certain strip-tease intellectuel auquel on se livre souvent avec complaisance dans les premières œuvres. Ma vie personnelle n'a rien en commun avec mes héroïnes.[602]

She goes on to specify the difference between herself and her heroines, stating: "Je n'ai pas de conflit avec ma famille, je n'ai jamais fait de fugue".[603] These statements allude to a fear of direct and personal self-representation as an Algerian woman in the late-colonial period, though the last citation also leads one to infer that Djebar perhaps did feel a certain proximity to her characters, that the difference between them lies rather in their emotional anguish, their moral ambiguity and the irrational and unproductive nature of their decisions and actions.

---

[601] Daniel Lançon: L'Invention de l'auteur: Assia Djebar entre 1957 et 1969 ou l'Orient second en français. In: Wolfgang Asholt/Mireille Calle-Gruber/Dominique Combe (eds.): *Assia Djebar: Littérature et transmission*. Paris: PSN 2010, p. 125.
[602] Debra Kelly: *Autobiography and Independence*, p. 256.
[603] Ibid, p. 256.

Many critics including Jean Déjeux and Nicholas Harrison have commented on the interdictions imposed as part of North African Islamic mores against the writing of autobiography, in particular feminine autobiography, whose potential authors, as has been explored by feminist thinkers like Fatima Mernissi, are expected to remain a selfless part of the *Ummah* (community). However one might speculate as to Djebar's motivations for cutting autobiographical ties, it remains clear that her first two texts, in particular *La Soif*, through the inconsistencies and irrationalities of their narrating feminine protagonists, invite the reader to view their representations of women as being in conflict with ideals of feminine representativity. Indeed *La Soif* and *Les Impatients* even contain subjective responses from their protagonists that are blackly amusing in their closed-mindedness and lack of self-awareness.

To begin with *La Soif*, the novel is presented from an advanced temporal position by the now older Nadia who recounts as a narrating-I the story of her twenty-year old self, the experiencing-I.[604] One might understand this separation of self as echoing the distance between Djebar and the woman she is principally depicting, as representing a split in perspective between more enlightened and less developed figures. Certainly one can cite numerous occasions in the narrative where Nadia's reactions to events are drawn and positioned such that her perspective is undermined. The narrative centres on Nadia's encountering Jedla, a former schoolmate with whom she has fallen out, and Ali, Jedla's husband. Nadia attempts to seduce Ali and manipulate the emotions of another male protagonist, Hassein, whom she marries at the novel's conclusion.

Because of her self-obsession and her avowal that, with regards to men, "ils m'amusaient quelquefois ; je les amenais alors tout doucement à mes pieds, bien ficelés", many of her subsequent reported thoughts appear amusingly absurd in their hypocrisy.[605] For example, after Jedla has possibly attempted to commit suicide, Nadia's self-involvement is emphasised by a proliferation of personal pronouns as she considers Ali's reaction to the event:

> Il ne *me* voyait pas, il ne *me* parlait pas, et sa distraction même *me* semblait bizarrement un abandon. Quand il pénétrait dans la chambre de Jedla et que *j*'étais là, *je me* levais. Il *me* retenait d'un geste las, auquel *je* ne savais que répondre.[606]

---

604 In Focalization in Graphic Narrative. In: *Narrative* Vol. 19, No. 3 (October 2011), p. 330–357 Silke Horstkotte and Nancy Pedri define the narrating-I as a version of the experiencing-I that exists at a different moment in time or level of consciousness.
605 Assia Djebar: *La Soif.* Paris: R. Julliard 1957, p. 65.
606 Ibid, p. 42 (emphasis added).

Ironically, however, she then immediately comments critically on Jedla's apparent self-involvement, stating that "[e]lle avait la liberté. Non ! – et ma rancune parlait alors – elle n'était pas libre, mais sèche, mais égoïste ; elle manquait de cœur".[607] Another choice example among many of Nadia's overtly hypocritical statements comes where she learns of Jedla's plan to have Ali fall in love with her (Nadia), so that their marriage can be broken off and so that Jedla will consequently not have to suffer the pain of a separation that is out of her control. Despite her reported enjoyment derived from playing with men's emotions, here she appreciates a moral bankruptcy in Jedla's manipulation:

> Elle n'avait pas le droit de disposer de sa vie, de leur vie. Après tout, Ali n'était pas un objet, mais un être libre.[608]

What is particularly interesting for this study of Djebar's representation of Algerian women as a whole is how the reader is encouraged to understand her protagonists' flaws and positive qualities, in differing ways, as in part historically and culturally determined. It is thus initially through the representation of women whose subjectivities are radically inconsistent and underdeveloped, and who are thus presented as non-autobiographical figures, that Djebar's novels find a literary expression for Algerian women's challenges and sufferings, past and contemporary, in which her identity holds a stake. Moreover, while Djebar seemingly determines that an autobiographical stance is unacceptable for her entry into discourse on women, her texts externalise, outsource, the work of introspection to her depicted characters. This is to say that while Djebar refuses the act of overt confession, of direct self-examination as a representative figure, her feminine protagonists engage in constant self-assessment, allowing Djebar to interrogate aspects of her socially determined femininity at a distance. This distancing from the represented alters somewhat in *Les Impatients* and significantly in *Les Enfants du nouveau monde* where more sympathetic portraits are drawn, inviting greater identification, but what is a constant within all three novels under discussion, as the next section will demonstrate, is a developing, though not always productive, tension between historical and cultural determination and the saying of I, of no, by women, a gesture that can be related in some ways to the notion of *Thanatos* discussed in my chapters on Feraoun and Mammeri, and indeed to Antigone and to Fatima, "Celle qui dit non à Médine", in Djebar's *Loin de Médine*.[609] The repetition of terms such as "rejet" and "ré-

---

607 Ibid, p. 43.
608 Ibid, p. 109.
609 Assia Djebar: *Loin de Médine: filles d'Ismaël*. Paris: A Michel 1991, p. 68.

volte" is conspicuous throughout and relates in complex ways to the determining socio-historical pressures exerted on the protagonists. Djebar thus produces a picture of socio-historical development among Algerian women that relates both to a changing socio-symbolic order to which her feminine protagonists are subjected and to an agency that seeks to break this order through radical subjective development that would permit a level of emancipation from masculinist Law.

6.2 Socio-historical Progression?

Focusing on *La Soif*, it should first be emphasised that the lives represented in the narrative are unusually and markedly Western and bourgeois in their quotidian content. As Clarisse Zimra writes, "*La Soif* had everything: beautiful females, well-off males, fast cars, lazy days at the beach [...] To the Parisian pundits, the resemblance to young Françoise Sagan's 1954 scandalous *Bonjour tristesse*, published by the same press (Julliard), was unmistakable".[610] One might add to this list "le jazz, et les cigarettes", "l'alcool" and "le Casino", amongst other signifiers of a Western bourgeois *mode de vie*.[611] The bourgeois nature of the narrative events is acknowledged in the text where Nadia tells of the "scandale de bourgeois" provoked by her conduct whilst engaged to her ex-fiancé, Saïd.[612] Her Western social parameters are attributed to her mother being French and to her father raising her "comme ils disaient, 'à l'européenne'".[613] Certainly then, *La Soif* develops a portrait of feminine figures, Nadia and Jedla, whose reported thoughts and actions are conditioned by a social backdrop that is, for the most part, only representative for a historically specific small class of Algerian women, the problematically termed *évoluées*. Nevertheless, it can be argued that *La Soif* develops an image of young Algerian women, in particular of the narrator Nadia, who attempt, albeit largely unsuccessfully, to come to terms with a subjective relationship to developing social mores that are representative of a commixture of different influences. The concoction of norms that the women of the text ingest is dominated by Western bourgeois ingredients, though not exclusively. Thus, though the narrative alludes, for example, to Nadia's jealousy of

---

610 Clarisse Zimra: Writing Woman: The Novels of Assia Djebar. In: *SubStance* No. 69 (1992), p. 68.
611 Assia Djebar: *La Soif*, p. 12, 14, 81.
612 Ibid, p. 24.
613 Ibid, p. 17.

her sister's enjoyment of regular sexual intercourse: "On m'avait appris à classer les femmes en trois catégories : les femmes de tête, les femmes de cœur, et les femelles, comme Myriem, au sexe avide",[614] or to a Camusian ennui provoked by the apparent emptiness of "les surprise parties les dimanches pluvieux, les courses folles au vent dans des voitures nerveuses comme de jeunes chevaux racés",[615] it also engages with masculinist socio-symbolic parameters that are determined by Algerian traditionalist values predicated on the maintenance of symbolic capital under the guise of "honour". These values are not assigned a specific genesis (Islam, nationalist politics etc.) but exist rather as an amalgamation of native masculinist symbolic content. Thus we read about the "jeune tante [...] qui s'était mariée à l'intérieur, dans une riche famille de marabout. Elle était tout le temps enceinte. Cinq fois, elle eut des filles ; la sixième fois, son mari, excédé, l'obligea à se faire avorter" and, in another regularly cited section, about "toutes les autres femmes de ce pays, nos mères, nos grand-mères : pourvu qu'elles aient leur foyer, qu'elles puissent servir, obéir à leur époux, c'est tout ce qu'elles demandent [...] Elles sont calmes, sages, soumises".[616] In the case of the latter citation, we find that Nadia's ability to resist the submissive stereotype that she has come to understand is limited, as she states that "[c]'est peut-être elles qui ont raison".[617] And indeed, though the narrative is largely determined by Nadia's revolt; by her enjoyment of her body: "Je jouissais de la souplesse de mes jambes, de tout mon corps",[618] by her rejection of a social attachment to men, and indeed by the emergence of a queer relationship with Jedla which, as Clarisse Zimra has commented, might "shortcircuit the patriarchal trajectory of desire", Nadia remains cloistered, crushed, and largely controlled by the society in which her rebellion is staged.[619]

In *The Psychic Life of Power*, Judith Butler discusses the notions of agency and subjectivity, writing the following in a summation of Foucauldian notions outlined in *Surveiller et punir*:

> The term "subjectivation" carries [a] paradox in itself: *assujettissement* denotes both the becoming of the subject and the process of subjection – one inhabits the figure of autonomy only by becoming subjected to a power, a subjection which implies a radical dependency.[620]

---

614 Ibid, p. 67.
615 Ibid, p. 11–12.
616 Ibid, p. 130, 145–146.
617 Ibid, p. 146.
618 Ibid, p. 51.
619 Clarisse Zimra: Writing Woman, p. 72.
620 Judith Butler: *The Psychic Life of Power: Theories in Subjection*. Stanford: SUP 1997, p. 83.

Concordantly, Nadia's revolt is itself dependent on an individualism and a social theatre located in an emergent social class. This individualism is assigned an atomising role by Djebar's text which prevents the production of an authentic, socially progressive feminine subject who would be aware of the determining importance of the Other as a shared socio-symbolic backdrop, and might therefore stage a symbolic revolt proper. The dependency of her revolt is perhaps most clearly articulated through Nadia's embodiment of differing *rôles* which one can read as reflections of emergent Western literary and social types. Nadia talks about, for example, "le beau rôle, celui de l'indulgence fatiguée",[621] the role of "une coquette",[622] and the role of "la petite fille ingénue, provocante à peine".[623] And, as Jane Hiddleston has noted, Nadia's understanding of masquerade, of role embodiment, resembles that of Emma Bovary as she acknowledges her reference to "des souvenirs de roman et de films".[624] Consequently, Nadia's development as a feminine subject, her revolt against the past, is to be understood as historically, culturally, symbolically conditioned, lacking in unmediated agency. Despite this, Djebar's text does allude to a development in the life possibilities for Algerian women by the very evocation of an individualist subject who appears relatively "free" to choose her conduct, in contrast with the "femmes soumises" referred to as a traditional standard in the text. For every feminine revolt, however radical, requires subsequent articulation in order to become a functioning part of the socio-symbolic order, a norm in discourse with which subsequent imaginary identifications can be made. Thus though *La Soif* articulates a largely inert, determined feminine protagonist, her status as an *évoluée* alludes obliquely to previous, perhaps somewhat limited revolts staged by others in a Western milieu.

Les Impatients places greater emphasis precisely on a contrast between traditional constricting mores and the will of the feminine subject, in evoking a compulsion to leave the sequestration of the home which repeats within its narrator, Dalila. The narrative centres on her desire to run away with the object of her affection, Salim, a desire that she eventually sates with unsatisfying consequences. Contemporary imaginary parameters still determine aspects of the protagonist's "révolte", a term upon which the narrator appears fixated, as she admits when questioned about her intentions regarding her love interest: "C'était vrai, c'était du romanesque. Je le savais et j'en étais heureuse".[625] Indeed, one

---

[621] Assia Djebar: *La Soif*, p. 93.
[622] Ibid, p. 21.
[623] Ibid, p. 68.
[624] Ibid, p. 68.
[625] Assia Djebar: *Les Impatients*. Paris: R. Julliard 1958, p. 107.

detects a kind of Proustian disappointment where her romantic wanderings in Algiers with Salim do not live up to her imaginings and one bears witness to a particularly troubling engagement with social theatre when Salim assaults her in Paris. Dalila comments that "[u]n calme étrange filtrait en moi goutte à goutte et j'essayais malgré ma fatigue de le comprendre [...] C'était plutôt l'avide plaisir que je ressentais d'avoir été au cœur d'un vrai drame".[626] Furthermore, one can argue that, to a large extent, Dalila's rebellion is predicated on her naïve frustrations with her stepmother Lella's refusal to reveal the details of her own troubled past. Nevertheless, partly because the novel's social context is less peculiarly Western than *La Soif* and more evocative of a representative subjective crisis undergone by colonised Algerian women, the tension generated between tradition and rebellion alludes to a more radical and productive desire to reject "the symbolic pact which regulates social exchange".[627]

Furthermore, Djebar's protagonist has a degree of self-awareness with respect to her own "romanesque" interpellation and is a more sympathetic character, narrowing the gap between author, reader and object. There are still scenes where identification with the narrator is deliberately and, again, amusingly stymied. One particularly comical example comes at the end of a letter written by Dalila to her friend, Mina. She closes the letter, explaining her situation, by simply and haughtily writing "P.s. ne cherche pas à comprendre".[628] However, after "révolté", the term that appears most repeated in the text is "puérile", used self-referentially, and though there is not a clear division between an advanced narrating-I and a flawed experiencing-I, the text works as a cautionary tale while obliquely maintaining the possibility of a positive feminine agency.

Moreover, *Les Impatients* provides richer testimony of women's suffering at the hands of masculinist traditional values. For example, Dalila's communal home is populated by downtrodden characters like Zohra, who maintains the vain hope that Thamani, the community's fixer, will provide her with a husband, and Dalila herself provides social commentary, stating, for example:

> Un sentiment étrange de fatalité m'avait emplie d'une exaltation telle que j'y étais allée, comme nos trop jeunes mariées se laissent entraîner à la chambre nuptiale, soumises et graves.[629]

---

626 Ibid, p. 217.
627 Slavoj Žižek: From Desire to Drive, p. 5.
628 Assia Djebar: *Les Impatients*, p. 168.
629 Ibid, p. 83.

At the same time, there is an evocation of a subjective resistance, similar to the notion of Thanatos, of a drive to break oppressive symbolic commitments, explored in my chapters on Feraoun and Mammeri. As an example of Dalila's incorporation of the drive, she states: "J'écoutais une houle déferler en moi ; je la reconnaissais. C'était cette même fièvre qui me dressait contre Lella, contre la maison fermée, contre tous ; c'était elle qui me délivrerait".[630] This kind of expression of a will to revolt against established symbolic norms is repeated throughout the text but its productivity is for the most part restricted because of a lack of subsequent direction. In some ways Dalila's repeating unfulfilled compulsions to revolt are evocative of Žižek's problematic of the morning after. In *The Indivisible Remainder*, he writes that "it is easy to suspend the big Other by means of the act *qua* real, to experience the "non existence of the big Other" in a momentary flash – however, what do we do *after* we have traversed the fantasy?".[631] Dalila is repeatedly portrayed as feeling this suspension of the big Other, of a spirit representing the conditioning pressures of cultural and historical context, but is shown to then be ill-equipped to answer Žižek's follow-up question. She is beset by a "fièvre qui [la] dress[e] contre Lella, contre la maison fermée, contre tous",[632] and continually embodies a notion of "révolte" against the socio-symbolic confines of her existence.[633] However, despite feeling "la houle" time and again, she doesn't find an emancipatory outlet in which to concretize rebellion in the morning after, but rather ponders as to the target of her next revolt: "ma seule lâcheté était la peur de ne pas trouver un jour qui affronter, contre qui me révolter".[634] A potential answer to *this* fear, however, is alluded to through the articulation of a metonymical revolt at the conclusion of the narrative. Dalila, after the deaths of her step-mother and Salim, encounters a young Algerian child being arrested and physically assaulted by the colonial police. The child repeatedly cries out "Ils mentent", echoing Dalila's own repeated revolts throughout the text, in particular those against her stepmother. However, Dalila then asks herself whether "c'était seulement la jeunesse qui prêtait à cette joie les accents de la haine, du désespoir. Si ce n'était pas plutôt une sorte de *grâce* que méritent certains êtres, *certains peuples*".[635] She then says: "J'ai pensé à moi. Avais-je perdu cette grâce ?".[636] Here, then, Dje-

---

630 Ibid, p. 92–93.
631 Slavoj Žižek: *The Indivisible Remainder*. London: Verso 1996, p. 133.
632 Assia Djebar: *Les Impatients*, p. 93.
633 Ibid, p. 38, 56, 83 et passim.
634 Ibid, p. 220.
635 Ibid, p. 238 (emphasis added).
636 Ibid, p. 238.

bar's text seems to tentatively probe the possibility of a subjectivity critical of colonial socio-symbolic structures, which her female protagonist might embody. The probing remains tentative, however, despite the prominence that this introspection is given at the conclusion of the text, as Dalila and the text's treatment of the possibility of revolution fluctuates in "pessimistic" fashion. Dalila still views the act of provocation as "inutile" and the text suggests that the children's symbolic revolt will inevitably be absorbed by colonial space through its description of the reestablishment of the flow of pedestrians: "le flux de la rue s'était refermé sur cette déchirure. Il coulait de nouveau, opaque".[637] Nevertheless, the final lines of the text can be interpreted as indirectly alluding to a colonial trauma, referred to as "un echo", that subjects will compulsively return to, leaving the notion of revolt charged with possibility: "Je venais de comprendre que les villes sont comme les êtres : les passions que l'on croit mortes et l'orgueil qu'on croit vaincu, laissent sur leur visage un écho qu'on ne sait définir".[638]

Thus one does note a progression from *La Soif* to *Les Impatients* in the evocation of a potentially resistant feminine subjectivity. Both texts allude to evolutions in the social status of women but *Les Impatients* seemingly gives a greater, though still limited, sense of women's potential to effect these evolutions in a productive manner. Of course, part of the evolution to which I am referring is political/anticolonial evolution and where *Les Impatients* begins to hint at this factor in the constitution of an emerging feminine subject, *Les Enfants du nouveau monde* draws realist sketches of women's coming to revolutionary consciousness. Furthermore, so far we have seen that Djebar has sought to engage in a reflexive representation of femininity from a distance, through the establishment of deeply flawed protagonists whose tales tell the reader about the socio-symbolic establishment of women without allowing Djebar to perform the "strip-tease intellectuel" that she equates with autobiography. Part of this strip-tease would include, it would seem, revolutionary/anti-colonial significance. For as Djebar stated in an interview in 1968, for her, "Il aurait été indécent de ma part d'utiliser cette vie comme thème. C'était pour moi alors plus que de la politique, plus que la littérature, oh bien plus, la vie la plus quotidienne possible. Erreur, peut-être ? Je n'en sais rien".[639] *Les Enfants du nouveau monde*, then, develops Djebar's representational stance, permits her both to incorporate a greater variety of personal and communal feminine concerns and, as we shall see, produces a continued focus on feminine introspection and socio-historical develop-

---

637 Ibid, p. 238.
638 Ibid, p. 238.
639 Assia Djebar: Le Romancier dans la cité arabe. In : *Europe* No. 474 (October 1968), p. 119.

ment and progression with an elevated sense of agency connected to a skilfully rendered subjective development.

6.3 Psychic/Subjective Progression and Emancipatory Learning

Though as a whole, in its following of the fictional events of 24th May 1956 in the small town of Blida, *Les Enfants du nouveau monde* develops a range of feminine perspectives that facilitate an investigation of a feminine society in flux far more effectively than the articulations of singular narrators' turmoil in *La Soif* and *Les Impatients*, in its earliest scenes the text produces a strong dichotomy between masculine agents and feminine spectators, as the women shelter from a French bombardment in their homes whilst keeping sight of the combat taking place on the mountainside: "il se trouve toujours une femme, jeune, vieille, peu importe, qui prend la direction du chœur : exclamations, soupirs, silences gémissants quand la montagne saigne et fume, couplets passionnés : 'Cette fois, ils ne les auront pas !'".[640] However, women's discursive consignment to passivity is then almost immediately overthrown by an illumination of the agency of women whom one might first consider precisely to be passive spectators. This monograph has illuminated in its introduction and in the chapter on Mohammed Dib, with, for example, the help of Djamila Amrane's and Natalya Vince's studies, the scale of women's involvement in active combat and in other revolutionary activities during the Algerian war. What is particularly engaging about *Les Enfants* is that while Djebar does not shy away from representing women as revolutionary *militantes*, she also produces an unprecedented focus on the difficulty and bravery associated both with women's entry into the war and, interestingly, with the activation of an emancipatory feminine agency which can be read as constitutive of this ingress. This focus takes as its initial nucleus poignant third person testimony of feminine suffering and sequestration stemming from traditionalist and masculinist symbolic divisions and violence. One of the more intriguing instances of this kind of evocation can be noted in an early conversation between Chérifa, a subdued and thoughtful protagonist who will later discover a will to act, and Youssef, her revolutionary second husband. First, a masculine inner uncertainty is evoked by an intimate omniscient narrator who employs increasing shades of free indirect discourse, intensifying the proximity

---

[640] Assia Djebar: *Les Enfants du nouveau monde*. Paris: Points 2012 (Originally published 1962), p. 14.

between reader and figure to a point where we have direct access to Youssef's thoughts:

> C'est Youssef qui, du vivant de Lla Aicha, a dû marier ses trois sœurs pour leur assurer la sécurité ; maintenant, il est libéré de toute obligation. Sa dernière sœur, Zineb, lui avait causé quelque souci: parce qu'elle avait pu faire des études, apprendre le français, aller au collège jusqu'à seize ans, elle avait difficilement accepté ensuite de se retrouver cloîtrée comme les autres, puis un jour, mariée à un inconnu... des tiraillements, c'était normal... Non, inutile de se mentir, pense Youssef, cela avait été plus grave [...][641]

Youssef then asks himself, à propos of Zineb whom societal norms have forced him to marry off, "'Suis-je vraiment responsable ?' [...] 'Ai-je vraiment gâché la vie de cette sœur que j'aime ?'".[642] The cause of his subjective disturbance is then given greater depth and resonance by his subsequent musing on Chérifa's allusions to her first marriage, in particular on the communal aspect of her suffering under the conjugal yoke:

> Il l'avait comprise ensuite, il se le rappelait, lorsque Chérifa lui avait tant parlé d'elle, de son premier mari, avec cette voix absente qu'elle prenait alors et ces yeux durs qui lui faisaient mal, lui qui croyait apercevoir dans leur eau profonde l'image de femmes multiples auxquelles on avait pris, à jamais, leur destin et qui se débattaient....[643]

Here the scale of a structural oppression to which a feminine community has been submitted is poignantly alluded to, while the possibility of emancipation is delicately maintained both by the verb "se debattre", which is intensified by the inclusion of an ellipsis, and subsequently by the awareness of suffering that Chérifa embodies. For it is Chérifa's increasing comprehension of the nature of the symbolic pacts that condition the parameters of women's behaviour, and of the shared feminine implication in the struggle against them, that represents the basis for acts that would demonstrate true agency in socio-historical progression. As the narrative progresses, Djebar's text makes clearer the linkage between emancipation and awareness as Chérifa wrestles with the decision of leaving the house, the *haram*, to seek out her husband in order to inform him that the colonial police are seeking to have him arrested. Indeed, like some of the women of Feraoun's novels, Chérifa can be interpreted as a feminine agent who begins to discern in the Phallus, in the presumed rectitude of the desire of the Other, the filler of its very inconsistency; the fact, in Žižek's words, that "the field of the

---

641 Idem, p. 47.
642 Idem, p. 48.
643 Idem, p. 48.

Other is inherently inconsistent", that the rules of social exchange are not coherent or fixed and are thus permissive of authentic acts of autonomy.[644] Indeed, Chérifa's decision to act is evocative of Sartre's ethics of authenticity in *Cahiers d'un morale* where he states that "originellement, l'authenticité consiste à refuser la quête de l'être, parce que je ne suis jamais *rien*".[645] As Yvan Salzmann writes, "l'exigence de l'authenticité ne porte pas sur la nature propre, mais sur les actes créateurs de chacun".[646] Chérifa begins to act in subjective evolution only where she realises that her "essence" in a Sartrian sense, the belief in her belonging to a group characterised by their structural oppression, does not determine her existence. At the same time, Djebar's text makes clear that this movement to authenticity is fraught with existential struggle and also works ultimately toward a communal goal:

> Pour une épouse heureuse vivant au cœur d'une maison d'où elle ne sort pas, selon les traditions, comment prendre, pour la première fois, la décision d'agir ? Comment "agir ?" Mot étrange pour celle qu'emprisonne l'habitude (et cette habitude, la ressentir tel un instinct, comme si toutes les femmes de sa famille, des maisons voisines, des générations précédentes la lui avaient léguée en héritage, sous forme de sagesse impérative) [...][647]

Despite her profound quandary, Chérifa does act: "Elle a décidé. Immobile, elle vibre pourtant: une flèche au début de sa trajectoire".[648] In acting, she forms the beginning of a fresh arc of self-construction, leaving behind the physical and psychic bonds of domestic space and venturing out into the public space of Blida to warn Youssef.

Thus, in its articulation of Chérifa's subjective evolution, Djebar's novel develops a complex image of women's emancipatory development that depends on a tension between the individual's act and her awareness of its difficulty stemming from the embedding of the individual in a community whose symbolic limits have been determined by masculinist discourses. In so doing, Djebar's text sheds light on the importance of subjective revolutions, of individual emancipations from symbolic determination, that do not pertain directly to active engagement in the war of independence. At the same time, the text forms connections between liberatory acts and perspectives like those of Chérifa, and acts and perspectives that may be perceived as more conventionally revolutionary. The pro-

---

644 Slavoj Žižek: Woman is One of the Names-of-the-Father, p. 27.
645 Jean-Paul Sartre: *Cahiers pour une morale*. Paris: Gallimard 1983, p. 492.
646 Yvan Salzmann: *Sartre et l'authenticité: vers une éthique de la bienveillance réciproque*. Geneva: Labor et Fides 2000, p. 120.
647 Assia Djebar: *Les Enfants du nouveau monde*, p. 120.
648 Idem, p. 121.

tagonist Salima, as an official agent of revolutionary politics, is arrested by the colonial police and the reader is invited to draw parallels between her introspection in prison and the tension between individual and community that act as a foundation for conceptions of Chérifa's socio-historical and subjective progression as a feminine agent.

Whilst in prison, Salima considers the pride she feels at her deviation from social norms as she avoids becoming "comme tant d'autres une femme effacée et douce".[649] Her "orgueil", however, is not derived in isolation but stems from a bond engaged principally with a feminine community but also with fellow revolutionary agents who are male, breaking down a dichotomy which might subtend women's symbolic relegation:[650]

> Un orgueil, elle s'en rend compte, quelque peu anonyme, qui ne lui vient pas du fond d'elle-même (car si elle avait écouté son être secret, ce n'était sans doute qu'une eau calme, passive qui aurait reflué en elle, qui l'aurait engloutie, qui sait), mais des autres : de sa mère veuve, usée par les multiples travaux qu'elle acceptait autrefois dans les demeures bourgeoises, de son frère dans sa prison, condamné depuis six ans et transporté quelque part en France, de toutes les femmes muettes qu'elle connaissait.[651]

Indeed, the text included in brackets would make clear that without an antithesis from which to set the self apart (an oppressive feminine positionality), and without the knowledge of the struggles of others, the self would undergo no evolution, would be "engloutie", drowned. Indeed, Salima goes on to affirm: "Je ne suis qu'un maillon de la chaîne".[652] This statement's self-diminishing tone belies the fundamental importance of women's entering into a metonymic relation with the symbolic nation whilst also demonstrating the capacity for women's symbolic participation to counter previous arrangements, going beyond the submissive symbolic participation that I outlined in my chapter on Feraoun.

Moreover, in contrast to these progressive protagonists, Djebar's text also produces a figure whose egotism sees her complicit with colonial rule and whose disinterest regarding others, in particular her countrywomen and men, sees her achieve no authentic emancipatory act. Though she purports to reject the dominion of the society in which she lives: "Je m'en moque ! Insultes, malédictions, je m'en moque ! Les gens comme toi, la ville entière, je m'en moque !",

---

649 Idem, p. 93.
650 One can see Salima's "orgueil" as initially echoing Dehbia's "égoïsme" in Feraoun's *Les Chemins qui montent*.
651 Idem, p. 94.
652 Idem, p. 94.

she exists, like Nadia of *La Soif*, in subjection to Western colonial mores.[653] She appears as trapped in a reflective relationship, a fascination with an unsustainable and inauthentic ideal-ego of individualist rebellion. As illustration of this, the reader notes echoes of Fanon's *Peau noire, masques blancs*, where she exclaims: "Les Arabes, je les hais",[654] having just determined her wish to be seen as an *évoluée:* "'[...] elle pourrait être de Marseille, ou d'Arles...'). Touma aime que les hommes la voient ainsi ; elle y voit une forme d'estime".[655] Furthermore, *Les Enfants* complicates a progressive/regressive dichotomy in its drawing of female protagonists by attaching a degree of sympathy to descriptions both of Touma's aimless "rebellion", as we read for example that "elle veut vivre, vivre... épuiser l'ardeur qui l'étouffe",[656] and of her persecution by her brother Tawfik. And, even more effective in this complication, is the inclusion of the protagonist Lila, whose initial inertia resulting from the departure of her revolutionary husband Ali is overturned, producing a "réveil" which is itself ambiguous in its psychic/subjective grounding.[657] For despite Lila's eventual arrest for harbouring the young revolutionary Bachir, whose intervention seemingly provokes a final break from an ego fixation where we read that "'Le réel', cela avait été si longtemps pour elle un homme qu'elle aimait, cet amour lui-même ; pour Bachir, il était l'avenir, avec ses hésitations",[658] the text alludes to a naivety which continues to subtend her subjectivity, even at the close of the novel:

> *Elle se trompe:* elle croit réapprendre le défi alors que tout, brusquement, derrière elle, a retrouvé son cours ; devant l'épreuve qui commence, elle pense qu'une seule certitude l'attend : le triomphe de son orgueil et la fierté du duel, alors qu'il s'agit désormais de sa naissance, – ou d'un véritable réveil.[659]

Thus even at the apotheosis of her revolutionary involvement, the text undermines Lila's comprehension of the charged dynamic at play in subjective development between an individual focus, "son orgueil", and her "naissance" into a contiguous relationship with other revolutionary subjects. Consequently, it can be argued that whilst *Les Enfants* alludes to the radical importance of an awareness of the mechanics of resistance and the import of the Other, the figure of the

---

653 Idem, p. 175.
654 Idem, p. 129.
655 Idem, p. 128.
656 Idem, p. 174.
657 Idem, p. 271.
658 Idem, p. 254.
659 Idem, p. 271 (emphasis added).

Symbolic order, it does not make the rose-tinted claim that all Algerian women possess a special and perfected understanding of their development during the late-colonial period.[660] Jane Hiddleston writes that "[t]he transformations undergone by characters such as Lila and Chérifa constitute not a straightforward celebration of individual agency and emancipation, but rather a gradual process of negotiation between the singular self and various collective demands".[661] I would go further and argue that *Les Enfants* investigates precisely the fraught production of individual agency, and, echoing Feraoun's evocations of *Mitsein*, alludes to the notion that a true expression of individual agency can only exist precisely when in tension with collective demands, with the Other. It is with regards to this investigation that one can understand *Les Enfants* as a epistemologically "revolutionary" step forward in women's writing on Algerian women. Indeed, one might be tempted to view the characters of Touma, Lila, and Salima as signifiers for the different levels of productive subjective emancipation present in *La Soif*, *Les Impatients* and *Les Enfants* respectively, with Salima's developed comprehension of the productive tension between self and Other representing the telos for the feminine subject. Though all three representatives are individuals subject to social formation, they each display, like their corresponding novels, varying degrees of awareness of the importance of the Other and of others for the emancipation of the feminine individual. As this chapter moves its focus back to Djebar's novels as formal expressions of reflexive representation, it will be seen to be productive to think through her representation of subjective evolution in relation to a progression in literary form which is metaphorically concordant with the Lacanian production of the subject, from the mirror stage to entry into and relation with the Symbolic order.

6.4 Shattered Mirrors

In Djebar's two earliest works, as this chapter has been investigating, the narratives offer protagonists with whom reader identification is deliberately stymied and through whom the text generates meaning with recourse largely to invited symptomatic readings, prompting the reader to conceive of "remedies", of

---

[660] Interestingly, Djebar also seemingly implicates herself in this status of continuing, imperfect self-conception as Jeanne-Marie Clerc on page 56 of *Assia Djebar: écrire, transgresser, résister* reports that Djebar understood an autobiographical bond between herself and Lila: "La position de Lila, à côté et, en même temps dedans et témoin, c'est un peu moi".

[661] Jane Hiddleston: *Assia Djebar: Out of Algeria*. Liverpool: Liverpool University Press 2006, p. 38–39.

more productive modes of subjectivity. The resistance, or lack thereof, that the characters of Nadia and Dalila embody implies a dominion of social determinants in their constitution which renders a will for rebellion somewhat inert. Nonetheless, both texts function to produce an intimacy between reader and central protagonist that is based on their continual introspection, on a focus on the self. Thus Djebar's literary beginnings perform reflexive representation by denying an authorial connection with their protagonists whilst simultaneously reproducing an autobiographical stance, a first-person reflexive narration. It is interesting to note therefore that despite the denial constituted by the severance of identification with the protagonists Nadia and Dalila, there are strong autobiographical resonances that can nonetheless be detected. Beyond the obvious connections (socio-economic standing, youth etc.), one might note the focus on an enjoyment of languorous relaxation in the texts and Djebar's admission in a 1962 interview that "journées indolentes" and "longues rêveries" constitute her ideal *mode de vie*.[662] More interestingly one might also point to the similarities between Dalila's road accident in *Les Impatients* and the autobiographical evocation of her suicide attempt in her 2007 work *Nulle part dans la maison de mon père*.[663] The similarities that one may note between the two incidents are particularly striking when on considers that Djebar herself stated of her own attempt that "[c]ette crise a éclaté en 1953, tout juste un an avant le début de la guerre d'Algérie. Depuis, je l'avais complètement occultée".[664] If one thinks of *Les Impatients* as part of Djebar's initial fervent rejection of autobiographical representativity it is interesting to think of the evocation of a similar incident as the return of the repressed, both in the sense of a re-emergence of the specific event in the text and also the drive to incorporate implication in the feminine community which Djebar's texts allude to. The fashion in which Djebar's literarity evolves from *Les Impatients* to *Les Enfants* can be understood as a productive displacement of this drive to incorporate implication, in that a privileged specular speaking subject is removed in favour of a multitude of perspectives on others which nonetheless permit reflexive representation with greater richness and sincerity. In *Les Enfants* we read a representation of Algerian women in which seemingly disparate members of the community play mutually-enriching roles in the development of a conception of identity which marks separated individuals. Indeed, what is at stake in this evolution is a movement from a specular mode of repre-

---

662 Gabrielle Rolin: Une femme du nouveau monde: interview with Assia Djebar. In: *Jeune Afrique* No. 87 (June 1962), p. 28.
663 Assia Djebar: *Nulle part dans la maison de mon père*. Paris: Fayard 2007.
664 Hamid Barrada/Tirthankar Chanda: Assia Djebar Interview. In: *Jeune Afrique* (30 March 2008). Available at http://www.jeuneafrique.com/57084/archives-thematique/assia-djebar/.

sentation in which we gaze upon flickers of Djebar's reflection, and a shattering of a singular mirror, forming glittering representative shards in *Les Enfants*.

The specular nature of Djebar's literary form in *La Soif* and *Les Impatients* is mirrored in the myriad references to reflective surfaces and the characters' engagement with them. *La Soif* begins with Nadia's consideration of herself in a mirror after Hassein mocks her for her interstitial identity, stating that "[à] cette frontière entre deux civilisations, vous ne savez que faire, en pauvre petit produit de fabrication mixte que vous êtes !".[665] We subsequently read that "[à] la maison, intriguée, j'ai contemplé dans la glace mon nouveau visage : il pleuvait".[666] In *Les Impatients*, Dalila spends an even greater amount of the text looking at herself in mirrored surfaces, from the murky waters of the docks where she spends time with Salim, to the eyes of her lover, to actual looking glasses. Dalila even performs a sustained meditation on mirrors and their importance for her in her subjective development:

> J'ai d'abord pensé à me contempler dans la glace ; je le faisais toujours dans ce que je croyais être les grands moments de ma vie. Je pense maintenant à tous les miroirs des chambres oubliées, qui réfléchirent mes différents visages : celui de la gaieté, de l'insouciance ; celui de la gravité et celui du rêve.[667]

Indeed, it should not be overlooked that the articulation of feminine protagonists who self-scrutinise, literally and metaphorically, itself represents an important first step in the development of an Algerian feminine literature that seeks to represent a community long excluded from the symbolic agora. Similarly it should be remembered that though the Imaginary register of the mirror stage is considered a regressive, non-productive order when set alongside the privileged Symbolic, it remains the primordial stage of subjectivation. As Lacan's famous title makes clear, "[l]e stade du miroir" must firstly be considered "comme formateur de la fonction du Je",[668] as the organisation of a discrete subject position from which one may begin to make utterances about the world and oneself. Furthermore, it is interesting to note that though the major change in representational form that *Les Enfants* incorporates consists of an expansion of a singular focus, the figure of Lila allows Djebar a degree of personal self-inscription. Beyond Djebar's own declaration cited in footnote 660, one can read, for example, a charming intertext with the famous autobiographical *Fillette arabe*

---

665 Assia Djebar: *La Soif*, p. 31.
666 Ibid, p. 32.
667 Assia Djebar: *Les Impatients*, p. 218.
668 Jacques Lacan: *Écrits*, p. 93.

scene from *L'Amour, la fantasia* where the narrator reports that "Lila se souvient de son père qui lui portait son cartable et la conduisait, main dans la main, à l'école primaire [...]".[669]

However, the movement away from a singular specular form to a collection of perspectives delivered by a third person narrator remains Djebar's central formal evolution and echoes Lacan's understanding of the subject as revealed in an unconscious that is Other. If we think of the location and mode of narration in *Les Enfants* as metaphor for the unconscious subject of Lacan's theory we can argue that its movement between and into different characters – through free indirect speech, for example, – recreates the identification of key signifiers in simple, displaced, and condensed forms, in the analysis of the analysand. And, Djebar's form amplifies this productive understanding of subjectivity through other narrative techniques that highlight the dependence of the self on the Other. Firstly, each chapter is headed with the name of a protagonist, foregrounding the divergence of perspectives in the text and the importance of each to the narrative, literary and socio-historical, of all "les enfants du nouveau monde". Moreover, Djebar's focus on a feminine community is maintained in the chaptering of the text as five of the nine chapters are headed with the names of feminine protagonists, including the first four. However, Djebar also incorporates masculine signifiers and indeed markers of colonial influence, including the name of Touma's young French suitor, Bob. Thus, *Les Enfants*, though focusing on the subjective and socio-historical evolution of women, formally acknowledges the importance of all figures in the symbolic domain to the generation of an Other that feeds the unconscious of subjects in a community. As Samo Tomšič writes in his Lacanian/Deleuzian criticism of Ferdinand de Saussure's presumed dichotomy between the unity of *lalanguage*, the system of language, and "the multiplicity of 'private' languages (*lalangue*)", "linguistics has done a lot of harm, notably when it separated language from production".[670] The unsteady production of language, attempts to generate meaning with shifting signifiers, cannot be separated from the reigning structure of the language of the Symbolic order, which in turn constitutes the Other for individual subjects.

What's also interesting about these headings is that they subvert the reader's assumption that the signifier will indicate the subject to be focused on. On the contrary, with the exceptions of chapters II (Lila) and V (Hakim) which begin with an investigation of the subjectivity of the protagonist stated in the heading, the other chapters do not begin with a direct connection between title signifier

---

[669] Assia Djebar, *Les enfants du nouveau monde*, p. 182.
[670] Samo Tomšič: *The Capitalist Unconscious: Marx and Lacan*. London: Verso 2015, p. 38.

and protagonist to be articulated in their evocation of a plurality of actors. One can thus compare the mode of narration to the location of signifiers in analysis specifically in relation to the mechanism of metonymy that Freud first established as displacement and that Lacan later translated through the work of Roman Jakobson to a linguistic domain. The protagonists of the text are presented as linked by implication in a shared symbolic structure or "language" by their juxtaposition with each other and with the dominant signifier that is the chapter heading. Though the reader does note metaphorical resonances where in particular the feminine subject "s'est substitué à l'autre en prenant sa place dans la chaîne signifiante",[671] it is in le *"mot à mot"* of connections,[672] the contiguity of differing individual actions and personal signifiers that the text encourages the reader to see a development of an understanding of feminine subjectivity in the text's historical context.

This contiguity is also reflected in the coming together of protagonists' narrative threads, in their unconscious adjacency. An early example of this comes where Lila's gazing out of her apartment windows alights upon the "file d'hommes" that constitutes the funeral cortège of Youssef's mother.[673] Other examples include Touma's noticing but not identifying Chérifa as the latter makes her way to Youssef, and Bachir's meeting Lila after setting fire to Ferrand's colonial farm. This final meeting of narrative threads results in a knot of understanding, a retrospective *point de capiton* for Lila of whom we read the following:

> [...] la nuit, cette halte merveilleuse, signifiait pour elle le bonheur, l'oublie et quoi d'autre encore... peut-être cet instant secret où l'on se retrouve dans une unité profonde, dans un mouvement de soi-même où tous les courants si désordonnés, si divers se rejoignent soudain, flux unique de l'âme – mais aussi où l'on se découvre en même temps qu'un autre, plus tard elle pensa "les autres".[674]

Can this prise de conscience not be taken precisely as metaphor for the formal evolution at stake in Djebar's early novels, from the specular to the Symbolic, discovering aspects of the self through a range of others whose generation of signification itself constitutes an Other that partially and necessarily determines the self?

Two pages after Lila's confrontation with the inherent connection between self-discovery and the uncovering of "les autres", one finds a metatextual allu-

---

[671] Jacques Lacan: *Écrits*, p. 507.
[672] Jacques Lacan: *Écrits*, p. 506.
[673] Assia Djebar, *Les Enfants du nouveau monde*, p. 61.
[674] Ibid, p. 251.

sion which focuses the reader's attention on Lila's proximity to Djebar as a reflexive scribe of a feminine community as one reads:

> On parlait tant, dans les livres qu'elle avait lus, du plaisir, de l'amour, de la solitude, du sexe, de toutes ces glaces déformantes où les auteurs choisissent de prolonger leurs personnages. Elle se mit à rêver à l'expérience que pourrait réserver la tentative de saisir ces ombres à travers un prisme différent : celui de la faim, de ses dents, de son ventre, de tous ses lyrismes.[675]

This metatextuality also, however, suggests an awareness of the inability of one subject, irrespective of her belonging to a certain community, feminine or other, to articulate, to represent, all members of that community, thus replicating a common concern in the texts that this study has investigated. What is also interesting about the above citation, however, is that it obliquely begins to suggest the danger inherent in a concretisation of a belief in the self's implication in the Other. For the condition of writing through a prism of perspective is evocative of the understandings of Althusser and Žižek in their writings on ideology as "the primordial form of *narrative*, which serves to occult some original deadlock".[676] This is to say that ideology, in its production of psychic coherence as a primordial fantasy, stabilizes the Symbolic, acts as a kind of epistemological fly-paper for circulating signifiers, reducing the incoherence of the world to a comprehensible narrative. Thus, as the next section will explore, it is important to analyse whether the decentering that Djebar's literary development in *Les Enfants* produces runs the risk nevertheless of reproducing a unifying fiction where all members are necessarily bound to an inchoate, though stable, sense of an ideal future nationhood. The question to be asked is to what extent is "le nouveau monde" a stable and unproblematised function of ideology and to what degree does it overshadow the texts' comprehension of "les enfants"? If the Other itself begins to become conflated with the ideal of a nation to come, and if this nation is insufficiently problematised, do allusions to its determination of the self fall back into an unproductive specular relation?

6.5 Ideological Evolution

As has been previously mentioned, it is surprising when reading *La Soif* and *Les Impatients* to discover that so little attention is paid by the texts to immediate

---

675 Ibid, p. 253.
676 Slavoj Žižek: *The Plague of Fantasies*. London: Verso 2008, p. 11.

and physical colonial violence. Despite the texts' allusions to the potentially pernicious effects of colonial mimicry and the latter briefly hinting at political rebellion at its close, their deficit in this regard is puzzling. At the same time, as has been noted above, this deficit can be attributed to a motivated decision taken by Djebar, rather than to a lack of knowledge or interest, with her political precocity at the time being well documented. Consequently, when analysing an ideological progression legible in Djebar's early works, the focus must be on her discovery and production of a literary form in which to articulate a positive feminine relationship with politics and the nation. The decentering at work in *Les Enfants*, the displacement of the primacy of a specular subject, seemingly allows Djebar to incorporate more content, more experiences, perspectives and attributes which encourage reader–protagonist and protagonist–author identification as it eschews the "strip-tease intellectuel" that she equates with autobiography. Part of this content is the political, the revolutionary, and thus the movement from *La Soif* and *Les Impatients* to *Les Enfants* represents a radical expansion of the representation of women's interaction with political ideology. However, while the displacement brought about by a mobile multiplicity of interconnected figures, by an articulation of a representative socio-symbolic order, represents a productive evolution in Djebar's form, it remains important to think through the extent to which this notion of an Other is itself, in Kirsten Campbell's terms, a "social fiction" and whether this "social fiction" leaves room for an important "pessimism", for a disruption that we can locate in the majority of the works explored in this monograph.

Kirsten Campbell through her notion of "social fictions", articulates a relationship between the Imaginary and the Symbolic that is particularly germane here. Herself citing John Lechte, Campbell writes that "[s]ocial fictions are both imaginary and symbolic. In social fictions, the Symbolic order is given content by the Imaginary: 'at the level of the Imaginary, the subject believes in the transparency of the Symbolic; it does not recognise the lack of reality in the Symbolic...in effect, the Imaginary is where the subject mis-recognises (*méconnait*) the nature of the Symbolic'".[677]

Where Lechte is referring to the Symbolic as a whole, including the innumerable possibilities for identification, with Djebar what is under investigation is an inchoate notion of a socio-symbolic order itself and whether it is invested with the referent of a unitary and unified revolutionary nation, or whether this social telos is in fact undermined in the text itself. Again, as has been alluded to on

---

[677] Kirstin Campbell: *Jacques Lacan and Feminist Epistemology.* London: Routledge 2004, p. 120–121.

several occasions in this book, this kind of a discussion about the presence or otherwise of a rose-tinted outlook on a coherent post-colonial future is particularly important for the study of the representation of Algerian women during the period leading up to independence considering the failures of the revolution to deliver a promised social justice. Dib, Kateb, Mammeri, and Feraoun all use literary form to suggest the possibility of failure in the literary and future socio-political representation of women within their evocations of the nascent nation.

Initially when one reads *Les Enfants*, however, especially considering the stark difference between its concerns and those of *La Soif* and *Les Impatients*, the teleology that the text displays and that the different protagonists share, causes one to read the text as following a dynamic of rationalization and a conception of historical development as outlined by Dipesh Chakrabarty and applied to the text by Gordon Bigelow. Bigelow writes that "[t]his breaking and remaking [of social structures found in the text] is a model for the emergence of the "new world" of Djebar's title, a new world of autonomous horizontally affiliated subjects, linked through rational participation in the structures of citizenship".[678] One can also more precisely understand the goal of the "new world" as a marker for a renewed mode of subjective comprehension of a shared socio-symbolic order, which might reify solidarity based on inter-dependence in identity and subjectivity. Indeed, one notes this renewed subjective mode's omnipresence as the text's telos and its reflection in the texts' fragmented yet unified form. Consequently one might perhaps suggest that *Les Enfants* represents the pinnacle of Djebar's interpellation into a revolutionary ideology of the nation to come. For one can make the argument that *Les Enfants* unveils, in the logic of its progression and its emphatic implication of the self in the Other, a notion of a feminine community that is tied up with an ideal of future nationhood which to some extent betrays its pre-independence conception, which subscribes somewhat to the hype that the FLN would establish "l'édification d'une République Algérienne, libre, démocratique et sociale, qui ne soit pas en contradiction avec les principes islamiques".[679] Within this conception of "une République Algérienne, libre, démocratique et sociale", lie the seeds of belief in women's future equality, bolstered by unprecedented implication in national struggle. The echoes of Fanon's feminine remodelling that are present in the description of Chérifa's emergence into the outside world, allude to this specific interpellation which would, to a large extent, be disappointed in post-independence Algeria.

---

[678] Gordon Bigelow: Revolution and Modernity: Assia Djebar's "Les Enfants du nouveau monde", p. 18.
[679] Idem, p. 18.

Nevertheless, one can also argue that Djebar's project does maintain aspects of what might be considered a traumatic "real" kernel that might disrupt the free-flow of evolving yet coherent social relations that constitute the ideal of the nation. While it would seem that the feminine community, perhaps with the exception of Touma, acts within the logic of a national quest to confront and overcome the symbolic and physical challenges associated with revolutionary emancipation, there are numerous figures of masculinity whose conduct and perspectives demonstrate the text's rejection of a notion of an uncomplicated post-revolutionary socio-symbolic exchange. One might first cite, for example, the reaction to Chérifa's Fanonian entry into public space encapsulated in the figure of Chicou-le-vrai, one of the two town drunks:

> "Je voudrais qu'elle me regarde !" répète en écho son cœur, comme si, à travers les premières limbes d'alcool, cette ombre de femme voilée qui passe avec majesté est venue pour éteindre ses rages. "Qu'elle me regarde !" gémit-il en s'arrêtant de jouer.[680]

Here we have echoes of the obsessional mode of desire evoked in Kateb's *Nedjma*, wherein the subject ignores the desire of the Other, including the bearer of the *objet petit a*. A similarly pernicious masculine approach to women is critically outlined by the behaviour and reported thoughts of Tawfik and Yahia in relation to Tawfik's sister. Where Chicou-le-vrai's conduct is not presented as a function of a specific tradition, Tawfik and Yahia appear to be driven by an interpellation into masculinist and pseudo-religious structures. Tawfik murders his sister for a perceived disregard of familial honour, or *nif*, due to her relationships with European men. In the aftermath of the murder, the text outlines a brief history of the effect of manifestations of masculinist honour structures on Tawfik's logic, encapsulated in the phrase "J'avais une tache sur moi, et je l'ai effacée... Je portais une souillure sur moi, je m'en suis purifié".[681] The phrase is revealed to be the echo of a phrase overheard in childhood: "'J'avais une tache sur moi... Je portais une souillure', ainsi a parlé, lui a-t-on raconté quand il était enfant, celui dont l'honneur s'est trouvé offensé par sa fille qui s'est donnée à un étranger, sur la route".[682] One might compare the continuing influence of honour structures here to the inner suffering of Amer in Feraoun's *Les Chemins qui montent*, or to the unsteady conclusions in the work of Kateb, and one might also see Salim's assault on Dalila in *Les Impatients* as a result of a concomitant sense of entitlement as regards control of a feminine other. As to Yahia's reaction to Tou-

---

680 Assia Djebar, *Les Enfants du nouveau monde*, p. 124.
681 Idem, p. 261.
682 Idem, p. 261.

ma's murder, Djebar produces a troubling representation laced with irony where we read the following:

> "L'heure de la justice" grommelle-t-il encore ; puis il chasse tout de son esprit : cette mort, un incident ; ces jours de peur et de trouble qui commencent, moments éphémères ; "seul Dieu... l'Unique... le *Miséricordieux*..." commence-t-il devant son tapis [...][683]

The contrast drawn between justice and pity underlines the sad state of contradiction which characterises the episteme of the fanatical religious figure. Moreover, the prevalence of a belief in symbolic justice and the disturbing, unethical misinterpretation of a religious imperative to pity is emphasised in the reaction of the crowd surrounding her body: "('son frère ! – oui, c'est son frère ! – il a vengé son honneur ! – Dieu ait pitié de lui !')."[684] It is also interesting to note how this crowd scene is immediately preceded by Amna's beating at the hands of her collaborator husband Hakim and how a secondary equivalence is also drawn with Hakim's killing of the revolutionary Saidi: "Hakim frappe le corps au sol. Il a tué un homme aujourd'hui".[685]

The presence of these kinds of regressive attitudes and behaviours towards women who are to be equated, as indicated in the above citation, with the figures of a nascent revolution, implies a competition of symbolic arrangements in an independent nation, of which a number risk provoking pernicious interpellations, deviations from the happy comprehension of a shared symbolic destiny that *Les Enfants* seemingly extolls. Their positioning at the conclusion of the novel whose chapter headings become dominated by masculine signifiers, as with the positioning of Salim's violence in *Les Impatients*, implies the likely possibility of their continuation alongside the subjective blossoming of figures like Lila, Hassiba and Salima. Indeed, it is interesting to consider their continuation in light of a passage from the novella "Il n'y a pas d'exil", which was constructed from Djebar's personal interactions with Algerian refugees in Tunisia and originally published in January 1960 in *La Nouvelle Critique*, later becoming a section of *Femmes d'Alger dans leur appartement*, the first work published after her literary hiatus. While the text refers repeatedly to the social upheavals engendered by anti-colonial struggle, its narrator remains caught in a web of retrograde social links, an object for exchange through marriage. She states: "Oui, je songeais que tout avait changé et que, pourtant, d'une certaine façon, tout restait par-

---

[683] Idem, p. 213 (emphasis added).
[684] Idem, p. 245.
[685] Idem, p. 242.

eil".[686] At the same time, the text continues to invoke a feminine resistance that appears as an alternate, underdetermined voice, as a disruption to dominant discourse, similar to Dib's Kristevan evocations of feminine voices. Indeed, at the close of the novella we read of the repetition of "une voix de femme qui, par la fenêtre ouverte, montait claire comme une flèche vers le ciel, qui se développait, déployait son vol, un vol ample comme celui de l'oiseau après l'orage [...]".[687]

In the introduction to this chapter, I made reference to Catherine Brun's rejection of the Mostefa Lacheraf complex theory which would claim that the remarkable change in focus from *La Soif* and *Les Impatients* to *Les Enfants* was brought about by her being criticised for a lack of engagement. In *Ces voix qui m'assiègent* Djebar famously refers to her treatment by ideologically motivated critics at the beginning of her literary career:

> Après que j'ai débuté à vingt ans dans la création romanesque avec une tranquille insouciance de jeune fille qui dut paraître à certains des miens scandaleuse, j'ai eu droit, longtemps après, aux attaques des Jdanov, en l'occurrence tel ou tel "penseur" – procureur, égaré sur le terrain laissé alors vacant de la critique littéraire maghrébine.[688]

The satirical moniker "les Jdanov" compares these ideologically motivated critics to the followers of the cultural policies of one of the founders of Soviet Socialist Realism, Andrei Zhdanov. Jonathon Green and Nicholas Karolides report that in 1946, under the direction of Zhdanov, the Central Committee issued a decree on literature, "Resolutions on the Journals *Zvezda* and *Leningrad*". The decree stated that "the task of Soviet literature is to aid the state to educate the youth correctly and to meet their demands, to rear a new generation strong and vigorous, believing in their cause, fearing no obstacles and ready to overcome all obstacles".[689] The repetition of "obstacles" is interesting here in an analysis of ideological progression in Djebar's early works for though her use of "Jdanov" probably referred first and foremost to the didacticism exhorted by her critics, one can come to understand Djebar's work as anti-Jdanov precisely in its important maintenance of these obstacles. It is this maintenance that alludes to a growing

---

[686] Assia Djebar: *Femmes d'Alger dans leur appartement*. Paris: Librairie générale française 2004 [1980], p. 156.
[687] Idem, p. 159.
[688] Assia Djebar: *Ces voix qui m'assiègent*, p. 87.
[689] Jonathon Green/Nicholas Karolides: *The Encyclopedia of Censorship*. New York: Facts on File 2014, p. 667.

productive questioning and maturity in Djebar's literary representation of interactions between individuals, communities and conceptions of the nation.

We have seen that Djebar's pre-independence works, with differing degrees of success, sought to explore women's negotiations of the tensions between rebellion and unity, between the personal and the national, between the self and the Other. We have also noted that the complexity and nuance applied to the exploration of these tensions evolved alongside a stylistic development that arguably existed to permit Djebar greater implication in the community that she depicted. However, just as Djebar rejects the role of *porte-parole*, her early texts, which build to an evocation of the self's implication in and dependence on the Other, maintain subjective distinctions, imply that not all agents will dream the same post-colonial nation-dream and that therefore more progressive feminine voices, literary and political, are needed. This questioning of the stability of a national ideal can be argued to represent the foundation of a profoundly influential literary career in which the undermining of rigid social and historical discourses was a centrepiece. Despite Djebar's discomfort as a singular representative, her importance as a scribe of Algerian femininity whose writing attempted to redress a discursive imbalance in which a weight of masculine testimony rendered female voices imperceptible, is undeniable. In the context of the period under study, Djebar's voice remains the only canonical counterpart to the works of our masculine authors and as such, as a reflexive attempt to come to terms with an inscription of a primordial aspect of identity (gender), is, despite and because of its imperfections, of central importance to the study of Algerian women's representation in the late-colonial period.

7 Conclusion – Women's Postcolonial Representation

Throughout this work it has been intimated that the masculine writers whose late-colonial works have been investigated deployed representational modes that suggested the necessity for Algerian women to themselves inaugurate a literature of feminine self-/representation. That is to say that the undermining of their own *Vertretung* positionality, of their authority and capacity as masculine writers to act as representatives who represent (*darstellen*) women, whether through formal destablisation of narrative voice, depictions which problematise masculine subjectivity, or evocations of masculinist socio-symbolic structures and their resistance to progressive change, constituted an exhortation to Algerian women to address the Bourdieusian dissymmetry in representation first referred to in my introduction. Indeed, as the preceding chapter noted, even Djebar, from the beginning of her literary career, avoided both an autobiographical posture and in particular a *porte-parole* status, populating *Les Enfants du nouveau monde* with a feminine community that might one day represent Algerian womanhood. Concordantly, though the nature of our writers' post-colonial literary production varies greatly, as a whole it retains a tentative and uneasy interest about what remains seemingly, for them, a *necessary* symbolisation, or evocation, of "the Algerian woman".[690]

Mohammed Dib's first novel following independence, for example, *Cours sur le rive sauvage* (1964),[691] extended, to a large extent, the oneiric investigation of feminine otherness in an Algerian milieu commenced in *Qui se souvient de la mer*, whilst once more incorporating masculine confusion and epistemic disarray in the face of womanhood. And, throughout the development of his literary career, from the 1970s up to his death in 2003, his texts continued to investigate femininity whilst rejecting a narrative subjective positioning of privilege or authority.[692] In this way one detects resonances in these texts with the statements made about the ruling, symbolically dominant male "homunculi" of Algeria in his famous congratulatory message to Djebar upon her winning of the Neustadt

---

[690] With the exception, of course, of Feraoun who, as was mentioned before, was assassinated by the OAS in 1962.

[691] Mohammed Dib : *Cours sur le rive sauvage*. Paris: Éditions du Seuil 1964.

[692] See in particular works like *La Danse du roi*. Paris: Éditions du Seuil 1968 and its theatrical rendering *Mille hourras pour une gueuse*. Paris: Éditions du Seuil 1980, *Habel*. Paris: Éditions du Seuil 1977 and *Le Sommeil d'Eve*. Arles: Sindbad 1989.

prize in 1996.[693] In the short tribute he rails against the unwillingness of the Algerian patriarchy to accept a feminine subject position that writes back, ironically stating that "had we suspected the nature of what she [Djebar] was to reveal, we would have blinded ourselves well in advance".[694] He simultaneously articulates his belief in a continuing deficit in the representation of Algerian women by emphasising the singular impact of Djebar's literary interventions, and foregrounds his own implication in a gendered sociological stratum that should perhaps retire from representing the Algerian woman. Indeed, beginning with *Habel* in 1977, Dib's textual movement away from an Algerian milieu altogether, towards European and in particular Finnish novelistic backdrops,[695] can be interpreted as a further yielding of representativity, another allusion to his comprehension of the dangers of *speaking for*.

As for Kateb, he stated, in a 1972 interview with El Hassar Benali, entitled 'Parce que c'est une femme' and published in a 2004 collection of the same name, that "[a]vec *Nedjma*, quand j'ai voulu camper le personnage, je me suis rendu compte à quel point nous ignorons pratiquement tout de nos femmes, de nos propres sœurs. Et avec la mère, la rupture a lieu dès l'enfance".[696]

Nonetheless, in part as a reaction to the political repression of forms of progressive ideational discourse in the public sphere, notably regarding women's position in society; as a riposte to what Benali himself terms "l'interdit qui frappait l'écrivain dans son propre pays, parce qu'il avait des idées considérées comme gênantes sur des sujets politiques qui étaient tabous à l'époque: les femmes, la langue et l'écriture de l'histoire",[697] and in the face of censorship and sabotage,[698] Kateb continued to seek to subvert dominant social fictions through literary form, in particular by staging theatrical productions centring on the deeds of historical Algerian heroines. More specifically, in Zebeïda Chergui's comments in the 'Présentation' to *Parce que c'est une femme*, one can detect

---

693 Mohammed Dib: Assia Djebar, or Eve in Her Garden. In: *World Literature Today*, 70.4 (1996), p. 788.
694 Ibid, p. 788.
695 See Dib's "Nordic Trilogy" of *Les Terrasses d'Orsol*. Arles: Sindbad 1985, *Le Sommeil d'Eve*. Arles: Sindbad 1989 and *Neiges de marbre*. Arles: Sindbad 1990.
696 Kateb Yacine: *Parce que c'est une femme*. Paris: Des Femmes 2004, p. 38.
697 Ibid, p. 21.
698 Kateb notes in a 1982 interview, an extract of which is also included in *Parce que c'est une femme*, that while he was trying to stage his play about the Amazigh leader *La Kahina ou Dihya*, "[c]omme par hasard [...] on a fait passer en même temps à la radio un feuilleton où il était question de La Kahina. Mais elle y était montrée comme une femme assoiffée de sang qui voulait détruire le pays, comme une sorcière." Ibid, p. 18.

a split rationale behind Kateb's historical focus, whose elements are enacted by his post-colonial texts:

> Parce que l'histoire d'autrefois montre à quel point l'histoire présente est petite quand elle prétend prouver les progrès réalisés au regard du passé, parce que les anciennes entreprises de terreur ressemblent à celles d'aujourd'hui et que les expériences se répètent de façon troublante à des siècles ou des kilomètres de distance, Kateb Yacine a consacré toute son œuvre, dès 1968, à porter l'Histoire au théâtre.[699]

On the one hand, then, Kateb seeks to disinter a history of emancipatory struggle that exceeds the confines of "l'histoire présente", highlighting Algerian precedents to those contemporary egalitarian scenarios that might be sought by progressive social agents. Thus, in plays like 1972's *Saout Ennissa, La voix des femmes* and *La Kahina ou Dihya*, eventually performed in 1975 as the prelude to *La guerre de 2000 ans*, the audience is presented with the influence and deeds of celebrated and powerful Algerian women from the thirteenth and seventh centuries respectively. At the same time, however, Kateb's decision to deploy a theatrical form, to, in a sense, have women speak for themselves, albeit through the medium of his scripts, perhaps demonstrates a continued reluctance to produce definitive representations of women, while his post-colonial plays continue to present a connection between masculine symbolic determination and masculinist socio-political control which tallies with both his previous work and the coordinates of post-colonial Algerian society. In both plays cited above the voice of the chief female protagonist is cut short: Dihya is killed and the remainder of her eponymous play proceeds through predominantly masculine articulation building to the affirmation of the 'premier paysan' that a feminine legacy will be received "qu'à nos mains sales, nous les derniers des paysans",[700] while Saout Ennissa ends up taking a back seat in an eventual return to masculine articulation and pernicious political control. Moreover, *Saout Ennissa* also echoes the "pessimistic" tone of Kateb's earlier theatre where one notes the repetition of the famous lines from *Les Ancêtres redoublent de férocité* :

> Dois-je égorger la rose
> Ou consentir
> À sa profanation ?[701]

---

699 Ibid, p. 8.
700 Ibid, p. 66.
701 Ibid, p. 104.

The other side of Kateb's historical rationale thus seems in tune with a continued "pessimistic" stance that is wary of repeated failures in the literary and social symbolisation and representation of gender, where men reduce the agency of women through symbolic objectification.

Mouloud Mammeri's post-colonial work also continues to bear the marks of a pessimistic stance, as the opening lines to his lone post-1962 novel *La Traversée* (1982) make clear:

> Ce qu'ils voulaient, c'était la grande – la grande vie pour tous et, si ce n'était possible, au moins pour eux: il fallait bien commencer par un bout. Au début ils manquaient de références. La grande vie c'est quoi? Puis les plus vieux se rappelèrent celle que jadis ils voyaient mener aux européens, les plus jeunes préférèrent apprendre dans les films ou à la télé. Danser, boire, manier de grands jouets, faire semblant de n'être pas jaloux de sa femme. Parce que la grande vie c'était bien, *mais ils ne pouvaient la mener avec les paysannes boueuses et analphabètes, qui leur avaient servi jusque là d'épouses et d'exutoires. Alors après la guerre, les uns après les autres, ils avaient divorcé. Ils avaient épousé des bourgeoises ripolinées, avec des cheveux eau–oxygénés, plein de bijoux et qui parlaient français en grasseyant les "r"* [...][702]

Indeed, Mammeri's inceptive evocation of a class-based post-colonial relegation suffered by women still ultimately subject to the politico-symbolic power of men, closely echoes the analyses of historians like Djamila Amrane-Minne and Natalya Vince while underlining the late-colonial perspicacity of the writers of our corpus in their embodiment of a "pessimistic" posture that subtends the imperative for a continuing critical search for gender equality.[703]

For though tracking the evolution of a writer like Djebar after Algerian independence demonstrates a magnificent coming to fruition of a call to feminine self-inscription extolled by the abdication from authority present in the writings of our male writers, and while writers like Maïssa Bey, Malika Mokeddem, Leïla Sebbar, Nina Bouraoui and Nawel Louerrad continue a developing feminine Algerian literary tradition today,[704] an expansion and evolution in "women's writing" has not tallied with a mass expansion in feminine social emancipa-

---

[702] Mouloud Mammeri: *La Traversée*. Paris: Plon 1982, p. 7 (emphasis added).
[703] Furthermore, Mammeri's words resonate specifically with this observation recorded by Buthaina Shaaban in an interview with a female veteran of the Algerian war of independence found in *Both Right and Left Handed: Arab Women Talk about their Lives*. London: Women's Press 1998, p. 200: "There were lots of men who married their women comrades in the mountains. Once they came down, however, and got good positions or good jobs in the towns, they divorced their comrades and got married to younger, more presentable, women."
[704] A feminine Algerian literary tradition arguably began in earnest with Djebar's return after hiatus in 1980 with *Femmes d'Alger dans leur appartement*.

tion.[705] This disconnect can at first be viewed as a result of a gap between women's representation and political power structures that have not undergone gendered democratization but have indeed promulgated inequality.[706] Among numerous examples of political regression in egalitarian representation, one often cites the proclamation of the Code de la Famille of 1984 as a milestone in the abrogation of Algerian women's rights. The piece of legislation, though being subject to minor reforms in 2005, made the following requirements law, amongst others:

> [It] makes it a legal duty for Algerian women to obey their husbands, and respect and serve them, their parents, and relatives (Article 39). It institutionalized polygamy and made it the right of men to take up to four wives (Article 8). Women cannot arrange their own marriage contracts unless represented by a matrimonial guardian (Article 11), and they have no right to apply for divorce.[707]

Each provision effectively acts as a reduction of women's symbolic power and a reinforcement of the Bourdieusian gendered dissymmetry that the literary interventions analysed in this monograph have sought to subvert. Thus, in a sense, the "pessimistic" stance identified in our corpus can be argued to have seen the fruits of its labours perish as the warning that it imparted, time and again, was insufficient to militate against the repetition of those structures whose return it would have the reader anticipate and fear.

Furthermore, the subversive potential of literature and of literary and social movements was, of course, severely afflicted by the climate of repression instituted by Algeria's "décennie noire" of the 1990s, during which the country was ravaged by civil war between Islamist and incumbent government factions. One area where this has been particularly emphasised in a non-gender specific sense is in the field of la bande dessinée as comics artists faced the threat of vi-

---

[705] See Jane Hiddleston: *Assia Djebar: Out of Algeria*. Liverpool: Liverpool University Press 2006 for an overview of Djebar's remarkable literary career and analyses of her evocations of Algerian femininity.

[706] Establishing the nature of this gap, in my opinion, certainly represents important future work that is, alas, beyond the scope of this study. However, on one level, just as Natalya Vince has emphasised the importance of class structures for the divisions in women's post-colonial advancement, perhaps one might argue that the field of women's literature, in particular the francophone novel, has not represented a sufficiently effective tool for the dissemination of emancipatory ideas into the public sphere, across all classes.

[707] Zahia Smail Salhi: Algerian Women, Citizenship, and the 'Family Code', p. 30.

olence and even assassination.⁷⁰⁸ Interestingly, however, a recent resurgence of this "minor" form in Algeria, highlighted in a dedicated exposition at the Festival d'Angoulême, 2013 as well as in a pan-Arabic bande dessinée exhibition at le musée de la bande dessinée d'Angoulême in 2018, now presents a particularly inventive and potentially subversive imago-literary framework for progressive ideational discourse generated by women. I mentioned above the artist Nawel Louerrad whose works, in particular *Les Vêpres algériennes* (2012), *Bach to black* (2013) and *Regretter l'absence de l'astre* (2015) have garnered much praise for their investigations of historical trauma and interpersonal histories through an accessible and immediately affective form that retains a great symbolic profundity.⁷⁰⁹ Other female artists whose multi-modal work might augur a future subversive literary movement also include Rim Laredj, Soumeya and Safia Ouarezki and Rym Mokhtari, whose cartoon "Épines", playful yet pertinent for this study, I include below. Dalila Nadjem, *commissaire* of the Festival International de BD d'Alger (FIBDA), which has taken place every year in October from 2008, remarked in 2013 that this new wave of writers/artists "ont une colère, une déchirure, qui ne s'est pas encore extériorisée".⁷¹⁰

Confronted with an electronically interconnected public sphere that privileges the image and the rapid dissemination of enjoyable information, perhaps the sweetened pill of la bande dessinée represents an unusual opportunity for an interaction between a youthful feminine force of creation, progressive ideals, complex literary form and socio-symbolic exchange.

For though the youthful association and organisation that brought about the Arab Spring, in its opposition to the structures and symbols of North Africa's dictatorships, did not result in the unproblematic democratization of its participating nations, its democratization of public symbolic participation and connection, whether through social media, graffiti, slam poetry, or indeed comics, highlights the subversive potential of domains of symbolisation that permit

---

708 See Lazhari Labter's *Panorama de la bande dessinée algérienne 1969–2009*. Algiers: Lazhari Labter Editions 2009, especially Chapter 2, for a particularly informative rendering of the terrorism faced at the time by comics artists.
709 See, for example, my forthcoming chapter '"Monstrez-vous en tutu": Obsessional Identity and Interpersonal Histories in the Post-Traumatic Bandes Dessinées of Nawel Louerrad' in Michael Goodrum/David Hall/Philip Smith, (eds.): *Drawing the Past: Comics and the Historical Imagination*. Jackson: Mississippi University Press 2019.
710 Article and Interview with Dalila Nadjem by Priscille Lafitte: Une nouvelle BD naît en Algérie et s'expose au festival d'Angoulême. In: *France24* (2013): http://www.france24.com/fr/20130131-bande-dessinee-nouvelle-bd-nait-algerie-expose-festival-angouleme .

mass participation.⁷¹¹ Coupled with international participation in forums like FIBDA and collaborative publications like *Monstres* (2011), *Waratha 1 and 2* (2012), *Déchaînés: 12 Aventures du Quotidien* (2013) and *La Nouvelle bande dessinée arabe* (2017) perhaps a future more horizontal, less hierarchical structure of literary production and consumption will contribute to the dissolution of symbolic dissymmetries, including our fundamental gendered division. Indeed, perhaps in this way la bande dessinée can lead by literary example in activating the participative potential of art, famously invoked by another Algerian woman, the Jewish writer Hélène Cixous, in her essay *Le Rire de la Méduse*. As Cixous puts it:

> Il faut que la femme s'écrive: que la femme écrive de la femme et fasse venir les femmes à l'écriture, dont elles ont été éloignées aussi violemment qu'elles ont été de leur corps [...] Il faut que la femme se mette au texte – comme au monde, et à l'histoire – de son propre mouvement.⁷¹²

---

711 In particular, the dissemination, form and content of the incisive social commentary enacted by the slam poetry and rapidly disseminated poetic videos of Taous Aït Mesghat, Toute Fine and Sihem Beniche, in particular their treatments of masculinist structures which interact with the Algerian notion of *hogra* or social injustice, merit further study.
712 Hélène Cixous: Le Rire de la Méduse. In: *L'Arc*, 61 (1975), p. 39.

7 Conclusion – Women's Postcolonial Representation

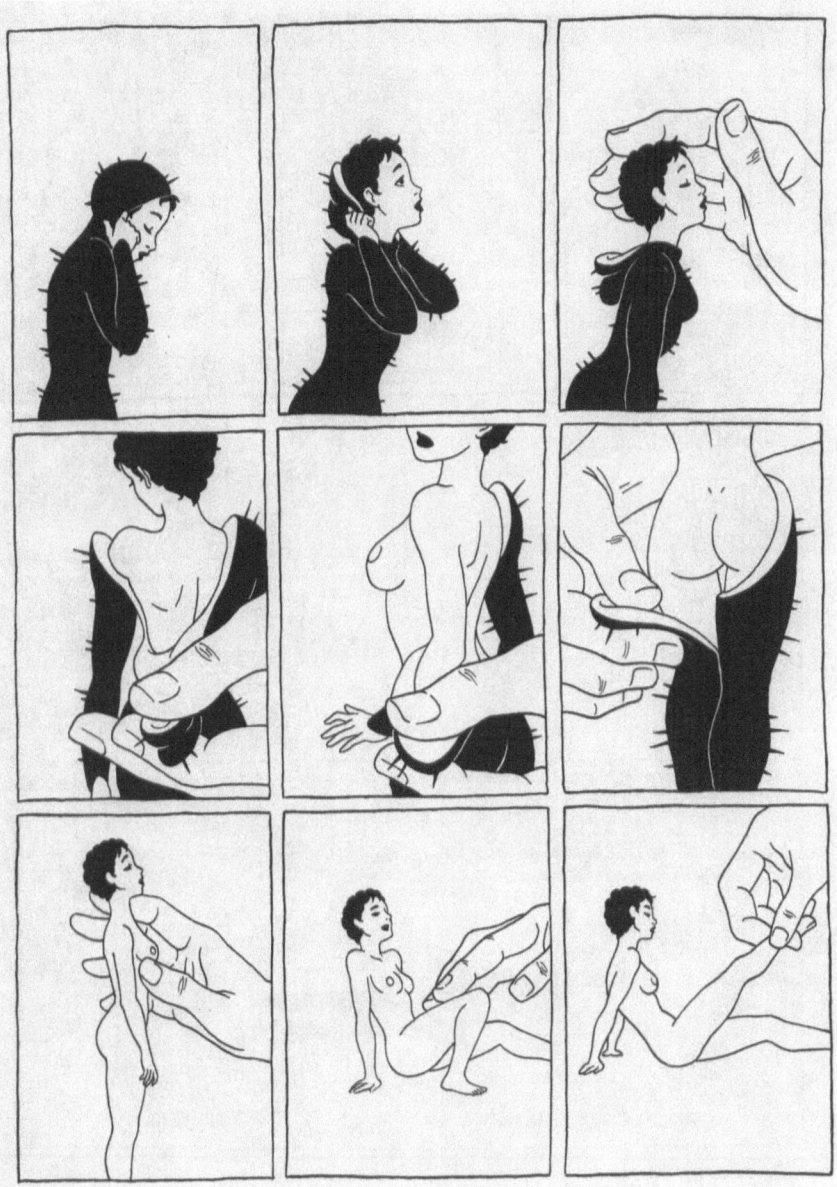

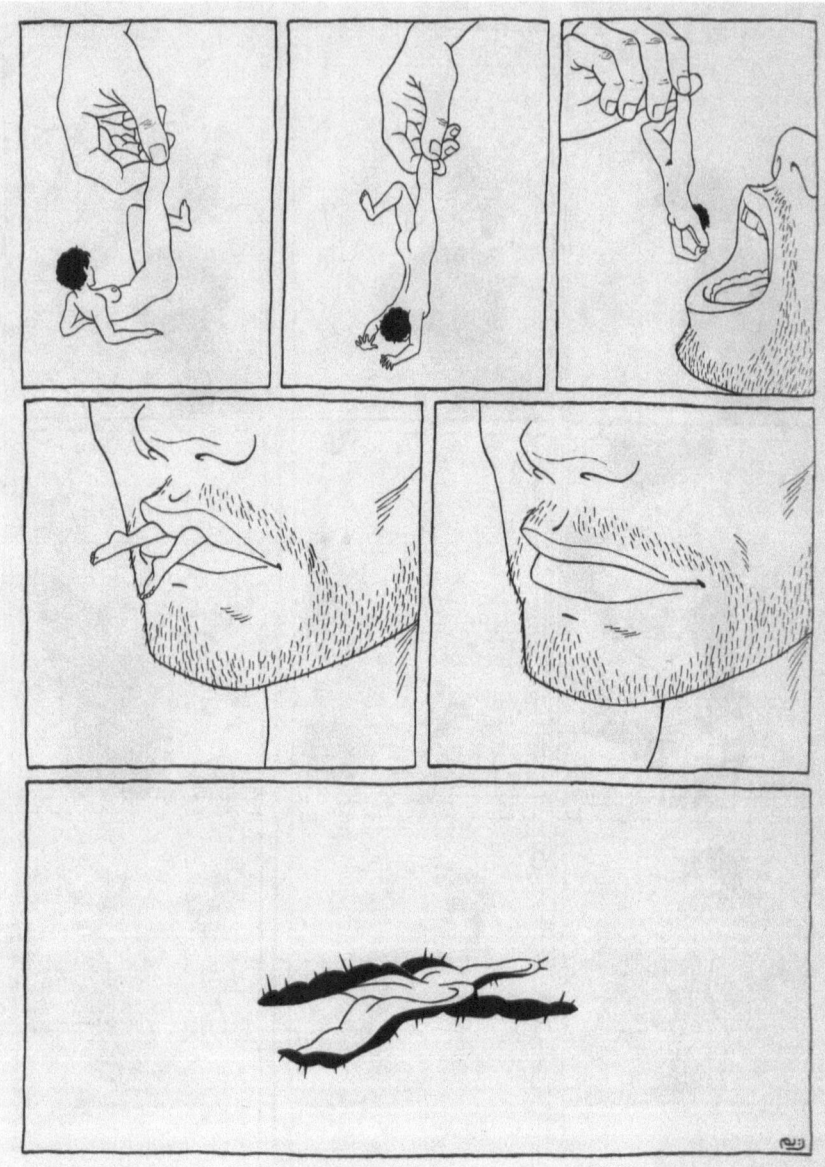

Images by R. Mokhtari © Dalimen are reproduced with the kind authorisation of the author and of Editions Dalimen.[713]

---

713 Rym Mokhtari: Épines. In: Étienne Schréder (ed.): *Monstres*. Algiers: Dalimen 2011, p. 15–18.

8 Bibliography

8.1 Primary Sources

Arnaud, Jacqueline (ed.)/Yacine, Kateb: *L'Œuvre en fragments*. Paris: Actes Sud 1986.
Dib, Mohammed: *La Grande Maison*. Paris: Points 1996 [1952].
Dib, Mohammed: *L'Incendie*. Paris: Points 2002 [1954].
Dib, Mohammed: *Le Métier à tisser*. Paris: Points 2001 [1957].
Dib, Mohammed: *Qui se souvient de la mer*. Paris: Éditions de la Différence 2007 [1962].
Dib, Mohammed: *Cours sur le rive sauvage*. Paris: Éditions du Seuil 1964.
Dib, Mohammed: *La Danse du roi*. Paris: Éditions du Seuil 1968.
Dib, Mohammed: *Habel*. Paris: Éditions du Seuil 1977.
Dib, Mohammed: *Mille hourras pour une gueuse*. Paris: Éditions du Seuil 1980.
Dib, Mohammed: *Les Terrasses d'Orsol*. Arles: Sindbad 1985.
Dib, Mohammed: *Le Sommeil d'Eve*. Arles: Sindbad 1989.
Dib, Mohammed: *Neiges de marbre*. Arles: Sindbad 1990.
Djebar, Assia: *La Soif*. Paris: R. Julliard 1957.
Djebar, Assia: *Les Impatients*. Paris: R. Julliard 1958.
Djebar, Assia: *Les Enfants du nouveau monde*. Paris: Points, 2012 [1962].
Djebar, Assia: *Femmes d'Alger dans leur appartement*. Paris: Librairie générale française 2004 [1980].
Djebar, Assia: *L'Amour, la fantasia*. Paris: J. C. Lattès 1985.
Djebar, Assia: *Loin de Médine: filles d'Ismaël*. Paris: Albin Michel 1991.
Djebar, Assia: *Le Blanc de l'Algérie*. Paris: Albin Michel 1995.
Djebar, Assia: *Ces voix qui m'assiègent*. Paris: Albin Michel 1999.
Djebar, Assia: *Nulle part dans la maison de mon père*. Paris: Fayard 2007.
Feraoun, Mouloud: *Le Fils du pauvre*. Paris: Points 1995 [1950, 1954].
Feraoun, Mouloud: *La Terre et le sang*. Paris: Points 2010 [1953].
Feraoun, Mouloud: *Les Chemins qui montent*. Paris: Éditions du Seuil 1957.
Feraoun, Mouloud: *Lettres à ses amis*. Paris: Éditions du Seuil 1969.
Feraoun, Mouloud: *L'Anniversaire*. Paris: Éditions du Seuil 1972.
Gabison, Thomas/Parfenov, Michel (eds.): *La Nouvelle bande dessinée arabe*. Arles: Actes Sud 2017.
Louerrad, Nawel: *Les Vêpres algériennes*. Algiers: Dalimen 2012.
Louerrad, Nawel: *Bach to black*. Algiers: Dalimen 2013.
Louerrad, Nawel: *Regretter l'absence de l'astre*. Algiers: Dalimen 2015.
Mammeri, Mouloud: *La Colline oubliée*. Paris: Gallimard 1992 [1952].
Mammeri, Mouloud: *Le Sommeil du juste*. Paris: Plon 1955.
Mammeri, Mouloud: *L'Opium et le bâton*. Paris: Éditions La Découverte 1992 [1965].
Mammeri, Mouloud: *La Traversée*. Paris: Plon 1982.
Mokhtari, Rym: Épines. In Schréder, Étienne (ed.): *Monstres*. Algiers: Dalimen 2011.
Schréder, Etienne (ed.): *Waratha 1 + 2*. Algiers: Dalimen 2012.
Yacine, Kateb: *Nedjma*. Paris: Éditions du Seuil 1956.
Yacine, Kateb: *Le Cercle des représailles*. Paris: Éditions du Seuil 1959.
Yacine, Kateb: *Le Polygone étoilé*. Paris: Éditions du Seuil 1966.
Yacine, Kateb: *Parce que c'est une femme*. Paris: Des Femmes 2004.

8.2 Secondary Sources

Abdel-Jaouad, Hédi: "Too Much in the Sun": Sons, Mothers and Impossible Alliances in Francophone Maghrebian Writing. In: *Research in African Literatures* Vol. 27, No. 3, (1996), p. 15–33.

Achour, Christiane: *Mouloud Feraoun: une voix en contrepoint*. Paris: Silex 1986.

Al Qur'an, (Quran.com).

Ali-Benali, Zineb: 'La fiancée du soir': un appel de femme dans 'La Colline oubliée'. In: Tassadit Yacine (ed.): *Le Genre dans les littératures postcoloniales. Feraoun, Mammeri, Belamri*. Paris: Éditions de la Maison des Sciences de L'Homme 2008, p. 77–86.

Amrane-Minne, Djamila, *La Femme algérienne et la guerre de libération nationale (1954–62)*. Actes du Colloque d'Oran 1980.

Amrane-Minne, Djamila: *Les Femmes algériennes dans la guerre*. Paris: Plon 1991.

Anderson, Benedict: *Imagined Communities: reflections on the origin and spread of nationalism*. London: Verso 2006.

Aquien, Michèle/Molinié, Georges: *Dictionnaire de rhétorique et de poétique*. Paris: Le Livre de Poche 1996.

Arnaud, Jacqueline: *Recherches sur la littérature maghrébine de langue française: le cas de Kateb Yacine*. Université de Paris III (Doctoral Thesis) 1978.

Bailly, Lionel: *Lacan*. Oxford: Oneworld publications 2009.

Barrada, Hamid/Chanda, Tirthankar: Assia Djebar Interview. In: *Jeune Afrique* (30 March 2008). Available at http://www.jeuneafrique.com/57084/archives-thematique/assia-djebar/.

Beckett, Samuel: *Molloy*. Paris: Éditions de Minuit 1982 [1951].

Benabdessadok, Chérifa: *Pour une analyse du discours sur la femme algérienne*. University of Algiers (Diplôme d'Études Avancées en Linguistique) 1977.

Benhaimi, Loubna: *Le Mythe de la femme fatale dans Nedjma de Kateb Yacine*. In: *Synergies Algérie* No. 13 (2011), p. 129–139.

Bensmaïa, Réda: *Experimental Nations, or, The Invention of the Maghreb*. Princeton: Princeton University Press 2003.

Bigelow, Gordon: Revolution and Modernity: Assia Djebar's "Les Enfants du nouveau monde". In: *Research in African Literatures* Vol. 34, No. 2 (Summer 2003), p. 13–27.

Boehmer, Elleke: Stories of Women and Mothers: Gender and Nationalism in the Early Fiction of Flora Nwape. In: Nasta, Susheila (ed.): *Motherlands: Black Women's Writing from Africa, the Caribbean and South Asia*. London: The Women's Press 1991, p. 3–23.

Boehmer, Elleke: *Stories of Nation: Gender and Narrative in the Postcolonial Nation*. Manchester: Manchester University Press 2005.

Bonn, Charles: *Lecture présente de Mohammed Dib*. Algiers: Entreprise nationale du livre 1988.

Bonn, Charles: *Kateb Yacine: Nedjma*. Paris: PUF 1990.

Bonn, Charles: De l'ambigüité tragique chez Feraoun, écrivain réputé "Ethnographique". In: *Nouvelle Revue Synergies Canada* No. 6 (2013).

Bonn, Charles: Preface. In: Elena Chiti/Touriya Fili-Tullon/Blandine Valford (eds.): *Écrire l'inattendu : Les 'printemps arabes' entre fictions et histoire*. Paris: L'Harmattan 2015, p. 22–32.

Bouhdiba, Abdelwahab : *La Sexualité en Islam*. Paris: Presses Universitaires de France 1975.

Bourdieu, Pierre: The Sentiment of Honour in Kabyle Society. In: Peristiany, Jean (ed.): *Honour and Shame*. London: Weidenfeld and Nicholson 1966.
Bourdieu, Pierre: *La Domination masculine*. Paris: Éditions du Seuil, 1998.
Bourdieu, Pierre: *Esquisse d'une théorie de la pratique précédé de trois études d'ethnologie kabyle*. Paris: Éditions du Seuil, 2000.
Boutayeb, Rachid: *La violence du texte fondateur: Abdelkébir Khatibi et la question du corps en Islam*. In: Gronemann, Claudia and Pasquier, Wilfried (eds.): *Scenes des genres au Maghreb, Masculinités, critique queer et espaces du féminin/masculin*. New York: Rodopi 2013.
Brahimi, Denise: *Nedjma, complexités du personnage*. In Julien, Anne-Yvonne/Camelin, Colette/Authier, François-Jean (eds.): *Kateb Yacine et l'étoilement de l'œuvre*. Rennes: Presses Universitaires de Rennes 2010.
Brennan, Timothy: The National Longing for Form. In: Ashcroft, Bill/Griffiths, Gareth/Tiffin, Helen (eds.): *The Post-colonial Studies Reader*. London: Routledge 1995.
Butler, Judith: Melancholy Gender-Refused Identification. In: *Psychoanalytic Dialogues: The International Journal of Relational Perspectives* Vol. 5.2 (1995) p. 165–180.
Butler, Judith: *The Psychic Life of Power: Theories in Subjection*. Stanford: SUP 1997.
Butler, Judith: *Gender Trouble, Feminism and the Subversion of Identity*. London: Routledge, 2002.
Campbell, Kirstin: *Jacques Lacan and Feminist Epistemology*. London: Routledge 2004.
Calle-Gruber, Mireille: *Comment en toucher un mot ? La Voix féminine de Kateb Yacine ou le pari de la littérature, une lecture de Nedjma*. In: Julien, Anne-Yvonne/Camelin, Colette/Authier, François-Jean (eds.): *Kateb Yacine et l'étoilement de l'œuvre*. Rennes: Presses Universitaires de Rennes 2010.
Camus, Albert: *Le Premier Homme*. Paris: Gallimard, 1994.
Cixous, Hélène: Le Rire de la Méduse. In: *L'Arc* Vol. 61 (1975), p. 39–54.
Clerc, Jeanne-Marie: *Assia Djebar: écrire, transgresser, résister*. Paris: L'Harmattan 1997.
Cooke, Miriam: *Women and the War Story*. Berkeley: University of California Press 1996.
Daly, Glyn/Žižek, Slavoj: *Conversations with Žižek*. Cambridge: Blackwell 2004.
De Beauvoir, Simone: *Le Deuxième sexe I*. Paris: Gallimard 1986 [1949].
Déjeux, Jean: À l'origine de *L'Incendie* de Mohammed Dib. In: *Presence Francophone* No. 10, (Spring 1975), p. 3–8.
Déjeux, Jean: *Littérature maghrébine de langue française*. Sherbrooke: Naâman 1978.
Déjeux, Jean: *La Colline oubliée* de Mouloud Mammeri. Un prix littéraire, une polémique politique. In: *Œuvres et Critiques* No. 4: 2, (1979), p. 69–80.
Dib, Mohammed: Interview. In: *L'Afrique littéraire et artistique* No. 18 (August 1970), p. 14.
Dib, Mohammed: Assia Djebar, or Eve in Her Garden. In: *World Literature Today*, 70.4 (1996), p. 788.
Djebar, Assia: Le Romancier dans la cité arabe. In: *Europe* No. 474 (October 1968), p. 114–20.
Djebnoun, Hédi: Naissance d'un "air de flûte". In: *Arabies* No.2 (February 1987), p. 83–84.
Dottin-Orsini, Mireille: *Femme Fatale*. In: Brunel, Pierre (ed.): *Dictionnaire des mythes littéraires*. Monaco: Éditions du Rocher 1988.
Elbaz, Robert/Mathieu-Job, Martine: *Mouloud Feraoun ou l'émergence d'une littérature*. Paris: Karthala 2001.
Evans, Dylan: *An Introductory Dictionary of Lacanian Psychoanalysis*. Hove: Routledge 1996.

Fanon, Frantz, *Sociologie d'une révolution (L'an V de la révolution algérienne)*. Paris: Maspero 1972 [1959].
Fanon, Frantz: *Peau noire, masques blancs*. Paris: Éditions du Seuil 1992 [1952].
Fanon, Frantz: *Les Damnés de la terre*. Paris: Éditions La Découverte 2002 [1961].
Faulkner, Rita: Assia Djebar, Frantz Fanon, Women, Veils and Land. In: *World Literature Today* Vol. 70, No. 4 (Autumn 1996), p. 847–855.
Felman, Shoshana: *What Does a Woman Want?* Baltimore: Johns Hopkins University Press 1993.
Feraoun, Mouloud: Lettres de Mouloud Feraoun à Emmanuel Roblès. In: *Esprit* No. 12, (1962), p. 966–981. http://www.samuelhuet.com/kairos/34-doxai/517-feraoun_3.html
Foucault, Michel: Qu'est-ce qu'un auteur? [1969]. In: *Dits et écrits*. Paris: Gallimard 2001.
Gallop, Jane: *Feminism and Psychoanalysis: the Daughter's Seduction*. London: Macmillan 1984.
Geertz, Clifford: *The Interpretation of Cultures*. New York: Basic Books 1973.
Graebner, Seth: Kateb Yacine and the Ruins of the Present. In: *SubStance* Vol. 36, No. 1, Issue 112 (2007), p. 139–163.
Green, Jonathon/Karolides, Nicholas: *The Encyclopedia of Censorship*. New York: Facts on File 2014.
Haddour, Azzedine: *Colonial Myths*. Manchester: Manchester University Press, 2000.
Hallward, Peter: *Absolutely Postcolonial: Writing between the Singular and the Specific*. Manchester: Manchester University Press 2001.
Harrison, Nicholas: *Postcolonial Criticism: History, Theory and the Work of Fiction*. Cambridge: Polity Press 2003.
Harrison, Nicholas: Le Voile littéraire: la politique d'Assia Djebar. In: Jean Bessière (ed.): *Littératures francophones et politiques*. Paris: Karthala 2009.
Hayes, Jarrod: *Queer Nations: Marginal Sexualities in the Maghreb*. Chicago: University of Chicago Press 2000.
Hélie-Lucas, Marie-Aimée: Women, Nationalism, and Religion in the Algerian Struggle. In: Badran, Margot/Cooke, Miriam: *Opening the Gates: A Century of Arab Feminist Writing*. Bloomington: Indiana University Press 2004.
Hiddleston, Jane, *Assia Djebar: Out of Algeria*. Liverpool: Liverpool University Press 2006.
Hiddleston, Jane: That Obscure Object of Desire. In: *French Forum* Vol. 38, No. 3 (2013), p. 133–145.
Hiddleston, Jane: *Decolonising the Intellectual, Politics, Culture, and Humanism at the End of the French Empire*. Liverpool: Liverpool University Press 2014.
Himeur, Ouarda: Le permis et l'interdit chez Mouloud Feraoun et Mouloud Mammeri. In: Yacine, Tassadit (ed.): *Le Genre dans les littératures postcoloniales. Feraoun, Mammeri, Belamri*. Paris: Éditions de la Maison des Sciences de L'Homme 2008, p. 31–43.
Horne, Alistair: *A Savage War of Peace*. New York: Viking 1977.
Horstkotte, Silke/Pedri, Nancy: Focalization in Graphic Narrative. In: *Narrative* Vol. 19, No. 3 (October 2011), p. 330–357.
Johnston, Adrian: Jacques Lacan. In: Zalta, Edward. N (ed.): *The Stanford Encyclopedia of Philosophy* (Winter 2016 Edition), forthcoming URL = <http://plato.stanford.edu/archives/win2016/entries/lacan/>.
Kelle, Michel: Mouloud Feraoun, romancier de l'honneur, de l'amour et de la jalousie. In: *Algérie Littérature/Action* No. 57 (Jan–Feb 2002), p. 78–89.

Kelly, Debra: *Autobiography and Independence: Selfhood and Creativity in North African Postcolonial Writing in French*. Liverpool: Liverpool University Press 2005.
Khadda, Naget: L'Allégorie de la féminité: Deuil d'une civilisation et mutation d'identité dans Le Fils du pauvre de M. Feraoun. In: *Peuples méditerranéens* No. 44–45 (July–December 1988), p. 73–88.
Khadda, Naget: *Mohammed Dib, cette intempestive voix recluse*. Aix-en-Provence: Edisud 2003.
Khanna, Ranjana: Post-Palliative; Coloniality's Affective Dissonance. In: *Postcolonial Text* Vol. 2, No. 2 (2006), p. 1–13.
Khanna, Ranjana: *Algeria Cuts: Women and Representation, 1830 to the Present*. Palo Alto: Stanford University Press 2008.
Khatibi, Abdelkebir: *Le Roman maghrébin: essai*. Rabat: Société marocaine des éditeurs réunis 1979 [1968].
Khelladi, Khedidja: *Archétypes et paradigmes littéraires dans l'œuvre de Kateb Yacine*. In: Julien, Anne-Yvonne/Camelin, Colette/Authier, François-Jean (eds.): *Kateb Yacine et L'Étoilement de L'œuvre*. Rennes: Presses Universitaires de Rennes 2010.
Kristeva, Julia: *Desire in Language: a Semiotic Approach to Literature and Art*. New York: Columbia University Press 1980.
Labter, Lazhari: *Panorama de la bande dessinée algérienne 1969–2009*. Algiers: Lazhari Labter Editions 2009.
Lacan, Jacques: *Écrits*. Paris: Éditions du Seuil 1966.
Lacan, Jacques: *Le Séminaire, livre VII, L'éthique de la psychanalyse, leçon du 6 juillet 1960*. Paris: Éditions du Seuil 1986.
Lacan, Jacques: *Le Séminaire. Livre XVII. L'Envers de la psychanalyse*. Paris: Éditions du Seuil 1991.
Lacheraf, Mostefa: La Colline oubliée ou les consciences anachroniques. In: *Le jeune musulman* No. 15 (1953), p. 4–6.
Lacheraf, Mostefa: L'Avenir de la culture algérienne. In: *Les temps modernes* No. 209 (October 1963), p. 733–734.
Lacoste-Dujardin, Camille: *Le Conte Kabyle: étude ethnologique*. Paris: Maspero 1970.
Lafitte, Priscille: Une nouvelle BD naît en Algérie et s'expose au festival d'Angoulême: *France 24* (2013): http://www.france24.com/fr/20130131-bande-dessinee-nouvelle-bd-nait-algerie-expose-festival-angouleme.
Lançon, Daniel: L'Invention de l'auteur: Assia Djebar entre 1957 et 1969 ou l'Orient second en français. In: Asholt, Wolfgang/Calle-Gruber, Mireille/Combe, Dominique (eds.): *Assia Djebar: Littérature et transmission*. Paris: PSN 2010.
Lazreg, Marnia, *The Eloquence of Silence: Algerian Women in Question*. New York: Routledge 1994.
Lechte, John: *Fifty Key Contemporary Thinkers*. London: Routledge 1994.
Lévi-Strauss, Claude: *Les Structures élémentaires de la parenté*. Berlin: Walter de Gruyter 2002 [1949].
Macey, David: *Frantz Fanon: a biography*. London: Verso 2012.
Mammeri, Mouloud: Ce sont les témoignages qu'il faudrait consigner. In: *Révolution africaine* No. 128 (10 juillet 1965), p. 24.
Marx, Karl: *Capital, Vol. 1*. London: Penguin Books 1992.

McClintock, Anne, No Longer in a Future Heaven: Gender, Race and Nationalism. In: McClintock, Anne/Mufti, Aamir/Shohat, Ella (eds.): *Dangerous Liaisons: Gender, Nation, and Postcolonial Perspectives*. Minneapolis: University of Minnesota Press 1997.
Merad, Ali: *Nedjma (review)*. In: IBLA No. 76 (1956), p. 438.
Mernissi, Fatima: *Women's Rebellion and Islamic Memory*. London: Zed Books 1996.
Messaoudi, Khalida/Schemla, Elizabeth: *Unbowed: An Algerian Woman Confronts Islamic Fundamentalism*. Philadelphia: University of Pennsylvania Press 1998.
Miller, Jacques-Alain: Interview with Hanna Waar. In: *Psychologies Magazine* No. 278 (2008).
Mitchell, Juliet/Rose, Jacqueline (eds.): *Feminine Sexuality*. Basingstoke: Macmillan 1982.
Monette, Pierre (ed.): *No. 49: Mouloud Mammeri: langues et langages d'Algérie*. Montréal: Dérives 1985.
Mortimer, Mildred: *Mouloud Mammeri, écrivain algérien*. Sherbrooke: Naâman, 1982.
Mortimer, Mildred: Le Monde traditionnel: *La Colline oubliée*. In: *CELFAN [Special Issue on Mouloud Mammeri]* Vol. 3, No. 2 (1984), p. 23–26.
Mosteghanemi, Ahlam: *Algérie, femmes et écritures*. Paris: L'Harmattan 1985.
M'Rabet, Fadéla: *La Femme algérienne: suivi de les algériennes*. Paris: Maspero 1983.
Mulvey, Laura: Visual Pleasure and Narrative Cinema. In: *Screen* Vol. 6, Issue 3 (1975), p. 6–18.
Poole, Sarah: Women and boundaries in the fiction of Mouloud Feraoun. In: *International Journal of Francophone Studies* Vol. 5, Issue 3 (2003), p. 157–164.
Roche, Anne: Tradition et subversion dans l'œuvre de Mouloud Mammeri. In: *Revue de l'Occident musulman et de la Méditerranée* Vol. 22, No. 1 (1976), p. 99–107.
Rolin, Gabrielle: Une femme du nouveau monde: interview with Assia Djebar. In: *Jeune Afrique* No. 87 (June 1962), p. 28–29.
Roumani, Judith: Mohammed Dib's *Qui se souvient de la mer*: Literary Technique and the Drama of Algeria. In: *Revue CELFAN* No. 2.2 (1983), p. 8–11.
Sahli, Mohammed Cherif: La Colline oubliée ou la colline du reniement. In: *Le jeune musulman* No. 15 (1953), p. 2.
Salhi, Zahia Smail: Algerian Women, Citizenship, and the 'Family Code'. In: *Gender and Development* 11.3 (2003), p. 27–35.
Salah Dembri, Mohammed: Querelles autour de *La Colline oubliée*. In: *Revue algérienne des lettres et des sciences humaines* No. 1 (1969), p. 171–173.
Sartre, Jean-Paul: *Cahiers pour une morale*. Paris: Gallimard 1983.
Salzmann, Yvan: *Sartre et l'authenticité: vers une éthique de la bienveillance réciproque*. Geneva: Labor et Fides 2000.
Sbouaï, Taïeb: *La Femme sauvage de Kateb Yacine*. Paris: Editions de l'Arcantère 1985.
Shaaban, Buthaina: *Both Right and Left Handed: Arab Women Talk about their Lives*. London: Women's Press 1998.
Sigurdson, Ola: Slavoj Žižek, The Death Drive, and Zombies: a Theological Account. In: *Modern Theology* Vol. 29, Issue 3 (July 2013), p. 361–380.
Slemon, Stephen: Modernism's Last Post. In: *ARIEL* Vol. 20, No. 4 (1989), p. 3–17.
Spivak, Gayatri: Can the Subaltern Speak? In: Morris, Rosalind (ed.): *Can the Subaltern Speak: Reflections on the History of an Idea*. New York: Columbia University Press 2010.
Stone, Martin: *The Agony of Algeria*. London: C. Hurst & Co. 1997.
Stora, Benjamin/Mitsch, R. H.: Women's Writing between Two Algerian Wars. In: *Research in African Literatures* No. 30.3 (1999), p. 78–94.

Stratton, Florence: *Contemporary African literature and the Politics of Gender.* London: Routledge 1994.
Tomšič, Samo: *The Capitalist Unconscious: Marx and Lacan.* London: Verso 2015.
Tremaine, Louis: The absence of Itinerary in Kateb Yacine's "Nedjma". In: *Research in African Literatures* Vol. 10, No. 1 (Spring, 1979), p. 16–39.
Tremaine, Louis: Psychic Deformity in Mohammed Dib's *Qui se souvient de la mer.* In: *Research in African Literatures* Vol. 19, No. 3 (1988), p. 283–300.
Vince, Natalya: *Our Fighting Sisters.* Oxford: Oxford University Press 2016.
Woodhull, Winifred: *Rereading "Nedjma":* Feminist Scholarship and North African Women. In: *SubStance* Vol. 21, No. 3, Issue 69: Special Issue: Translations of the Orient: Writing the Maghreb (1992), p. 46–63.
Woodhull, Winifred: *Transfigurations of the Maghreb, Feminism, Decolonization, and Literatures.* Minneapolis: University of Minnesota Press 1993.
Woodhull, Winifred: Unveiling Algeria. In Lewis, Reina/Mills, Sara (eds.): *Feminist Postcolonial Theory: A Reader.* New York: Routledge 2003.
Yacine, Kateb: (Interview) Les intellectuels, la révolution et le pouvoir. In: *Jeune Afrique* (26 March, 1976), p. 26–33.
Yacine, Kateb: *Le Poète comme un boxeur: Entretiens 1958–1989.* Paris: Éditions du Seuil 1994.
Zaoui, Amin: Assia Djebar: Pourquoi le prix Nobel de littérature est raté? In: *Liberté* (19th October 2013): https://www.facebook.com/notes/amin-zaoui/assia-djebar-pourquoi-le-prix-nobel-de-litt%C3%A9rature-est-rat%C3%A9-/476184062479346).
Zimra, Clarisse: Writing Woman: The Novels of Assia Djebar. In: *SubStance* No. 69 (1992), p. 68–84.
Žižek, Slavoj: Woman is One of the Names-of-the-Father, or How Not to Misread Lacan's Formulas of Sexuation. In: *Lacanian ink* No. 10 (1995), p. 24–39.
Žižek, Slavoj: From desire to drive: Why Lacan is not Lacaniano. In: *Atlántica de Las Artes* No. 14 (1996), p. 1–7.
Žižek, Slavoj: *The Indivisible Remainder.* London: Verso 1996.
Žižek, Slavoj: *On Belief.* London: Routledge 2001.
Žižek, Slavoj: *The Silent Partners.* London: Verso 2006.
Žižek, Slavoj: *The Sublime Object of Ideology.* London: Verso 2008 [1989].
Žižek, Slavoj: *Enjoy Your Symptom!* London: Routledge 2008.
Žižek, Slavoj: *The Plague of Fantasies.* London: Verso 2008.

Name Index

Achour, Christiane   17, 100f.
Amrane-Minne, Djamila   2f., 7f., 69f., 203
Amrouche, Taos   12, 170
Anderson, Benedict   5
Arnaud, Jacqueline   15, 20f., 25, 32, 52f.

Bachi, Salim   17, 158–163, 187, 192
Beckett, Samuel   78
Ben Bella, Ahmed   4
Ben Bouali, Hassiba   3
Benhaimi, Loubna   26, 35
Bensmaïa, Réda   125
Bigelow, Gordon   171, 195
Boehmer, Elleke   14, 47, 111
Bonn, Charles   15, 18f., 30, 32f., 47f., 61, 68–71, 74, 77, 79, 100, 123, 137, 149
Bouhired, Djamila   3
Boumédiène, Houari   4, 136
Boupacha, Djamila   3
Bourdieu, Pierre   8–10, 18, 41–43, 52, 56, 64f., 103–105, 108f., 113, 118, 140, 162
Brahimi, Denise   24, 27
Brennan, Timothy   63f.
Butler, Judith   50, 80, 89f., 93f., 178

Calle-Gruber, Mireille   27f., 32, 174
Campbell, Kirstin   194
Camus, Albert   62, 172
Cixous, Hélène   206
Cooke, Miriam   3, 7, 12, 33f., 85, 137, 158

De Beauvoir, Simone   141
Debèche, Djamila   12, 170
Déjeux, Jean   15, 19, 44, 70, 101, 137–139, 175
Dib, Mohammed   13f., 60–91, 93–96, 98–100, 102, 108, 121, 131, 136f., 146, 148f., 162, 165, 170f., 183, 195, 198, 200f.
Djebar, Assia   1, 12f., 15, 22, 60, 135f., 167–177, 179–186, 188–201, 203f.
Dottin-Orsini, Mireille   27
Drif, Zohra   3

Elbaz, Robert   101, 109, 124, 131
Ennissa, Saout   202

Fanon, Frantz   1, 5, 7, 62f., 70, 93, 187, 195
Faulkner, Rita   1
Felman, Shoshana   29
Feraoun, Mouloud   13–15, 29, 66, 72, 87, 100–110, 112–116, 118–138, 142, 149f., 152, 158, 160, 170, 176, 181, 184, 186, 188, 195f., 200
Foucault, Michel   167

Gallop, Jane   14, 79
Geertz, Clifford   138
Graebner, Seth   49f.

Haddour, Azzedine   62
Halimi, Gisèle   3
Hallward, Peter   61–63, 89f., 93
Hamidou, Maliha   3
Harrison, Nicholas   172, 175
Hayes, Jarrod   72, 82, 99, 103, 113, 116
Hélie-Lucas, Marie-Aimée   6f., 12
Hiddleston, Jane   29f., 43f., 103, 110, 127, 179, 188, 204
Horne, Alistair   4

Kelly, Debra   100, 102, 129, 174
Khadda, Naget   65, 68, 75, 77, 93, 95, 103f., 115, 121
Khanna, Ranjana   3, 60, 98, 171
Khatibi, Abdelkebir   60, 101, 124, 137
Khelladi, Khedidja   27, 45f., 48
Kristeva, Julia   14, 61, 74–77, 80, 99, 165, 198

La Kahina   201f.
La Pointe, Ali   3
Labter, Lazhari   205
Lacan, Jacques   14, 18, 36f., 63, 74, 82, 87, 96f., 104, 114, 118f., 130f., 151, 154, 164f., 190–192, 194
Lacheraf, Mostefa   135, 137, 168, 198

Lacoste-Dujardin, Camille 29
Lançon, Daniel 168, 174
Lazreg, Marnia 1f., 4, 6, 8
Lévi-Strauss, Claude 9, 143f., 149
Louerrad, Nawel 203, 205

Macey, David 62
Mammeri, Mouloud 13–15, 64, 96, 100, 135–139, 141, 143–155, 157–159, 162–166, 168, 170f., 174, 176, 181, 195, 203
Marx, Karl 10f., 191
Mathieu-Job, Martine 101, 109, 124, 131
McClintock, Anne 4f., 43
Mernissi, Fatima 34, 115, 175
Messaoudi, Khalida 6
Mitchell, Juliet 97
Mokhtari, Rym 205, 210
Mortimer, Mildred 136, 146, 158
Mosteghanemi, Ahlam 90, 111, 123
M'Rabet, Fadéla 2, 4
Mulvey, Laura 137, 153, 155

Nadjem, Dalila 205

Roche, Anne 27, 146, 150, 162, 164
Rose, Jacqueline 97
Roumani, Judith 85f.

Salhi, Zahia Smail 4, 204
Salzmann, Yvan 185
Sartre, Jean-Paul 185
Schemla, Elizabeth 6
Slemon, Stephen 64
Spivak, Gayatri 1, 10f.
Stone, Martin 20
Stora, Benjamin 11f.
Stratton, Florence 170

Tomšič, Samo 191
Tremaine, Louis 24, 79, 85f., 89, 92

Vince, Natalya 2, 6, 8, 183, 203f.

Woodhull, Winifred 5, 22, 31f., 34, 57, 88, 95

Yacine, Kateb 1, 13–15, 17–37, 39–60, 62, 72, 80, 85, 96, 98–100, 102, 115, 121f., 129, 131f., 136, 138, 142, 148f., 162, 170, 195f., 201–203

Zimra, Clarisse 177f.
Žižek, Slavoj 13f., 63, 104, 114, 117–119, 165, 180f., 184f., 193

Index of Theoretical Terms

Bande Dessinée 204–206

Colonisation 2, 5, 10, 43, 47, 60, 66, 71, 80, 82, 90–92, 94, 101, 104, 138–141, 143, 145, 180

Darstellung 1, 10, 200
Death drive 14, 104f., 114, 116f., 152, 164, 176, 181
Desire 14, 23f., 27, 29, 35–40, 43, 48, 54–56, 58, 62, 74, 76, 80–82, 87, 91, 93f., 96, 99, 108, 114, 118f., 123, 127, 130, 141f., 165f., 178–180, 184, 196
– Feminine desire 27, 29, 40, 72
– Obsessional 14, 36–38, 43, 51, 58, 96, 196, 205

Ego-ideal 172
Ekphrasis 35
Ethnography 103, 105, 108, 137

Factitiousness 129, 131, 150
– Ventriloquism 129

Gendered dissymmetry 8, 41, 200, 204

Ideal-ego 187
Ideology 12–14, 63f., 104, 114, 122, 134, 139, 147–149, 151, 193–195
– Fantasy 36, 38, 46, 63f., 96f., 99, 131, 181, 193

Kabyle Sociology 137

Male Gaze 1, 14, 96, 131, 137, 153–158, 190
– Scopophilia 149, 154
Marriage 25, 108, 120, 137, 139, 141, 143–145, 147f., 151, 159f., 176, 184, 197, 204
Masculine Blindness 15, 149, 151f., 154f., 157
Masculinist 5, 12–15, 18, 24, 26–29, 48, 51, 53–55, 61–64, 68, 76f., 79, 98, 101–103, 105–113, 116, 118, 121f., 133, 137, 145–148, 151, 154, 157f., 160–162, 177f., 180, 183, 185, 196, 200, 202, 206

Melancholy 15, 61f., 80, 84f., 89f., 93f., 97–99, 162
Metaphor 22, 36f., 44f., 47, 50f., 87, 111, 132, 191f.
Metonymy 12, 14, 71, 74, 111, 186, 192
Displacement 94, 148, 166, 189, 192, 194
Mirror Stage 188, 190
Mitsein 127f., 134, 188

Pessimism 14f., 18, 51, 53–55, 57–59, 62, 80, 98f., 102, 121, 131, 136f., 148, 157, 162–164, 182, 194, 202–204
Phallus 15, 36f., 61f., 79, 83, 87, 94, 105, 119f., 122, 144, 159, 162, 184
– Not-all 87, 119

Realism 14, 60–62, 73f., 174, 198
Rebellion 34, 105, 114f., 122, 148, 159, 178, 180f., 187, 189, 194, 199
– Fitna 34f., 72, 115
– Nushuz 72, 105, 115, 142
Rivalry 23, 40–43, 55, 142–144

Semiotic 61, 74–76, 80, 93, 96, 99, 164f.
Socio-symbolic 4f., 14f., 17, 34, 41, 43, 51, 63, 77, 101, 105, 107f., 111, 114–117, 119f., 126, 140, 142, 145, 147, 150, 152, 154, 158–160, 162–164, 166, 169, 177–179, 181f., 194–196, 200, 205
– Social Fictions 139, 194, 201
Subjectivity 13f., 18, 23, 35f., 43, 62, 86, 117, 123, 127, 129, 152, 166, 178, 182, 187, 189, 191f., 195, 200
Supplements 15, 109, 137, 157
Symbolic capital 8–10, 12, 41–44, 48, 50, 52, 54f., 57, 61, 112f., 120, 141–143, 146, 160, 178

– Honour   1, 8f., 41, 43, 50, 53, 55f., 103, 105, 107f., 112, 115f., 118–122, 134, 141f., 144, 155, 160, 168, 178, 196
– Nif   118f., 122, 196
Symbolic order   4, 9, 36, 43, 63, 67, 75–77, 90, 93f., 104, 112, 114, 144, 154, 188, 191, 194

Trauma   20, 23, 25, 76, 93, 104, 131–133, 182, 196, 205

Vertretung   1, 10f., 13f., 19, 28, 51, 61, 80, 99, 101, 134, 149, 172, 200
– Porte-parole   172f., 199f.

www.ingramcontent.com/pod-product-compliance
Lightning Source LLC
Chambersburg PA
CBHW031812220426
43662CB00007B/611